Edmund Spenser, Mary Elizabeth Litchfield

Spenser's Britomart

From books III, IV, and V of the Faery queene

Edmund Spenser, Mary Elizabeth Litchfield

Spenser's Britomart
From books III, IV, and V of the Faery queene

ISBN/EAN: 9783337322779

Printed in Europe, USA, Canada, Australia, Japan

Cover: Foto ©ninafisch / pixelio.de

More available books at **www.hansebooks.com**

BRITOMART

FROM BOOKS III, IV, AND V
OF THE
FAERY QUEENE

EDITED, WITH INTRODUCTION AND NOTES
BY
MARY E. LITCHFIELD

BOSTON, U.S.A., AND LONDON
GINN & COMPANY, PUBLISHERS
The Athenæum Press
1896

PREFACE.

EXCEPT to the special student of literature, Britomart, the most charming of Spenser's heroines, is almost unknown. Indeed, she has for long years been wandering in the mazes of the poet's fairy-land, well-nigh lost to view. And yet no story in the *Faery Queene* is so romantic and none has such a strong human interest as that which tells of the "lady knight." As we read of her adventures we are reminded of Rosalind in the forest of Arden. In this little book the scattered portions of Spenser's interesting narrative have been taken out and re-united. It has been necessary to omit stanzas and occasionally lines from the parts selected, but the language of the poet has in no instance been tampered with. In the case of writers like Dante and Milton, the attempt to take out and re-unite scattered portions would be an evident impertinence. With Spenser, however, a genius whose constructive ability did not enable him to make of a long poem an artistic whole, the proceeding seems justifiable. The text is that of the best editions, but the spelling has been modernized except where the modern spelling would change the sound of the word. In the elucidation of difficult passages the highest authorities have been consulted. The notes, however, contain only such information as is necessary to the intelligent study of the poem. In order that this study may prove a delight rather than a task, the notes have been placed at the bottom of the page, and have been so arranged that any portion of the narrative may be read by itself. Except for a few suggestions, there has been no attempt at tracing the allegory.

INTRODUCTION.

Since every piece of literature is in a way the product of the age in which it is written, we must, if we would rightly estimate the poetry of Spenser, consider the circumstances amid which the poet lived and the events and movements that left their impress upon his character. And since Spenser's poetry has an important — though not the most important — place in the literature of the 16th century in England, it is well, before studying his works, to seek to know the causes that led to the unparalleled literary activity of the Elizabethan Age.

During the century that preceded the birth of Spenser, great events followed one another in quick succession: in 1453 Constantinople was taken by the Turks, and through the Greek scholars that fled to Italy the culture of Greece was carried into Western Europe; about 1475 Caxton set up his printing-press in England; Columbus discovered the New World in 1492; in 1517 Luther attacked the doctrine of indulgences; in 1534 Henry VIII declared himself head of the English church. However, not until the reign of Elizabeth, with its long years of internal peace, did the conditions resulting from these events find adequate expression in English literature. Caxton fortunately set up his printing-press just as the New Learning was making its way, bringing from Italy an enthusiasm for the classics and awakening among English scholars an interest in the study of the Bible in the original tongues. In the religious disturbances that darkened the reigns of Edward VI and Mary, the light of the New Learning seemed in danger of being quenched; but, with the coming of Elizabeth, herself a lover of Greek and Latin literature, the classics regained their supremacy, and the grammar schools, recently established, spread the love of learning among the people.

A spirit of inquiry in regard to natural phenomena was abroad in Elizabeth's time. The Copernican system was revolutionizing men's ideas in regard to the relations of the heavenly bodies, and, before many years, Francis Bacon was to give to the study of natural science an impulse such as it had never before received in England.

In the province of religion old barriers were swept aside and new forces were given full play. When Henry VIII threw off his allegiance to Rome and declared himself head of the English church, the national consciousness was no doubt quickened; but the event that did most during his reign toward developing the moral and religious sentiment of the nation was the translation of the Bible into English. In a few years the Bible, known already through the teachings of the clergy, became the one book of the mass of the people; the images of the Hebrew writers were in every mind, their phrases on every tongue. More than Homer to the Greek was the Bible to the Englishman;

for from it he gained that moral strength, that realization of his individual worth as the child of God, which made him battle with a stout heart against the dreaded power of Catholic Spain, and which, later, enabled him to resist successfully the tyranny of his own rulers. The translation of the Bible exercised an influence upon the development of English literature; and the influence was in part owing to the time at which the translation was made; that is, it was made just when the language was ripe for it. Not until the 16th century were the various elements that go to make up the English tongue thoroughly assimilated. While to-day the language of Chaucer needs to be studied, the speech of the 16th century, freed from its peculiarities in spelling, may easily be read by a person of ordinary intelligence; in fact, it is practically modern English. By the wide and rapid diffusion of the Bible, the people as a whole, even those speaking peculiar dialects, became familiar with a body of writings expressed in the literary medium of the period. Consequently the 16th-century writers when employing the current tongue could appeal to persons of various social conditions. This is one reason why the literature of the Elizabethan Age is the literature, not of a class, but of a nation.

While the influences just mentioned quickened the moral perceptions and refined the literary instincts of the people, the discovery of the New World awoke in them a sudden consciousness of their own force, and led them to realize in a slight degree the part they were destined to play on the great stage of the world. Up to the beginning of the 16th century Englishmen had been obliged to acknowledge that their small island had little weight in the affairs of Europe. She had heretofore looked to Rome for spiritual guidance and to Italy and France for inspiration and teaching in literary matters. Now at last she was to take her true place in the onward march of the nations. The discovery of America and the subsequent explorations of daring navigators sailing under English colors had given to England even more truly than to Castile and Leon a " New World." The spirit of the Vikings that had slumbered for centuries in their descendants awoke, and England felt her real power — the power of the conqueror and the colonizer; the power which was to make that "little body with a mighty heart" the greatest civilizing force of modern times.

As we consider these facts we begin to see why the man of the Elizabethan Age differed in many respects both from his predecessors and from his descendants. We can now account for his unruly passions, his lively imagination, his religious intolerance, and his love of adventure. We do not wonder that the finer spirits of the time were inspired by lofty and generous ideals. Fortunate, indeed, was the genius whose lot was cast in this remarkable century; if not heir of all the ages that have stored up their wealth for the 19th-century man, he was the possessor of a rich inheritance. If the genius were a Spenser, he looked beyond the material universe, out upon vast realms of the imagination peopled with those airy nothings to which the poet alone can give a local habitation and a name.

And yet, the poet is, after all, born into the hard, actual world, —

> ... the world
> Of all of us, — the place where in the end,
> We find our happiness, or not at all;

and he, like the commonest mortal, must grapple with facts, and gain strength and insight through experience.

Edmund Spenser was born in London near the Tower, some time between 1549 and 1554. 1552 is the date usually fixed upon, and this makes him six years old when Elizabeth came to the throne. He was evidently of good family, though his parents must have been in moderate circumstances. He was a pupil in the grammar school established by the Merchant Taylors' Company, and when sixteen or seventeen left school for the university of Cambridge. In 1573 he became B.A., and in 1576 left the university with the degree of M.A. His friendship with Gabriel Harvey, a fellow-student, had an important influence upon his future life, since Harvey introduced him to Sir Philip Sidney, who made him known to his uncle, the Earl of Leicester. After a short stay in the north of England, where he is supposed to have wooed unsuccessfully a certain fair Rosalind, the poet settled in London. In 1579 his first printed book, the "Shepherd's Calendar," was published. This production was dedicated to Sidney. In 1580 Spenser went to Ireland as secretary to Arthur, Lord Grey de Wilton. Since he was staying at Lord Leicester's house just before this event, it is probable that he obtained the position through Leicester's influence. Lord Grey was recalled in 1582, and

Spenser returned to England with him. In 1586 a large estate at Kilcolman, not far from the city of Cork, was granted Spenser by the queen; and it was in his new home that he composed the first three books of the *Faery Queene*. Sir Walter Raleigh, whose friendship he had gained during his former visit to Ireland, thought so highly of the work that he persuaded Spenser to accompany him to England that he might present him to the queen. Elizabeth received the poet with marked favor, and granted him a pension of fifty pounds a year. The three books were published in 1590 with an explanatory letter addressed to Raleigh. In 1591 a collection of Spenser's shorter poems appeared. In 1594 the poet married a "countrey lasse" named Elizabeth, and in honor of the occasion wrote his celebrated *Epithalamion*. A second edition of the first three books of the *Faery Queene* was printed in 1596, together with the next three books. Spenser was in London at this time. After his return to Ireland, in 1598, the Tyrone Rebellion broke out, and the castle of Kilcolman was sacked and burnt. The poet was obliged to flee with his family, and in the hurry and confusion one of the children was left to perish in the flames. Spenser managed to reach England, but died three months later, in January, 1599. His body lies beside that of Chaucer in Westminster Abbey.

In the *Prothalamion*, written when he was a little over forty, the poet speaks of his birthplace as

> . . . merry London, my most kindly nurse,
> That to me gave this life's first native source;

and in the same poem he alludes to

> . . . the shore of silver-streaming Thames;
> Whose rutty bank, the which his river hems,
> Was painted all with variable flowers,
> And all the meads adorned with dainty gems
> Fit to deck maidens' bowers.

It is interesting to picture Spenser as a boy in London — that strange London of the 16th century, with its filth and its splendor, its Puritanism and its license, its hatred of popery and its stanch loyalty to the queen, — above all, with its daring hopes and its world-wide interests. We see the schoolboy playing on the "rutty" banks of the river, or dodging as he runs from school to avoid the frequent holes and the heaps of filth that make the streets anything but ways of pleasantness. Now he gazes at the stuffed monkeys and parrots, the tomahawks and the Indian ornaments exposed to view in some shop. A live red man even may meet his gaze, for Indians were occasionally brought to London in those days. We see him listening breathless as some returned mariner tells the knot of boys gathered about him of Eldorados more wonderful than Mexico and Peru, of lands where the rivers run gold and the rocks are full of diamonds. At another time we see the future poet of fairy-land cheering on a street fight or following with the crowd that escorts an unfortunate victim to the stocks or to the gallows. Perhaps the boy's attention is arrested by a passing courtier, the willing cynosure of admiring eyes, fantastically arrayed as a Spanish grandee or as a French beau of the period. The plays given in the court-yards of the inns are sure to have aroused Spenser's enthusiasm; and tucked in among his burly elders he doubtless watched with keen delight the crude performances of the early Elizabethan stage. After the play would come the walk home in the quick coming darkness of the winter afternoon, the flaring light of the linkboy's torch making well-known objects strangely unfamiliar. But, above all, the shows! — processions, pageants, masks, mummeries, morality plays; every kind of spectacle that could delight the eyes of man might be seen in or near the London of Spenser's day. The queen never moved but in a show. The most trifling occasion was celebrated by allegorical representations. The vices and virtues became as familiar to the sight as they are in all ages to the inner consciousness of the people. The *Mask of Cupid* that Britomart witnesses in Busirane's castle is only a court mask of Spenser's time that has found its way into fairy-land.

If the imagination of the future poet was fed by the sights and sounds of the city, it must have been nourished by books as well. Stories from every land and every age found their way to the printing-presses of London: Italian poems, French romances, Spanish tales, and classical mythologies. Spenser read of the gods of Greece; and in the early red of the morning he saw Aurora coming to rejoice the slumbering world. He pored over Geoffrey of Monmouth and the *Morte d'Arthur* till in the clouds of sunset he could distinguish the shining spears and the crimson banners of the knights of the Round Table. With these romantic tales were mingled Scripture narratives; and back of all, — a dark, deep undercurrent, — whispers of popish plots and stories of Spanish cruelty. It is no wonder that the *Faery Queene* is at the first glance a strange medley; that Christian knights and fair ladies as they wander in Spenser's fairy-land meet with sorcerers and dragons, with Saracens and Amazons; while the vices and virtues personified live on terms of intimacy with the thinly disguised characters of the poet's own time.

Little is known of Spenser's life at Cambridge. It is known, however, that the university was at that time represented to the authorities in London as being in a state of dangerous excitement. Religious controversies were rife, and the more subtle doctrines of the various Puritanical sects were eagerly discussed. Gabriel Harvey, Spenser's college friend, in a letter written to the poet a short time after the latter had left Cambridge, says: "Every day spawns new opinions: heresy in divinity, in philosophy, in humanity, in manners, grounded upon hearsay; doctors contemn'd; the *devil* not so hated as the *pope;* many invectives but no amendment." However, in spite of the prevailing interest in religious controversies, the poet must have found at the university much that would tend to develop the intellectual side of his nature; and if he was, as some maintain, the most learned of the English poets after Milton (Gray should come first, probably), he owed much of his knowledge to the opportunities enjoyed at Cambridge. Certainly he possessed more than a cursory knowledge of Plato and Aristotle, and his acquaintance with the literatures of Greece, Rome, and Italy was wide if not accurate. In the poets and chroniclers of his own tongue he was deeply read, and Chaucer was his master, beloved and imitated. In addition to his intellectual gains, Spenser, while at the university, made friends whose sympathy and interest were a constant encouragement and stimulus.

A few years after leaving Cambridge the poet counted among his friends not only Edward Kirk and Gabriel Harvey, university men, but also Sir Philip Sidney, Sir Walter Raleigh, and Lord Grey; while Lord Leicester and Queen Elizabeth herself were among his patrons. It is important to consider his relations with the aristocracy, since these relations must have broadened his outlook and have added to his knowledge of men and of affairs; while the atmosphere of the court which surrounded him for short intervals several times during the course of his life doubtless quickened his perceptions and refined his tastes. In Sidney, Raleigh, and Grey he saw living examples of the knightly heroes whose valor and generosity had filled his boyish soul with admiration; and in the brilliant spectacles at court and at Lord Leicester's house he witnessed scenes that needed only the transmuting touch of genius to become worthy of fairy-land itself. The rapid development of his powers was doubtless due in part to his association with these cultivated men of the court and to the knowledge that their warm appreciation was sure to greet his best efforts. But if Spenser saw and profited by the better side of court life, he was not blind to the baser elements that went to make up that brilliant society. The following lines are from his poem, *Colin Clout's Come Home Again:*

> For, sooth to say, it is no sort of life,
>   For shepherd fit to lead in that same place,
> Where each one seeks with malice, and with strife,
>   To thrust down other into foul disgrace,
> Himself to raise : and he doth soonest rise
>   That best can handle his deceitful wit
> In subtle shifts, and finest sleights devise.

In his satire, *Prosopopoia, or Mother Hubbard's Tale*, Spenser makes us aware that his experience at court was not altogether a happy one :

> Most miserable man, whom wicked fate
>   Hath brought to Court, to sue for had ywist,[1]
> That few have found, and many one hath missed !
> Full little knowest thou, that hast not tried,
> What hell it is in suing long to bide :
> To lose good days, that might be better spent ;
> To waste long nights in pensive discontent ;
> To speed to-day, to be put back to-morrow ;
> To feed on hope, to pine with fear and sorrow ;
> To have thy Princes' grace, yet want her Peers' ;
> To have thy asking, yet wait many years ;
> To fret thy soul with crosses and with cares ;
> To eat thy heart through comfortless despairs ;
> To fawn, to crouch, to wait, to ride, to run,
> To spend, to give, to want, to be undone.
> Unhappy wight, born to disastrous end,
> That doth his life in so long tendance spend.

The years spent in Ireland — except for short visits to London, the last eighteen years of his life — must have seemed to the poet a period of exile. Taking into consideration the difficulty of communication in his time, he was doubtless farther from London, for him the cen-

---

[1] *Had ywist*, had I known ; that is, vain regret.

tre of the social and intellectual world, than is to-day the Englishman living in New Zealand. Ireland in the 16th century was peopled by barbarous, turbulent people — Catholics for the most part — who were, for sufficiently good reasons, bitterly opposed to English rule. Spenser speaks of the "good Lord Grey," whom he portrays in the *Faery Queene* as Artegall, the knight of Justice, as "most gentle, affable, loving, and temperate; always known to be a most just, sincere, godly, and right noble man, far from sternness, far from unrighteousness"; and yet, he admits that the Lord-Deputy left a terrible name behind him in Ireland. Church[1] says of Spenser's patron: "He was certainly a man of severe and unshrinking sense of duty, and like many great Englishmen of the time, so resolute in carrying it out to the end, that it reached, when he thought it necessary, to the point of ferocity." Were Spenser merely the gentle dreamer that some critics conceive him to be, he would, while with Lord Grey, have shut his eyes so far as he could to the barbarous scenes of English rule (or misrule), and have taken refuge in the more attractive world of the imagination. Instead of this, we find him some years later writing his "View of the Present State of Ireland," in which he proposes a plan for the reformation of the rebellious island. Like our greatest English writers, — Shakespeare, Milton, and Chaucer, — Spenser was, notwithstanding his poetic genius, a practical, clear-headed Englishman, with enough of hardness to enable him to hold his own among the ruling spirits of a turbulent age.

[1] *Spenser*, by R. W. Church, in the *English Men of Letters Series*.

Kilcolman, Spenser's home, was near the hill of Aharlo, a great fastness in the Desmond Rebellion, and to the north stretched a wild country, half forest, half bog. Here, except for short visits to London, the poet lived in retirement. He did, it is true, make occasional trips to Dublin, where he had a small circle of English friends who sympathized to a certain degree with his literary tastes. Painful as this banishment may have been for the man Spenser, the poet could hardly have found a place better calculated to develop his peculiar genius. A painter of contemporary manners like Pope would have suffered intellectual starvation amid these hills and bogs; but the man who was to create the fairy-land of Gloriana and then lose himself in its interminable mazes needed to be where outward things would not distract his mind. Bunyan wrote his allegory in Bedford jail; Milton saw the wonders of heaven and hell after his eyes were closed to the actual world; and Spenser, forgetting the loneliness of his position, could transform the scenes of violence and disorder, whose echoes reached him, into glorious knightly achievements, and could people the wild solitudes of Kilcolman with the varied creations of his fertile imagination. Speaking of the *Faery Queene*, Church says: "The realities of the Irish wars and of Irish social and political life gave a real subject, gave body and form to the allegory. . . . There in visible fact were the vices and falsehoods which Arthur and his companions were to quell and punish. . . . The allegory bodies forth the life of man in all conditions and at all times. But Spenser could never have seen in England such a strong and perfect image of the allegory itself — with the wild wanderings of its personages, its daily chances of battle and danger, its hairbreadth escapes, its strange encounters, its prevailing anarchy and violence, its normal absence of law and order — as he had continually and customarily before him in Ireland."

While we learn from the biographies of Spenser a good deal about the circumstances of the poet's life, we find in them little regarding his personal character. We know that he had the artist's feeling for beauty and that he was a seeker after the ideal. We know, too, that he loved his country and admired his queen, — for we cannot consider his extravagant expressions in regard to Elizabeth as mere adulation, — and that he felt the most cordial hatred for the pope, the Spaniard, and all whom he looked upon as England's enemies. From the *Epithalamion* we infer that he was able to invest those dearest to him with something of that ideal beauty which was always seeking expression in his writings. Perhaps, however, the most admirable trait that has been preserved for us is his chivalric constancy in friendship. Living as he did in an age of patronage, an age in which the struggling genius must look to those high in rank for the means that should enable him to prosecute his work, Spenser might easily, in the struggle for existence, have forgotten to be grateful. Eager for his own advancement, he might have sought always the favor of those whose smiles would insure success. This was not the case with the poet. Although his friend and patron, Lord Grey de Wilton, was recalled from Ireland to England and censured by the home government for his unsuccessful though strenuous efforts at ruling the turbulent island that had been placed under his control, Spenser, in his *View of the Present State of Ireland*, heartily commended the administration of the Lord-Deputy. Besides, he introduced him into the *Faery Queene* as Artegall, the knight of Justice. Earlier in his career, when writing the *Shepherd's Calendar*, the poet chose as the pattern of a true Christian pastor his former patron, Archbishop Grindal, — whom he denominated Algrind, — although at that very time the bishop was suffering under the displeasure of the court. One familiar with the jealousies and intrigues of Elizabeth's court will realize that the course pursued by Spenser in the instances referred to gives evidence not only of constancy in friendship but of high moral courage as well.

Besides the *Faery Queene*, Spenser wrote: the *Shepherd's Calendar*, a collection of pastoral poems, one for each month in the year; *Prosopopoia, or Mother Hubbard's Tale*, a satirical fable; *Colin Clout's Come Home Again*, a fanciful account of the poet's trip to England with Raleigh and of his presentation to the queen; *Astrophel, a Pastoral Elegy upon the Death of the most Noble and Valorous Knight, Sir Philip Sidney; Prothalamion, or a Spousal Verse; Epithalamion*, a poem celebrating the poet's own marriage; four *Hymns* in honor of *Love, Beauty, Heavenly Love*, and *Heavenly Beauty;* and numerous other poems, among them a large number of sonnets. In addition to these poetical works, he left behind him the prose treatise, *View of the Present State of Ireland*, and several letters.

The poet who can write interesting narratives, keen satires, fanciful allegories, and lyrics of marvellous beauty is certainly not a one-sided genius. At the same time Spenser has, with the exception of Britomart, created no living character; and on occasions Britomart, even, becomes shadowy, unsubstantial. The author of the *Faery Queene* lacks dramatic power and is wanting also in the constructive ability that goes to the making of great epics. He is, too, devoid of passion, unless an absorbing love for the good and the beautiful may be counted as passion. Not once in all his poems does he, like Shakespeare, touch those chords that awaken an echo in the deepest recesses of the human heart ; nor does he, like Wordsworth, find a new and hidden beauty in the " meanest flower that blows." And yet Milton calls him "a better teacher than Scotus or Aquinas," and Wordsworth in his *Prelude* says :

> And that gentle Bard,
> Chosen by the muses for their page of State,
> Sweet Spenser, moving through his clouded heaven
> With the moon's beauty and the moon's soft pace,
> I called him Brother, Englishman, and Friend.

Brother and friend he has in truth been to his fellow-craftsmen from his own time to ours, — and master as well. His title, "the poets' poet," is no empty phrase. When he began to write England had for a hundred and fifty years been without a great poet. Chaucer with his archaic forms could no longer serve as teacher and inspirer, and the verse-makers, lacking an English model, looked to Italy for instruction in their art. Spenser revealed to his contemporaries the capacities of the English tongue. A master of poetic form, and sensitive to the subtlest harmonies of language, he taught the writers of the 16th century how to use the resources at their command; and echoes of his melodious phrases may be detected in some of the latest productions of English literature. The Spenserian stanza — the stanza of the *Faery Queene* — still remains one of the chief forms of English verse. However, it is not simply because of his artistic qualities that Spenser has exercised an important influence upon the development of English poetry. His characteristic charm lies in the fact that better than any other poet of his nation he knows how to communicate to his readers the joy that comes from the contemplation of ideal beauty. His poetry, it is true, does not cause that ecstatic thrill which is akin to pain; rather it gives a calm and serene happiness, the result of long companionship with what is pure and high. "The noblest mind the best contentment has," Spenser tells us. In the *Faery Queene* life is represented as a conflict in which the good are often hard pressed. Still, we are not troubled; for the eternal forces are at work and the victory is sure. As we read, the sense of earthly limitations passes away, and we find ourselves in a new world where we gladly linger, charmed and detained by the long swell of the Spenserian stanza. Lowell has called this world, "the land of pure heart's ease, where no ache or sorrow of spirit can enter."

Spenser is, as we have seen, peculiarly the representative of his own age in its higher aspects. As in the more realistic of the Elizabethan dramatists we see pictured the actual life of the time, so in Spenser we find the beliefs, the dreams, the ideals of his contemporaries. The cultivated men of his day read Plato and Aristotle, and enjoyed Homer, Virgil, Boccaccio, and Ariosto; and we find reproduced in Spenser's poems the thoughts and images of these writers. Their own past had likewise its charm for the men of Elizabeth's court; and Spenser, an avowed disciple of Chaucer, steeped himself in old chronicles and romances, and found an irresistible attraction in the forms of a rapidly decaying feudalism. Spenser is the poet of the Renaissance with its love of learning, its feeling for the artistic in form and color, its new delight in life, its faith in the possibilities of human achievement. At the same time he never forgets that life is a struggle; and underneath his most glowing pictures may be found the noble aims and the high ideals of the Puritan. As we read his poetry, the past, touched with a glory not its own, lives once more in our imagination; and we gain the culture that comes through sympathy with interests remote from those of to-day. Our ears, trained by a skilled musician, learn to trace with delight the hitherto unsuspected harmonies of the great masters of verse. But more than this is won if the poet accomplishes his purpose; for in his letter to Raleigh he says, speaking of the *Faery Queene:* "The generall end, therefore, of all the booke is to fashion a gentleman or noble person in vertuous and gentle discipline"; and surely we must gain in virtue and in magnanimity if we associate with the generous and noble spirit of Spenser.

In his letter to Sir Walter Raleigh (which follows this chapter), Spenser tells the purpose and the plan of the *Faery Queene*. The plan, however, was never carried out; for but six of the twelve books proposed, and fragments of a seventh, were given to the world. Of these books, the first "containing the Legend of the Knight of the Red Cross, or of Holiness," is the most perfect in form, and as a narrative the most complete. The interest, however, depends largely upon the allegory underlying the poem. The second book, which contains "The Legend of Sir Guyon, or of Temperance," though less artistic than the first, has passages of surpassing beauty and possesses some interest as a narrative. In both these books, however, the characters are abstractions. The third book, "containing the Legend of Britomartis, or of Chastity," introduces a clearly defined character; for Britomart, while she represents an abstract quality, is herself a woman with the graces and the failings of her sex. Indeed, as he sees her searching for her unknown lover, accompanied by the gentle Amoret, the reader cannot fail to be reminded of Shakespeare's Rosalind and her faithful cousin, Celia. The story of Britomart's adventures is continued through the fourth book, containing the "Legend of Cambel and Triamond, or of Friendship," and the fifth which contains the "Legend of Artegall, or of Justice." In reading the three books, however, it is difficult to keep Britomart in view, so numerous are the characters introduced and so confusing the account of their adventures. Of course the careful student of Spenser will read the entire *Faery Queene*, will trace the underlying allegories, will seek the sources from which the poet derived many of his ideas and images, and will look up allusions to the events and the personages of the time. The general student of English literature, however, may find in the narrative here presented a production especially calculated to arouse his interest and to stimulate him to the further study of the poet. The poem has a peculiar value in connection with the study of the institutions of Chivalry; and on this account it may be classed with Chaucer's *Knightes Tale*, with Scott's romantic poems, and with Tennyson's *Idylls of the King*.

The stanza employed in the *Faery Queene* should be carefully examined. While it is said to be a modification of the Italian "ottava rima," it differs sufficiently from the Italian stanza to be considered Spenser's own creation. It will be noticed that the first eight lines consist each of five, and the ninth line of six iambic feet; and it will be observed that irregularities in metre are occasionally introduced for the sake of emphasis, or to break the monotony of the rythm. Mr. Corson in his *Primer of English Verse* has an excellent article on the Spenserian stanza.

Some attention should be paid to Spenser's peculiar use of language. He was for some reason attracted by the older rather than the newer forms of his day. Such old forms as *ydrad* for dreaded, *yclad* for clad, and *yold* for yielded occur frequently; he uses *ne* with not—the double negative; while old words not to be found in Shakespeare and other writers only a few years younger than himself, are at times employed by him.

It is said that his vocabulary, notwithstanding his occasional use of foreign idioms, is more Germanic than that of any other great English poet. It must be confessed that he sometimes uses language arbitrarily, twisting the meaning of a word, or altering the form or the accent to suit his artistic purposes. For this reason the philologist looks a little askance at his productions.

The student will do well to consult Mr. Frederic I. Carpenter's *Outline Guide to the Study of Spenser*, where he will find lists of books that may be used with advantage. The following works will be found useful : complete works of Spenser edited by Grosart ; the Globe edition of Spenser edited by Morris, with a memoir by Hales; Professor Child's edition of Spenser's poems ; Books I and II of the *Faery Queene* edited by Kitchin ; Book I of the *Faery Queene* edited by Percival ; *Selections from Spenser* by Professor Gummere, in the Athenæum Press series (announced) ; *Spenser* by R. W. Church, in the *English Men of Letters* series ; Green's *History of the English People;* Taine's *History of English Literature;* Brooke's *Primer of English Literature;* Corson's *Primer of English Verse;* Dowden's *Transcripts and Studies;* Craik's *Spenser and His Poetry;* and Lowell's *Among My Books*, 2d series (Vol. IV of the Riverside edition of his writings).

A LETTER of the Authors expounding his whole intention in the course of this worke [1]; which, for that it giveth great light to the reader, for the better understanding is hereunto annexed.

TO THE RIGHT NOBLE AND VALOROUS

SIR WALTER RALEIGH, KNIGHT,

Lo: Wardein of the Stanneries,[2] *and her majesties lieutenaunt of the countie of Cornewayll.*

SIR,

Knowing how doubtfully all Allegories may be construed, and this booke of mine, which I have entituled *The Faery Queene*, being a continued Allegorie, or darke conceit,[3] I have thought good, as well for avoyding of jealous[4] opinions and misconstructions, as also for your better light in reading thereof, (being so, by you commanded) to discover unto you the generall intention and meaning, which in the whole course thereof I have fashioned, without expressing of any particular purposes, or by-accidents therein occasioned. The generall end therefore of all the booke, is to fashion a gentleman or noble person in vertuous and gentle discipline. Which for that I conceived shoulde be most plausible and pleasing, beeing coloured with an historicall fiction, the

---

[1] This worke. The letter served as an introduction to the first three books of the *Faery Queene*.

[2] Stanneries, stannaries, tin mines or tin works.

[3] Darke conceit, mysterious or obscure conception or design.

[4] Jealous, suspicious.

which the most part of men delight to read, rather for varietie of matter than for profit of the ensample : I chose the historie of king Arthure, as most fit for the excellencie of his person, beeing made famous by many mens former workes, and also furthest from the danger of envie,[1] and suspicion of present time. In which I have followed all the antique poets historicall: first Homer, who in the persons of Agamemnon and Ulysses hath ensampled[2] a good governour and a vertuous man, the one in his Ilias, the other in his Odysseis : then Virgil, whose like intention was to doe in the person of Æneas: after him Ariosto comprised them both in his Orlando : and lately Tasso dissevered them againe, and formed both parts in two persons, namely, that part which they in philosophy call *Ethice*, or vertues of a private man, coloured in his Rinaldo : the other named *Politice*, in his Godfredo. By ensample of which excellent Poets, I laboure to pourtraict in Arthure, before he was king, the image of a brave knight, perfected in the twelve private morall vertues, as Aristotle hath devised : which if I find to be well accepted, I may be perhaps encoraged to frame the other part of pollitike vertues in his person, after he came to bee king.

To some I know this Methode will seem displeasant, which had rather have good discipline delivered plainly in way of precepts, or sermoned at large, as they use, then[3] thus clowdily enwrapped in Allegoricall devises. But such, mee seeme, should be satisfied with the use of these dayes, seeing all things accounted by their showes, and nothing esteemed of, that is not delightfull and pleasing to common sense. For this cause is Xenophon preferred before Plato, for that the one, in the exquisite depth of his judgement,

[1] Envie, ill will, hatred.
[2] Ensampled, given an example of.
[3] Then, than.

formed a Commune-wealth, such as it should be; but the other, in the person of Cyrus and the Persians, fashioned a government, such as might best be: So much more profitable and gracious is doctrine by ensample then by rule. So have I laboured to do in the person of Arthure: whom I conceive, after his long education by Timon (to whom he was by Merlin delivered to be brought up, so soone as he was borne of the Lady Igrayne) to have seen in a dreame or vision the Faerie Queene, with whose excellent beautie ravished, hee awaking, resolved to seek her out: and so, being by Merlin armed, and by Timon throughly instructed, he went to seeke her forth in Faery land. In that Faery Queene I mean *Glory* in my generall intention: but in my particular I conceive the most excellent and glorious person of our soveraine the Queene, and her kingdome in Faery land. And yet, in some places else, I doe otherwise shadow[1] her. For considering shee beareth two persons, the one of a most royall Queene or Empresse, the other of a most vertuous and beautifull lady, this latter part in some places I doe expresse in Belphoebe, fashioning her name according to your owne excellent conceipt of Cynthia,[2] (Phoebe and Cynthia being both names of Diana.) So in the person of Prince Arthure I sette forth magnificence in particular, which vertue, for that (according to Aristotle and the rest) it is the perfection of all the rest, and containeth in it them all, therefore in the whole course I mention the deeds of Arthure appliable to the vertue, which I write of in that booke. But of the twelve other vertues I make XII other knights the patrons, for the more varietie of the historie: Of which these three bookes contain three. The first, of the Knight of the Red crosse, in whom I expresse Holinesse: the second of Sir Guyon, in whome I set foorth Temperance: the

---

[1] Shadow, represent typically.
[2] Cynthia, an allusion to Sir Walter Raleigh's poem "Cynthia."

third of Britomartis, a Lady knight, in whom I picture Chastitie. But because the beginning of the whole worke seemeth abrupt and as depending upon other antecedents, it needs that yee know the occasion of these three knights severall adventures. For the Methode of a Poet historicall is not such as of an Historiographer. For an Historiographer discourseth of affaires orderly as they were done, accounting as well the times as the actions; but a Poet thrusteth into the middest, even where it most concerneth him, and there recoursing to the things forepast, and divining of things to come, maketh a pleasing analysis of all. The beginning therefore of my historie, if it were to be told by an Historiographer, should be the twelfth booke, which is the last; where I devise that the Faery Queene kept her annuall feast twelve daies; uppon which twelve severall dayes, the occasions of the twelve severall adventures hapned, which being undertaken by XII severall knights, are in these twelve books severally handled and discoursed.

The first was this. In the beginning of the feast, there presented him selfe a tall clownish younge man, who falling before the Queene of Faeries desired a boone (as the manner then was) which during that feast she might not refuse: which was that hee might have the atchievement of any adventure, which during that feast should happen; that being granted, he rested him selfe on the floore, unfit through his rusticitie for a better place. Soone after entred a faire Ladie in mourning weedes,[1] riding on a white Asse, with a dwarfe behind her leading a warlike steed, that bore the Armes of a knight, and his speare in the dwarfes hand. She falling before the Queene of Faeries, complayned that her father and mother, an ancient King and Queene, had bene by an huge dragon many yeers shut up in a brazen Castle, who thence suffered them not to issew: and therefore

[1] Weedes, garments.

besought the Faery Queene to assigne her some one of her knights to take on him that exployt. Presently[1] that clownish person upstarting, desired that adventure ; whereat the Queene much wondering, and the Lady much gaine-saying, yet he earnestly importuned his desire. In the end the Lady told him, that unlesse that armour which she brought would serve him (that is, the armour of a Christian man specified by Saint Paul, V. Ephes.) that he could not succeed in that enterprise: which being forth with put upon him with due furnitures thereunto, he seemed the goodliest man in al that company, and was well liked of the Lady. And eftesoones[2] taking on him knighthood, and mounting on that straunge Courser, he went forth with her on that adventure : where beginneth the first booke, viz.

 A gentle knight was pricking on the playne, etc.

The second day there came in a Palmer bearing an Infant with bloody hands, whose Parents he complained to have bene slaine by an enchauntresse called Acrasia : and therefore craved of the Faery Queene, to appoint him some knight to performe that adventure, which being assigned to Sir Guyon, he presently went foorth with the same Palmer: which is the beginning of the second booke and the whole subject thereof. The third day there came in a Groome,[3] who complained before the Faery Queene, that a vile Enchaunter, called Busirane, had in hand a most faire Lady, called Amoretta, whom he kept in most grevious torment. Whereupon Sir Scudamour, the lover of that Lady, presently tooke on him that adventure. But beeing unable to performe it by reason of the hard Enchauntments, after long

---

[1] Presently, immediately.
[2] Eftesoones, immediately.
[3] Groome, servant.

sorrow, in the end met with Britomartis, who succoured him, and reskewed his love.

But by occasion hereof, many other adventures are intermedled; but rather as accidents then intendments. As the love of Britomart, the overthrow of Marinell, the miserie of Florimell, the vertuousness of Belphoebe; and many the like.

Thus much, Sir, I have briefly-over-run to direct your understanding to the wel-head of the History, that from thence gathering the whole intention of the conceit, ye may as in a handfull gripe all the discourse, which otherwise may happely seem tedious and confused. So humbly craving the continuance of your honourable favour towards me, and th' eternall establishment of your happines, I humbly take leave.

     Yours most humbly affectionate,

             EDM. SPENSER.

23 Januarie, 1589.

BRITOMART.

1. It falls me[1] here to write of chastity,
   That fairest virtue far above the rest:
   For which what needs me fetch from Faëry[2]
   Foreign ensamples it to have expressed?
   Sith[3] it is shrinèd in my sovereign's breast,
   And formed so lively in each perfect part,
   That to all ladies, which have it professed,
   Need but behold the portrait of her heart;
   If portrayed it might be by any living art:

2. But living art may not least part express,
   Nor life-resembling pencil it can paint:
   All were it[4] Zeuxis[5] or Praxiteles,[6]
   His dædale[7] hand would fail and greatly faint,
   And her perfections with his error taint:

NOTE.—Britomart is the knight of chastity. The name denotes a martial Britoness, as Spenser uses it. It is really one of the names of Diana.

[1] *Falls me*, falls to me, falls to my lot.
[2] *Faëry*, faeryland, fairyland.
[3] *Sith*, since.
[4] *All were it*, although it were.
[5] *Zeuxis*, a celebrated Greek painter who lived during the latter half of the 5th century B.C.
[6] *Praxiteles*, a famous Greek sculptor who flourished about 350 B.C.
[7] *Dædale*, skilful.

Ne[1] poet's wit, that passeth painter far
In picturing the parts of beauty daint,[2]
So hard a workmanship adventure darre,
For fear through want of words her excellence to mar.

3 How then shall I, apprentice of the skill
That whilom[3] in divinest wits did reign,
Presume so high to stretch mine humble quill?
Yet now my luckless lot doth me constrain
Hereto perforce: but, O dread sovereign,
Thus far forth pardon, sith that choicest wit
Cannot your glorious portrait figure plain,
That I in colored shows may shadow it;
And ántique praises unto present persons fit.

4 But if in living colours, and right hue,
Thyself thou covet to see picturèd,
Who can it do more lively, or more true,
Than that sweet verse, with nectar sprinkelèd
In which a gracious servant[4] picturèd
His Cynthia, his heaven's fairest light?
That with his melting sweetness ravishèd,
And with the wonder of her beamës bright,
My senses lullèd are in slumber of delight.

5 But let that same delicious poet lend
A little leave unto a rustic muse

---

[1] *Ne*, nor.
[2] *Daint*, dainty.
[3] *Whilom*, formerly.
[4] *A gracious servant*, i.e. Sir Walter Raleigh who wrote a poem called "Cynthia." Queen Elizabeth, being unmarried, was often called Cynthia, — another name for the virgin goddess, Diana.

To sing his mistress' praise; and let him mend,
If ought amiss her liking may abuse:
Ne let his fairest Cynthia refuse
In mirrors more than one herself to see;
But either Gloriana[1] let her choose,
Or in Belphoebe[2] fashionèd to be;
In th' one her rule, in th' other her rare chastity.

[1] *Gloriana*, the queen of Faeryland, beloved by Prince Arthur.

[2] *Belphoebe*, a character in books III and IV of the "Faery Queene."

I.

Britomart encounters Prince Arthur and Sir Guyon. After separating from them, she passes on to Castle Joyous where she falls in with the Redcross knight.

1   THE famous Briton prince[1] and faery knight,[2]
   After long ways and perilous pains endured,
   Having their weary limbs to perfect plight
   Restored, and sorry wounds right well recured,
   Of the fair Alma[3] greatly were procured[4]
   To make there lenger sojourn and abode;
   But, when thereto they might not be allured
   From seeking praise and deeds of arms abrode,
   They courteous congé[5] took, and forth together yode.[6]

2   Long so they travellèd through wasteful ways,[7]
   Where dangers dwelt, and perils most did won,[8]
   To hunt for glory and renowmèd[9] praise:

[1] *The famous Briton prince*, Prince Arthur, the perfect knight, who is in love with Gloriana, the queen of Faeryland.

[2] *Faery knight.* All Gloriana's champions are called faery knights. The one here mentioned is Guyon, the knight of Temperance.

[3] *Alma*, the lady of the house of Temperance. The two warriors have been enjoying her hospitality after a perilous adventure.

[4] *Procured*, entreated.

[5] *Congé*, leave.

[6] *Yode*, went.

[7] *Wasteful ways*, waste places, desolate places.

[8] *Won*, dwell.

[9] *Renowmed*. Spenser seems to prefer the form renowm to the modern form.

Full many countries they did overrun,
From the uprising to the setting sun,
And many hard adventures did achieve;
Of all the which they honour ever won,
Seeking the weak oppressèd to relieve,
And to recover right for such as wrong did grieve.

3 At last, as through an open plain they yode,
They spied a knight that tówards prickèd[1] fair;
And him beside an aged squire there rode,
That seemed to couch[2] under his shield three-square,[3]
As if that age bade him that burden spare,
And yield it those that stouter[4] could it wield:
He, them espying, gan himself prepare,
And on his arm address his goodly shield
That bore a lion passant[5] in a golden field.[6]

4 Which seeing, good Sir Guyon dear besought
The prince, of grace, to let him run that turn.
He granted: then the Faery quickly raught[7]
His poignant[8] spear, and sharply gan to spurn[9]
His foamy steed, whose fiery feet did burn
The verdant grass as he thereon did tread;
Ne did the other back his foot return,

---

[1] *Pricked*, spurred onward.
[2] *Couch*, bend.
[3] *Three-square*, having three equal sides.
[4] *Stouter*, more boldly.
[5] *Passant*, walking.
[6] *Field*, term in heraldry for the surface of a shield. Britomart bore the legendary arms of Brute, her ancestor.
[7] *Raught*, reached.
[8] *Poignant*, sharp.
[9] *Spurn*, spur.

But fiercely forward came withouten dread,
And bent his dreadful spear against the other's head.

5 They been ymet, and both their points arrived ;
But Guyon drove so furious and fell,[1]
That seemed both shield and plate it would have rived[2] ;
Natheless[3] it bore his foe not from his sell,[4]
But made him stagger, as he were not well :
But Guyon self, ere well he was aware,
Nigh a spear's length behind his crouper fell ;
Yet in his fall so well himself he bare,
That mischievous mischance his life and limbs did spare.

6 Great shame and sorrow of that fall he took ;
For never yet, sith warlike arms he bore
And shivering spear in bloody field first shook,
He found himself dishonourèd so sore.
Ah ! gentlest knight that ever armour bore,
Let not thee grieve dismounted to have been,
And brought to ground, that never wast before ;
For not thy fault, but secret pow'r unseen ;
That spear enchanted was which laid thee on the green !

7 But weenedst thou what wight[5] thee overthrew,
Much greater grief and shamefuller regret
For thy hard fortune then thou wouldst renew,
That of a single[6] damsel thou wert met

[1] *Fell*, fiercely.
[2] *Rived*, torn apart.
[3] *Natheless*, nevertheless.
[4] *Sell*, saddle.
[5] *Wight*, person.
[6] *Single*, weak.

On equal plain, and there so hard beset :
Even the famous Britomart it was,
Whom strange adventure did from Britain fett [1]
To seek her lover, (love far sought, alas !)
Whose image she had seen in Venus' looking-glass.

8 Full of disdainful wrath, he fierce uprose
For to revenge that foul reproachful shame,
And, snatching his bright sword, began to close
With her on foot, and stoutly forward came ;
Die rather would he then [2] endure that same.
Which when his palmer [3] saw, he gan to fear
His tóward [4] peril, and untoward [5] blame,
Which by that new rencounter he should rear [6] ;
For death sat on the point of that enchanted spear :

9 And hasting towards him gan fair persuade
Not to provoke misfortune, nor to ween [7]
His spear's default to mend with cruel blade ;
For by his mighty science he had seen
The secret virtue of that weapon keen,
That mortal puissance mote [8] not withstand :
Nothing on earth mote always happy [9] been !
Great hazard were it, and adventure fond, [10]
To lose long-gotten honour with one evil hond. [11]

[1] *Fett*, fetch.
[2] *Then*, than ; this form occurs frequently in the poem.
[3] *Palmer*, a wandering religious votary. Palms were sometimes carried by a palmer, as a sign that he had been to the Holy Land.
[4] *Toward*, near at hand.
[5] *Untoward*, troublesome, vexatious.
[6] *Rear*, raise, bring upon himself.
[7] *Ween*, think.
[8] *Mote*, might.
[9] *Happy*, successful.
[10] *Fond*, foolish.
[11] *Hond*, act.

10 By such good means he him discounsellèd¹
   From prosecuting his revenging rage :
   And eke² the prince like treaty handelèd,³
   His wrathful will with reason to assuage ;
   And laid the blame, not to his carriäge,
   But to his starting steed that swarved aside,
   And to the ill purveyance of his page,
   That had his furnitures⁴ not firmly tied :
   So is his angry corage⁵ fairly pacified.

11 Thus reconcilement was between them knit,
   Through goodly temperance and affection chaste ;
   And either vowed with all their power and wit
   To let not other's honour be defaced
   Of friend or foe, whoever it embaste,⁶
   Ne arms to bear against the other's side :
   In which accord⁷ the prince was also placed,
   And with that golden chain of concord tied :
   So goodly all agreed, they forth yfere⁸ did ride.

12 O, goodly usage of those ántique times,
   In which the sword was servant unto right !
   When not for malice and contentious crimes,
   But all for praise, and proof of manly might,
   The martial brood accustomèd to fight :
   Then honour was the meed of victory,
   And yet the vanquishèd had no despite⁹:

---

¹ *Discounselled*, dissuaded.
² *Eke*, likewise.
³ *Like treaty handeled*, used the same argument.
⁴ *Furnitures*, equipment.
⁵ *Corage*, heart.
⁶ *Embaste*, insulted.
⁷ *Accord*, agreement.
⁸ *Yfere*, together.
⁹ *Despite*, malice, hatred.

Let later age that noble use envý,[1]
Vile rancour to avoid and cruel surquedry![2]

13 Long they thus travellèd in friendly wise,
Through countries waste, and eke well edified,[3]
Seeking adventurers hard, to exercise
Their puissance, whilom[4] full dernly[5] tried.
At length they came into a forest wide,
Whose hideous horror and sad trembling sound
Full grisly[6] seemed: therein they long did ride,
Yet tract[7] of living creature none they found,
Save bears, lions, and bulls, which roamèd them around.

14 All suddenly out of the thickest brush,
Upon a milk-white palfrey all alone,
A goodly lady did foreby[8] them rush,
Whose face did seem as clear as crystal stone,
And eke, through fear, as white as whalës bone:
Her garments all were wrought of beaten gold,
And all her steed with tinsel trappings shone,
Which fled so fast that nothing mote him hold,
And scarce them leisure gave her passing to behold.

15 Still as she fled her eye she backward threw,
As fearing evil that pursued her fast;
And her fair yellow locks behind her flew,
Loosely dispersed with puff of every blast:
All as a blazing star doth far outcast

---

[1] *Envy*, emulate.
[2] *Surquedry*, insolence.
[3] *Edified*, built.
[4] *Whilom*, formerly.
[5] *Dernly*, sadly, severely.
[6] *Grisly*, terrible.
[7] *Tract*, trace.
[8] *Foreby*, by.

His hairy beams, and flaming locks dispread,
At sight whereof the people stand aghast;
But the sage wizard tells, as he has read,
That it impórtunes[1] death and doleful dreryhed.[2]

16 So as they gazèd after her awhile,
    Lo! where a grisly[3] foster[4] forth did rush,

. . . .

His tireling jade[5] he fiercely forth did push
Through thick and thin, both over bank and bush,
In hope her to attain by hook or crook,
That[6] from his gory sides the blood did gush:
Large were his limbs, and terrible his look,
And in his clownish hand a sharp boar-spear he shook.

17 Which outrage when those gentle[7] knights did see,
    Full of great envy and fell jealousy,[8]
    They stayed not to avise[9] who first should be,
    But all spurred after, fast as they mote fly,
    To rescue her from shameful villainy.
    The prince and Guyon equally bylive[10]
    Herself pursued, in hope to win thereby
    Most goodly meed, the fairest dame alive:
    But after the foul foster Timias did strive.

[1] *Importunes*, portends.
[2] *Dreryhed*, sorrow.
[3] *Grisly*, frightful, dreadful.
[4] *Foster*, forester.
[5] *Tyreling jade*, hackney?
[6] *That*, so that.
[7] *Gentle*, high-born, noble.

[8] *Great envy and fell jealousy.* Prof. Child remarks that both envy and jealousy are here used in the sense of indignation. Fell means fierce.
[9] *Avise*, consider.
[10] *Bylive*, quickly.

18 The whiles fair Britomart, whose constant mind
   Would not so lightly follow beauty's chase,
   Ne recked of ladies' love, did stay behind;
   And them awaited there a certain space,
   To weet[1] if they would turn back to that place:
   But, when she saw them gone, she forward went,
   As lay her journey, through that perlous pace,[2]
   With steadfast courage and stout hardiment[3];
   Ne evil thing she feared, ne evil thing she meant.

19 At last, as nigh out of the wood she came,
   A stately castle far away she spied,
   To which her steps directly she did frame.
   That castle was most goodly edified,[4]
   And placed for pleasure nigh that forest side:
   But fair before the gate a spacious plain,
   Mantled with green, itself did spreaden wide,
   On which she saw six knights, that did darrayne[5]
   Fierce battle against one with cruel might and main.

20 Mainly[6] they all attonce upon him laid,
   And sore beset on every side around,
   That nigh he breathless grew, yet nought dismayed,
   Ne ever to them yielded foot of ground,
   All had he[7] lost much blood through many a wound;
   But stoutly dealt his blows, and every way,
   To which he turnèd in his wrathful stound,[8]

---

[1] *Weet*, know, learn.
[2] *Perlous pace*, perilous pass.
[3] *Hardiment*, boldness.
[4] *Edified*, built.
[5] *Darrayne*, wage.
[6] *Mainly*, strongly.
[7] *All had he*, although he had.
[8] *Stound*, moment, mood.

Made them recoil, and fly from dread decay,[1]
That none of all the six before him durst assay[2]:

21 Like dastard curs, that, having at a bay
The salvage[3] beast embossed[4] in weary chase,
Dare not adventure on the stubborn prey,
Ne[5] bite before, but roam from place to place
To get a snatch when turnèd is his face.
In such distress and doubtful jeopardy
When Britomart him saw, she ran apace[6]
Unto his rescue, and with earnest cry
Bade those same six forbear that single enemy.

22 But to her cry they list not[7] lenden ear,
Ne aught the more their mighty strokes surcease[8];
But, gathering him round about more near,
Their direful rancour rather did increase;
Till that she rushing through the thickest preasse[9]
Perforce disparted their compacted gyre,[10]
And soon compelled to hearken unto peace:
Tho[11] gan she mildly of them to inquire
The cause of their dissention and outrageous ire.

23 Whereto that single knight did answer frame:
"These six would me enforce, by odds of might,
To change my liefe,[12] and love another dame;

---

[1] *Decay*, destruction.
[2] *Before him durst assay*, dared attack him in front.
[3] *Salvage*, wild.
[4] *Embossed*, tired out.
[5] *Ne*, nor.
[6] *Apace*, quickly.
[7] *List not*, cared not to.
[8] *Surcease*, cause to cease.
[9] *Preasse*, crowd.
[10] *Gyre*, circle.
[11] *Tho*, then.
[12] *Liefe*, love.

That death me liefer[1] were then such despite,[2]
So unto wrong to yield my wrested right :
For I love one, the truest one on ground,
Ne list me[3] change ; she th' Errant Damsel[4] hight[5];
For whose dear sake full many a bitter stound[6]
I have endured, and tasted many a bloody wound."

24 "Certes,"[7] said she, " then been ye six to blame,
To ween[8] your wrong by force to justify :
For knight to leave his lady were great shame
That faithful is ; and better were to die.
All loss is less, and less the infamy,
Than loss of love to him that loves but one :
Ne may love be compelled by maistery[9];
For, soon as maistery comes, sweet love anon
Taketh his nimble wings, and soon away is gone."

25 Then spake one of those six : " There dwelleth here
Within this castle wall a lady fair,
Whose sovereign beauty hath no living pere[10];
Thereto so bounteous and so debonaire,[11]
That never any mote[12] with her compare :

---

[1] *Liefer*, preferable.
[2] *That death me liefer were then such despite, i.e.* I would rather die than do what I should so scorn to do.
[3] *Ne list me*, nor do I desire to.
[4] *Errant Damsel, i.e.* Una, the heroine of the first book of the "Faery Queene." This "single knight" is her champion, and he is called the Redcross knight because :

". . . on his breast a bloody cross he bore,
The dear remembrance of his dying Lord."

[5] *Hight*, is called.
[6] *Stound*, peril.
[7] *Certes*, certainly.
[8] *Ween*, think.
[9] *Maistery*, superior power.
[10] *Pere*, peer.
[11] *Debonaire*, gracious.
[12] *Mote*, may.

>She hath ordained this law, which we approve,
>That every knight which doth this way repair,
>In case he have no lady nor no love,
>Shall do unto her service, never to remove:

26 "But if he have a lady or a love,
>Then must he her forego with foul defame,[1]
>Or else with us by dint[2] of sword approve[3]
>That she is fairer than our fairest dame;
>As did this knight, before ye hither came."
>"Perdy,"[4] said Britomart, "the choice is hard!
>But what reward had he that overcame?"
>"He should advancèd be to high regard,"
>Said they, "and have our lady's love for his reward.

27 "Therefore aread,[5] sir, if thou have a love."
>"Love have I sure," quoth she, "but lady none;
>Yet will I not fro mine own love remove,
>Ne to your lady will I service done,[6]
>But wreak your wrongs wrought to this knight alone,
>And prove his cause." With that, her mortal[7] spear
>She mightily aventred[8] tówards one,
>And down him smote ere well aware he weare[9];
>Then to the next she rode, and down the next did bear.

28 Ne did she stay till three on ground she laid,
>That[10] none of them himself could rear again:

[1] *Defame*, dishonor.
[2] *Dint*, stroke.
[3] *Approve*, prove.
[4] *Perdy*, truly.
[5] *Aread*, declare.
[6] *Done*, do.
[7] *Mortal*, death-giving.
[8] *Aventred*, aimed.
[9] *Weare*, were.
[10] *That*, so that.

The fourth was by that other knight dismayed,
All were he[1] weary of his former pain;
That now there do but two of six remain;
Which two did yield before she did them smite.
"Ah!" said she then, "now may ye all see plain,
That truth is strong, and true love most of might,
That for his trusty servants doth so strongly fight."

29 "Too well we see," said they, "and prove too well
Our faulty weakness, and your matchless might:
Forthy,[2] fair sir, yours be the damosel,
Which by her own law to your lot doth light,
And we your liegemen faith unto you plight."
So underneath her feet their swords they mard,[3]
And, after, her besought, well as they might,
To enter in and reap the due reward:
She granted; and then in they all together far'd.[4]

30 Long were it to describe the goodly frame
And stately port of Castle Joyeous,[5]
(For so that castle hight[6] by common name),
Where they were entertained with courteous
And comely glee of many gracious
Fair ladies, and of many a gentle knight;
Who, through a chamber long and spacious,
Eftsoones[7] them brought unto their lady's sight,
That of them cleepèd[8] was the Lady of Delight.

[1] *All were he*, although he was.
[2] *Forthy*, therefore.
[3] *Mard*, debased.
[4] *Fared*, went.
[5] *Joyeous;* the final syllable is pronounced as two syllables. The same is true of *gracious* and *spacious*.
[6] *Hight*, was called.
[7] *Eftsoones*, speedily.
[8] *Cleeped*, called.

31 But, for to tell the sumptuous array
    Of that great chamber, should be labour lost;
    For living wit, I ween, cannot display
    The royal riches and exceeding cost
    Of every pillar and of every post,
    Which all of purest bullion framèd were,
    And with great pearls and precious stones
        embossed[1];
    That the bright glister of their beamës clear
    Did sparkle forth great light, and glorious did appear.

32 These stranger knights, through passing, forth
        were led
    Into an inner room, whose royalty
    And rich purveyance[2] might uneath[3] be read[4];
    Mote[5] prince's place beseem so decked to be.
    Which stately manner whenas they did see,
    The image of superfluous riotize,[6]
    Exceeding much the state of mean[7] degree,
    They greatly wond'red whence so sumptuous guise
    Might be maintained, and each gan diversely devise.[8]

33 The walls were round about apparellèd
    With costly cloths of Arras and of Toure[9];
    In which with cunning hand was portrayèd
    The love of Venus and her paramour,[10]

[1] *Embossed*, ornamented with raised work.
[2] *Purveyance*, furniture.
[3] *Uneath*, with difficulty.
[4] *Read*, imagined.
[5] *Mote*, might.
[6] *Riotize*, extravagance.
[7] *Mean*, moderate.
[8] *Devise*, imagine.
[9] *Cloths of Arras and of Toure* (*Tours*), tapestry woven at these places.
[10] *Paramour*, lover.

The fair Adonis,[1] turnèd to a flow'r;
A work of rare device and wondrous wit.
First did it show the bitter baleful stour,[2]
Which her essayed with many a fervent fit,
When first her tender heart was with his beauty smit:

34 Lo! where beyond[3] he lieth languishing,
Deadly engorèd of a great wild boar;
And by his side the goddess grovelling
Makes for him endless moan, and evermore
With her soft garment wipes away the gore
Which stains his snowy skin with hateful hue:
But, when she saw no help might him restore,
Him to a dainty flower she did transmew,[4]
Which in that cloth was wrought, as if it lively grew.

35 And all the while sweet music did divide
Her looser notes with Lydian harmony[5];
And all the while sweet birds thereto applied
Their dainty lays and dulcet melody,
Aye carrolling of love and jollity,
That wonder was to hear their trim consórt.[6]

. . . .

36 Thence they were brought to that great lady's view,
Whom they found sitting on a sumptuous bed

---

[1] *Adònis*, a beautiful youth beloved of Venus, who was killed while hunting a wild boar. The flower Adonis autumnalis — the pheasant's eye — was said to have sprung from his blood.

[2] *Stour*, distress.
[3] *Beyond*, at a distance.
[4] *Transmew*, change.
[5] *Lydian harmony;* Lydian music was said to be of a soft and voluptuous character.

[6] *Trim consort*, pleasing concert.

That glist'red all with gold and glorious shew,
As the proud Persian queens accustomèd.
She seemed a woman of great bountihead[1]
And of rare beauty, saving that askance
Her wanton eyes (ill signs of womanhead)
Did roll too lightly, and too often glance,
Without regard of grace or comely amenaunce.[2]

37 Long work it were, and needless, to devise[3]
    Their goodly entertainment and great glee:
    She causèd them be led in courteous wise
    Into a bow'r, disarmèd for to be,
    And cheerèd well with wine and spicery:
    The Redcross knight was soon disarmèd there;
    But the brave maid would not disarmèd be,
    But only vented up her umbrière,[4]
    And so did let her goodly visage to appear.

38 As when fair Cynthia,[5] in darksome night,
    Is in a noyous[6] cloud envelopèd,
    Where she may find the substance thin and light,
    Breaks forth her silver beams, and her bright head
    Discovers to the world discomfitèd,[7]
    Of the poor traveller that went astray
    With thousand blessings she is herièd[8];
    Such was the beauty and the shining ray
    With which fair Britomart gave light unto the day.

---

[1] *Bountihead*, goodness, generosity.
[2] *Amenaunce*, behavior.
[3] *Devise*, describe.
[4] *Vented up her umbrière*, raised her visor.
[5] *Cynthia*, the same as Diana, the goddess of the moon.
[6] *Noyous*, annoying, disagreeable.
[7] *Discomfited*, dejected.
[8] *Heried*, praised.

39 And eke[1] those six, which lately with her fought,
    Now were disarmed, and did themselves present
    Unto her view, and company[2] unsought;
    For they all seemèd courteous and gent,[3]
    And all six brethren, born of one parent,
    Which had them trained in all civility,
    And goodly taught to tilt and tournament;
    Now were they liegemen to this lady free,
    And her knight's service ought,[4] to hold of her in fee.[5]

40 The first of them by name Gardantè[6] hight,
    A jolly[7] person, and of comely view;
    The second was Parlantè, a bold knight;
    And next to him Jocantè did ensue[8];
    Basciantè did himself most courteous shew;
    But fierce Bacchantè seemed too fell[9] and keen;
    And yet in arms Noctantè greater grew:
    All were fair knights, and goodly well beseen[10];
    But to fair Britomart they all but shadows been.

---

[1] *Eke*, likewise.

[2] *Company*, become her companions.

[3] *Gent*, noble.

[4] *And her knight's service ought* (*owed*), *i.e.* they held land of her on condition that they should perform for her some noble or military service — such service being usually performed on horseback.

[5] *To hold of her in fee;* that is, to hold her land as a stipend for service performed, — the land so held being called a fief.

[6] *Gardantè* means a gazer or ogler; *Parlantè*, a prattler; *Jocantè*, a jester; *Basciantè*, one who kisses; *Bacchantè*, a drinker of wine; and *Noctantè*, a reveller by night.

[7] *Jolly*, handsome.

[8] *Ensue*, follow.

[9] *Fell*, fierce.

[10] *Beseen*, appearing.

41 For she was full of amiable grace
    And manly terror mixèd therewithal;
    That as the one stirred up affections base,
    So th' òther did men's rash desires appal,
    And hold them back that would in error fall:
    As he that hath espied a vermeil rose,
    To which sharp thorns and breres[1] the way forestall,
    Dare not for dread his hardy hand expose,
    But, wishing it far off, his idle wish doth lose.

42 Supper was shortly dight,[2] and down they sat;
    Where they were servèd with all sumptuous fare,
    Whiles fruitful Ceres[3] and Lyæus[4] fat
    Poured out their plenty, without spight[5] or spare;
    Nought wanted there that dainty was and rare:

    . . . .

After the meal was over, the knights and ladies amused themselves in various ways: —

43 Some fell to dance; some fell to hazardry[6];
    Some to make love; some to make merriment;
    As diverse wits to diverse things apply.

    . . . .

44 High time it seemèd then for every wight
    Them to betake unto their kindly rest:
    Eftsoones[7] long waxen torches weren light

---

[1] *Breres*, briars.
[2] *Dight*, prepared.
[3] *Ceres*, the goddess of corn and tillage.
[4] *Lyæus*, a surname given to Bacchus.
[5] *Spight*, grudge.
[6] *Hazardry*, gaming.
[7] *Eftsoones*, immediately.

Unto their bow'rs[1] to guiden every guest :
Tho,[2] when the Britoness saw all the rest
Avoided[3] quite, she gan herself despoil,[4]
And safe commit to her soft feathered nest ;
Where through long watch, and late day's weary toil,
She soundly slept, and careful thoughts did quite
    assoil.[5]

Before long, the warlike maiden waked to find herself in danger. There was a noise,—

45 . . . .

    And the whole family, therewith adread,[6]
    Rashly[7] out of their rousèd couches sprong,
    And to the troubled chamber all in arms did throng.

46 And those six knights, that lady's champions,
    And eke the Redcross knight ran to the stound,[8]
    Half armed and half unarmed, with them attons[9] :
    Where when confusèdly they came, they found
    Their lady lying on the senseless ground :
    On th' other side they saw the war-like maid
    All in her snow-white smock, with locks unbound,
    Threat'ning the point of her avenging blade ;
    That with so troublous terror they were all dismayed.

47 About their lady first they flocked around ;
    Whom having laid in comfortable couch,
    Shortly they reared out of her frozen swownd[10] ;

---

[1] *Bowers*, chambers.
[2] *Tho*, then.
[3] *Avoided*, departed.
[4] *Despoil*, unclothe.
[5] *Assoil*, put off.
[6] *Adread*, frightened.
[7] *Rashly*, hastily.
[8] *Stound*, alarm.
[9] *Attons*, together.
[10] *Swownd*, swoon.

And afterwards they gan[1] with foul reproach
To stir up strife, and troublous contecke[2] broach:
But, by ensample of the last day's loss,[3]
None of them rashly durst to her[4] approach,
Ne in so glorious spoil themselves emboss[5]:
Her succoured eke the champion of the bloody cross.[6]

48 But one of those six knights, Gardantè hight,[7]
Drew out a deadly bow and arrow keen,
Which forth he sent with felonous despite[8]
And fell intent against the virgin sheen[9]:
The mortal[10] steel stayed not till it was seen
To gore her side; yet was the wound not deep,
But lightly rasèd[11] her soft silken skin,
That[12] drops of purple blood thereout did weep,
Which did her lily smock with stains of vermeil[13] steep.

49 Wherewith enraged she fiercely at them flew,
And with her flaming sword about her laid,
That none of them foul mischief could eschew,[14]
But with her dreadful strokes were all dismayed:
Here, there, and everywhere, about her swayed
Her wrathful steel, that none mote[15] it abide;

[1] *Gan*, began.
[2] *Contecke*, contention.
[3] *By ensample of the last day's loss*, i.e. warned by the unfortunate experience of the preceding day.
[4] *Her*, i.e. Britomart.
[5] *Emboss*, fatigue.
[6] *Champion of the bloody cross*, the Redcross knight.
[7] *Hight*, called.
[8] *Despite*, malice, hatred.
[9] *Sheen*, radiant, fair.
[10] *Mortal*, deadly.
[11] *Rased*, rubbed, grazed.
[12] *That*, so that.
[13] *Vermeil*, vermillion.
[14] *Eshew*, escape from.
[15] *Mote*, might.

And eke[1] the Redcross knight gave her good aid,
Aye joining foot to foot, and side to side;
That in short space their foes they have quite
    terrified.

50 Tho[2] whenas all were put to shameful flight,
The noble Britomartis her arrayed,
And her bright arms about her body dight[3]:
For nothing would she lenger[4] there be stayed,
Where so loose life and so ungentle trade[5]
Was used of knights and ladies seeming gent[6]:
So, early, ere the gross earth's gryesy[7] shade
Was all dispersed out of the firmament,
They took their steeds, and forth upon their journey
    went.

---

[1] *Eke*, also.
[2] *Tho*, then.
[3] *Dight*, disposed.
[4] *Lenger*, longer.
[5] *Ungentle trade*, ignoble conduct.
[6] *Gent*, high-bred.
[7] *Gryesy*, moist, foggy.

II.

Britomart and the Redcross knight journey on together. Going back in his narrative, the poet tells how the maiden sees in a magic looking-glass the image of Arthegall, and how she falls in love with the unknown knight.

1 HERE have I cause in men just blame to find,
  That in their proper praise[1] too partial be,
  And not indifferent[2] to woman kind,
  To whom no share in arms and chivalry
  They do impart, ne maken memory
  Of their brave gests[3] and prowess martial:
  Scarce do they spare to one, or two, or three,
  Room in their writtes[4]; yet the same writing small
  Does all their deeds deface, and dims their glories all.

2 But by record of ántique times I find
  That women wont in wars to bear most sway,
  And to all great exploits themselves inclined,
  Of which they still the girlond[5] bore away;
  Till envious men, fearing their rule's decay,[6]
  Gan coin strait[7] laws to curb their liberty:
  Yet, sith[8] they warlike arms have laid away,

---

[1] *In their proper praise, i.e.* in praising themselves.
[2] *Indifferent*, impartial.
[3] *Gests*, deeds.
[4] *Writtes*, writings.
[5] *Girlond*, garland.
[6] *Their rule's decay, i.e.* the decline of their own authority.
[7] *Strait*, strict, rigorous.
[8] *Sith*, since.

They have excelled in arts and policy,
That[1] now we foolish men that praise gin[2] eke
   t' envy.[3]

3 Of warlike puissance in ages spent,[4]
Be thou,[5] fair Britomart, whose praise I write;
But of all wisdom be thou precedent,
O sovereign Queen,[6] whose praise I would endite,[7]
Endite I would as duty doth excite;
But ah! my rhymes too rude and rugged are,
When in[8] so high an object they do light,
And, striving fit to make, I fear do mar:
Thyself thy praises tell, and make them knowen far.

4 She, travelling with Guyon,[9] by the way
Of sundry things fair purpose[10] gan to find,[11]
T' abridge their journey long and ling'ring day:
Mongst which it fell into that Faery's[12] mind
To ask this Briton maid what uncouth[13] wind
Brought her into those parts, and what inquest[14]
Made her dissemble her disguisèd kind[15]:
Fair lady she him seemed, like lady dressed,
But fairest knight alive, when armèd was her breast.

[1] *That*, so that.
[2] *Gin*, begin.
[3] *Envy*, begrudge.
[4] *Spent*, passed.
[5] *Be thou*, i.e. be thou precedent or example.
[6] *O sovereign Queen;* Elizabeth, of course, is here referred to.
[7] *Endite*, indite.
[8] *In*, i.e. on.

[9] *Guyon;* this is a mistake; it should be the Redcross knight.
[10] *Purpose*, discourse.
[11] *Gan to find*, i.e. did find.
[12] *Faery's*, i.e. Faery knight's; *Faery* because he served the Faery Queen.
[13] *Uncouth*, strange.
[14] *Inquest*, quest or adventure.
[15] *Kind*, sex.

5 Thereat she sighing softly had no pow'r
   To speak awhile, ne ready answer make;
   But with heart-thrilling throbs and bitter stour,[1]
   As if she had a fever fit, did quake,
   And every dainty limb with horror shake;
   And ever and anon the rosy red
   Flashed through her face, as it had been a flake[2]
   Of lightning through bright heaven fulminèd[3]:
   At last, the passion past, she thus him answerèd:

6 "Fair sir, I let you weet,[4] that from the hour
   I taken was from nurse's tender pap,
   I have been trainèd up in warlike stour,[5]
   To tossen spear and shield, and to affrap[6]
   The warlike rider to his most mishap;
   Sithence[7] I loathèd have my life to lead,
   As ladies wont, in pleasure's wanton lap,
   To finger the fine needle and nice[8] thread;
   Me lever were[9] with point of foeman's spear be dead.

7 "All my delight on deeds of arms is set,
   To hunt out perils and adventures hard,
   By sea, by land, whereso they may be met,
   Only for honour and for high regard,
   Without respect of richesse or reward:
   For such intent into these parts I came,

---

[1] *Stour*, struggles.
[2] *Flake*, flash.
[3] *Fulmined*, the same as *fulminated*; to fulminate is to thunder, or to hurl lightning.
[4] *Let you weet*, inform you.
[5] *In warlike stour*, amid the din of war, amid warlike scenes.
[6] *Affrap*, strike.
[7] *Sithence*, since.
[8] *Nice*, delicate.
[9] *Me lever were*, I would rather.

Withouten compass or withouten card,[1]
Far fro my native soil, that is by name
The Greater Britain,[2] here to seek for praise and fame.

8 "Fame blazèd hath, that here in Faery-lond
Do many famous knights and ladies won,[3]
And many strange adventures to be fond,[4]
Óf which great worth and worship[5] may be won:
Which to prove, I this voyage have begun.
But mote I weet of you,[6] right courteous knight,
Tidings of one that hath unto me done
Late foul dishonour and reproachful spite,
The which I seek to wreak,[7] and Arthegall[8] he hight.[9]"

9 The word gone out she back again would call,
As her repenting so to have missaid,[10]
But that he, it uptaking ere the fall,[11]
Her shortly answerèd: "Fair martial maid,
Certes[12] ye misavisèd[13] been t' upbraid
A gentle[14] knight with so unknightly blame:

---

[1] *Card*, chart.

[2] *Greater Britain*. Church says that this means Wales, and is so called to distinguish it from Lesser Brittany in France. Fairy Land is England proper. Hillard.

[3] *Won*, dwell.

[4] *Fond*, found.

[5] *Worth and worship*, distinction and honor.

[6] *Mote I weet of you*, may I learn of you.

[7] *Wreak*, revenge.

[8] *Arthegall;* it has seemed best to follow the original and keep the two forms, Arthegall and Artegall.

[9] *Hight*, is called.

[10] *Missaid*, said wrongly.

[11] *Ere the fall*, i.e. before the words had fallen from her mouth.

[12] *Certes*, certainly.

[13] *Misavised*, inconsiderate.

[14] *Gentle*, noble.

For, weet[1] ye well, of all that ever played
At tilt or tourney, or like warlike game,
The noble Arthegall hath ever borne the name.[2]

10 " Forthy[3] great wonder were it, if such shame
Should ever enter in his bounteous[4] thought,
Or ever do that mote deserven blame[5]:
The noble corage[6] never weeneth[7] aught
That may unworthy of itself be thought.
Therefore, fair damsel, be ye well aware,
Lest that too far ye have your sorrow sought[8]:
You and your country both I wish welfare,
And honour both; for each of other worthy are."

11 The royal maid woxe[9] inly wondrous glad,
To hear her love so highly magnified;
And joyed that ever she affixèd had
Her heart on knight so goodly glorified,
However finely[10] she it feigned to hide.

. . . .

12 But to occasion him to further talk,
To feed her humour with his pleasing style,
Her list[11] in stryfull[12] terms with him to balk,[13]

[1] *Weet*, know.
[2] *Name*, i.e. of "gentle knight."
[3] *Forthy*, therefore.
[4] *Bounteous*, good, noble.
[5] *Or ever do that mote deserven blame*, i.e. or if he should ever do that for which he might deserve blame.
[6] *Corage*, heart.
[7] *Weeneth*, thinketh.
[8] *Lest that too far ye have your sorrow sought*, i.e. lest you have cause to repent of your rashness in seeking to avenge an imaginary wrong.
[9] *Woxe*, became.
[10] *Finely*, skilfully.
[11] *Her list*, it pleased her.
[12] *Stryfull*, contentious.
[13] *Balk*, deal in cross-purposes.

And thus replied: "However, sir, ye file
Your courteous tongue his praises to compyle,[1]
It ill beseems a knight of gentle sort,
Such as ye have him boasted, to beguile
A simple maid, and work so heinous tort,[2]
In shame of knighthood, as I largely[3] can report.

13 "Let be therefore my vengeance to dissuade,
And read,[4] where I that faytour[5] false may find."
"Ah! but if reason fair might you persuade
To slake your wrath, and mollify your mind,"
Said he, "perhaps ye should it better find:
For hardy thing it is, to ween by might
That man to hard conditions[6] to bind;
Or ever hope to match in equal fight,
Whose prowess' paragon[7] saw never living wight.

14 "Ne[8] soothlich[9] is it easy for to read[10]
Where now on earth, or how, he may be found;
For he ne wonneth[11] in one certain stead,[12]
But restless walketh all the world around,
Aye doing things that to his fame redound,
Defending ladies' cause and orphans' right,
Whereso he hears that any doth confound
Them comfortless, through tyranny or might;
So is his sovereign honour raised to heaven's height."

---

[1] *Compyle*, heap up.
[2] *Tort*, wrong.
[3] *Largely*, i.e. with full particulars.
[4] *Read*, declare.
[5] *Faytour*, deceiver.
[6] *Conditions;* pronounce *con-di-si-oons.*
[7] *Whose prowess' paragon*, i.e. the like of whose prowess.
[8] *Ne*, nor.
[9] *Soothlich*, truly.
[10] *Read*, declare, say.
[11] *Ne wonneth*, dwells not.
[12] *Stead*, place.

15 His feeling words her feeble sense much pleased,
   And softly sunk into her molten heart:
   Heart that is inly hurt is greatly eased
   With hope of thing that may allegge¹ his smart;
   For pleasing words are like to magic art,
   That doth the charmèd snake in slumber lay:
   Such secret ease felt gentle Britomart,
   Yet list the same efforce with feigned gainsay²:—
   So discord oft in music makes the sweeter lay:—

16 And said: "Sir knight, these idle terms³ forbear;
   And, sith⁴ it is uneath⁵ to find his haunt,
   Tell me some marks by which he may appear,
   If chance I him encounter paravaunt⁶;
   For perdy,⁷ one shall other slay, or daunt:
   What shape, what shield, what arms, what steed, what stead,⁸
   And whatso else his person most may vaunt."
   All which the Redcross knight to point aread,⁹
   And him in every part before her fashionèd.

17 Yet him in every part before she knew,
   However list her now her knowledge feign,¹⁰
   Sith him whilom¹¹ in Britain she did view,

---

¹ *Allegge*, allay.
² *Yet list the same efforce with feigned gainsay, i.e.* yet it pleased her to restrain this feeling and assume, instead, an air of opposition.
³ *Idle terms*, foolish remarks.
⁴ *Sith*, since.
⁵ *Uneath*, hard.
⁶ *Paravaunt*, peradventure.
⁷ *Perdy*, truly.
⁸ *Stead*, place.
⁹ *To point aread*, exactly described.
¹⁰ *However list her now her knowledge feign, i.e.* notwithstanding the fact that now she chose to conceal her knowledge.
¹¹ *Whilom*, formerly.

To her revealèd in a mirror plain;
Whereof did grow her first engraffèd¹ pain,
Whose root and stalk so bitter yet did taste,
That, but the fruit more sweetness did² contain,
Her wretched days in dolour³ she mote⁴ waste,
And yield, the prey of love, to loathsome death at last.

18 By strange occasion she did him behold,
And much more strangely gan⁵ to love his sight,
As it in books hath written been of old.
In Deheubarth, that now South-Wales is hight.⁶
What time King Ryence reigned and dealèd right,
The great magician Merlin had devised,
By his deep science and hell-dreaded might,
A looking-glass, right wondrously aguised,⁷
Whose virtues through the wide world soon were solemnized.⁸

19 It virtue⁹ had to show in perfect sight
Whatever thing was in the world contained,
Betwixt the lowest earth and heaven's height,
So that¹⁰ it to the looker appertained:
Whatever foe had wrought, or friend had feigned,
Therein discovered¹¹ was, ne aught mote pass,¹²
Ne aught in secret from the same remained;

---

¹ *Engraffed*, deeply fixed.
² *Did, i.e.* should.
³ *Dolour*, grief.
⁴ *Mote*, must.
⁵ *Gan*, began.
⁶ *Hight*, called.
⁷ *Aguised*, fashioned.
⁸ *Solemnized*, celebrated.
⁹ *Virtue*, power.
¹⁰ *So that*, provided that.
¹¹ *Discovered*, revealed, displayed.
¹² *Ne aught mote pass, i.e.* nothing could escape notice.

Forthy[1] it round and hollow shapèd was,
Like to the world itself, and seemed a world of glass.

20 Who wonders not, that reads[2] so wondrous work?
But who does wonder, that has read the tow'r
Wherein th' Egyptian Phao[3] long did lurk
From all men's view, that none might her discoure,[4]
Yet she might all men view out of her bow'r?
Great Ptolomæe[5] it for his leman's[6] sake
Ybuilded all of glass, by magic pow'r,
And also it impregnable did make;
Yet, when his love was false, he with a peaze[7] it brake.

21 Such was the glassy globe that Merlin made,
And gave unto King Ryence for his guard,[8]
That never foes his kingdom might invade,
But he it knew at home before he hard[9]
Tidings thereof, and so them still[10] debarred:
It was a famous present for a prince,
And worthy work of infinite reward,
That treasons could bewray,[11] and foes convince[12]:
Happy this realm, had it remainèd ever since!

[1] *Forthy*, therefore.
[2] *Reads*, reads of.
[3] *The tow'r wherein th' Egyptian Phao, etc.* The tower alluded to is probably the Pharos of Ptolemy Philadelphus. Spenser had evidently read some mediæval legend that confused matters. (From Prof. Child's note.)
[4] *Discoure*, discover.
[5] *Ptolomæe*, Ptolemy.
[6] *Leman's*, love's.
[7] *Peaze*, blow.
[8] *Guard*, protection.
[9] *Hard*, heard.
[10] *Still*, always.
[11] *Bewray*, reveal.
[12] *Convince*, conquer.

22 One day it fortunèd fair Britomart
    Into her father's closet¹ to repair;
    For nothing he from her reserved apart,
    Being his only daughter and his heir;
    Where when she had espied that mirror fair,
    Herself awhile therein she viewed in vain:
    Tho,² her avising³ of the virtues rare
    Which thereof spoken were, she gan again
    Her to bethink of that mote⁴ to herself pertain.

23 But as it falleth,⁵ in the gentlest hearts
    Imperious Love hath highest set his throne,
    And tyrannizeth in the bitter smarts
    Of them, that to him buxom⁶ are and prone:
    So thought this maid (as maidens use to done⁷)
    Whom fortune for her husband would allot;

    .   .   .   .

24 Eftsoones⁸ there was presented to her eye
    A comely knight, all armed in complete wise,
    Through whose bright ventail,⁹ lifted up on high,
    His manly face, that did his foes agrise¹⁰
    And friends to terms of gentle truce entize,¹¹
    Looked forth, as Phœbus'¹² face out of the east

---

¹ *Closet*, small room for retirement.
² *Tho*, then.
³ *Avising*, bethinking.
⁴ *Of that mote*, of that which might.
⁵ *Falleth*, happeneth.
⁶ *Buxom*, yielding.
⁷ *Use to done*, i.e. are in the habit of doing.
⁸ *Eftsoones*, immediately.
⁹ *Ventail*, the part of the helmet which could be lifted up, — the beaver.
¹⁰ *Agrise*, terrify.
¹¹ *Entize*, entice.
¹² *Phœbus*, Apollo, the sun god.

Betwixt two shady mountains doth arise :
Portly[1] his person was, and much increased
Through his heroic grace and honorable gest.[2]

25 His crest was covered with a couchant[3] hound,
And all his armour seemed of ántique mould,
But wondrous massy and assurèd sound,
And round about yfretted[4] all with gold,
In which there written was, with cyphers[5] old,
Achilles' arms[6] which Arthegall[7] did win :
And on his shield enveloped sevenfold
He bore a crownèd little ermilin,[8]
That decked the azure field[9] with her fair pouldred[10] skin.

26 The damsel well did view his personage,
And likèd well; ne further fast'ned not,[11]
But went her way; ne her unguilty age
Did ween, unwares, that her unlucky lot
Lay hidden in the bottom of the pot :
Of hurt unwist[12] most danger doth redound :
But the false archer, which that arrow shot

---

[1] *Portly*, stately.
[2] *Gest*, carriage.
[3] *Couchant*, lying down with the head raised.
[4] *Yfretted*, ornamented with raised work.
[5] *Cyphers*, characters.
[6] *Achilles' arms.* Achilles is the hero of Homer's "Iliad." His arms were forged by the god Hephæstus or Vulcan.
[7] *Arthegall* (Arthur's peer) is meant for Arthur, Lord Grey of Wilton, and the arms seem to be devised in allusion to his name. Upton.
[8] *Ermilin*, ermine.
[9] *Field*, surface of the escutcheon.
[10] *Pouldred*, spotted.
[11] *Ne further fast'ned not, i.e.* her thoughts dwelt no more upon it.
[12] *Unwist*, unknown.

So slyly that she did not feel the wound,
Did smile full smoothly at her weetless[1] woful
    stound.[2]

27 Thenceforth the feather in her lofty crest,
    Ruffèd[3] of love, gan lowly to availe[4];
    And her proud portance[5] and her princely gest,[6]
    With which she erst[7] triúmphèd, now did quail:
    Sad, solemn, sour,[8] and full of fancies frail,
    She woxe[9]; yet wist[10] she nether how, nor why;
    She wist not, silly maid, what she did ail,
    Yet wist she was not well at ease, perdy[11];
    Yet thought it was not love, but some meláncholy.

28 So soon as night had with her pallid hue
    Defaced the beauty of the shining sky,
    And reft[12] from men the world's desired view,
    She with her nurse adown to sleep did lie;
    But sleep full far away from her did fly:
    Instead thereof sad sighs and sorrows deep
    Kept watch and ward about her warily,
    That nought she did but wail, and often steep
    Her dainty couch with tears which closely[13] she did
        weep.

---

[1] *Weetless*, unconscious.
[2] *Stound*, plight.
[3] *Ruffed*, ruffled.
[4] *Availe*, sink.
[5] *Portance*, port, carriage.
[6] *Gest*, bearing.
[7] *Erst*, formerly.
[8] *Sour*, peevish.
[9] *Woxe*, grew.
[10] *Wist*, knew.
[11] *Perdy*, truly.
[12] *Reft*, taken away.
[13] *Closely*, secretly.

29 And if that any drop of slumb'ring rest
    Did chance to still[1] into her weary sprite,[2]
    When feeble nature felt herself oppressed,
    Straightway with dreams, and with fantastic sight
    Of dreadful things, the same was put to flight;
    That oft out of her bed she did astart,
    As one with view of ghastly fiends affright:
    Tho gan[3] she to renew her former smart,
    And think of that fair visage written in her heart.

30 One night, when she was tossed with such unrest,
    Her aged nurse, whose name was Glaucè hight,[4]
    Feeling her leap out of her loathèd nest,
    Betwixt her feeble arms her quickly keight,[5]
    And down again her in her warm bed dight[6]:
    "Ah! my dear daughter, ah! my dearest dread,[7]
    What uncouth[8] fit," said she, "what evil plight,
    Hath thee oppressed, and with sad drearyhead[9]
    Changèd thy lively cheer,[10] and living made thee dead?

31 "For not of nought these sudden ghastly fears
    All night afflict thy natural repose;
    And all the day, whenas thine equal peers
    Their fit disports with fair delight do chose,[11]
    Thou in dull corners dost thyself inclose;

---

[1] *Still*, drop.
[2] *Sprite*, spirit, mind.
[3] *Tho gan*, then began.
[4] *Hight*, called.
[5] *Keight*, caught.
[6] *Dight*, placed.
[7] *Dread*, one highly revered.
[8] *Uncouth*, strange.
[9] *Drearyhead*, sorrow.
[10] *Cheer*, countenance.
[11] *Chose*, choose.

Ne tastest prince's pleasures, ne dost spread
Abroad thy fresh youth's fairest flow'r, but lose
Both leaf and fruit, both too untimely shed,
As one in wilful bale[1] forever burièd.

32 "The time that mortal men their weary cares
Do lay away, and all wild beasts do rest,
And every river eke[2] his course forbears,
Then doth this wicked evil thee infest,
And rive[3] with thousand throbs thy thrillèd[4] breast :
Like an huge Ætn'[5] of deep engulfèd grief,
Sorrow is heapèd in thy hollow chest,
Whence forth it breaks in sighs and anguish rife,
As smoke and sulphur mingled with confusèd strife.

33 "Ay me ! how much I fear lest love it be !
But if that love it be, as sure I read[6]
By knowen signs and passions which I see,
Be it worthy of thy race and royal seed,[7]
Then I avow, by this most sacred head
Of my dear foster child, to ease thy grief
And win thy will. Therefore away do dread[8] ;
For death nor danger from thy due relief
Shall me debar ; tell me, therefore, my liefest lief[9]!"

34 So having said, her twixt her armës twain
She straitly[10] strained, and collèd[11] tenderly ;

[1] *Bale*, sorrow.
[2] *Eke*, likewise.
[3] *Rive*, rend.
[4] *Thrilled*, pierced.
[5] *Ætna*, a volcano in Sicily.
[6] *Read*, declare.
[7] *Seed*, race.
[8] *Away do dread*, i.e. fear not.
[9] *Liefest lief*, dearest dear.
[10] *Straitly*, closely.
[11] *Colled*, clasped about the neck.

And every trembling joint and every vein
She softly felt, and rubbèd busily,
To do[1] the frozen cold away to fly;
And her fair dewy eyes with kisses dear
She oft did bathe, and oft again did dry:
And ever her impórtuned not to fear
To let the secret of her heart to her appear.

35 The damsel paused; and then thus fearfully:
"Ah! nurse, what needeth thee to eke[2] my pain?
Is not enough that I alone do die,
But it must doubled be with death of twain?
For nought for me but death there doth remain!"
"Oh daughter dear," said she, "despair no whit:
For never sore but might a salve obtain:
That blinded god, which hath ye blindly smit,
Another arrow hath your lover's heart to hit."

36 "But mine is not," quoth she, "like other wound;
For which[3] no reason can find remedy."
"Was never such, but mote[4] the like be found,"
Said she[5]; "and though no reason may apply
Salve to your sore, yet love can higher stye[6]
Then[7] reason's reach, and oft hath wonders done."
"But neither god of love nor god of sky
Can do," said she, "that which cannot be done."
"Things oft impossible," quoth she, "seem, ere
    begun."

---

[1] *Do*, make.
[2] *Eke*, increase.
[3] *For which*, i.e. my wound is one for which, etc.
[4] *Mote*, might.
[5] *She*, i.e. Glauce.
[6] *Stye*, mount.
[7] *Then*, than.

37 "These idle words," said she, "do not assuage
　My stubborn smart, but more annoyance breed :
　For no, no usual fire, no usual rage
　It is, O nurse, which on my life doth feed,
　And sucks the blood which from my heart doth bleed.
　But since thy faithful zeal lets me not hide
　My crime, (if crime it be,) I will it read.[1]
　Nor prince nor peer it is, whose love hath gryde[2]
　My feeble breast of late, and launchèd[3] this wound wide :

38 Nor man it is, nor other living wight ;
　For then some hope I might unto me draw ;
　But th' only shade and semblant[4] of a knight,
　Whose shape or person yet I never saw,
　Hath me subjected to love's cruel law :
　The same one day, as me misfortune led,
　I in my father's wondrous mirror saw,
　And, pleasèd with that seeming goodlihead,[5]
　Unwares the hidden hook with bait I swallowèd.

39 "Sithens[6] it hath infixèd faster hold
　Within my bleeding bowels, and so sore
　Now rankleth in this same frail fleshly mould,
　That all mine entrails flow with pois'nous gore,
　And th' ulcer groweth daily more and more ;
　Ne can my running sore find remedy,
　Other then my hard fortune to deplore,

---

[1] *Read*, declare.
[2] *Gryde*, pierced.
[3] *Launched*, pierced as with a lance.
[4] *Semblant*, appearance.
[5] *Goodlihead*, goodliness.
[6] *Sithens*, since that time.

And languish as the leaf fall'n from the tree,
Till death make one end of my days and misery!"

40 "Daughter," said she, "what need ye be dismayed?
Or why make ye such monster of your mind?
Of much more uncouth[1] thing I was afraid;

. . . .

But this affection nothing strange I find;
For who with reason can you aye reprove
To love the semblant pleasing most your mind,
And yield your heart whence ye cannot remove?
No guilt in you, but in the tyranny of love.

The nurse mentioned some who had loved wrongly, and then said:—

41 "But thine, my dear, (well fare thy heart, my dear!)
Though strange beginning had, yet fixèd is
On one that worthy may perhaps appear;
And certes seems bestowèd not amiss:
Joy thereof have thou and eternal bliss!"
With that, upleaning on her elbow weak,
Her alabaster breast she soft did kiss,
Which all that while she felt to pant and quake,
As it an earthquake were: at last she[2] thus bespake:

The maiden declared that she had less comfort than those who loved wrongly; for,—

42 . . . .
"Short end of sorrows they thereby did find;
So was their fortune good, though wicked were
their mind.

---

[1] *Uncouth*, strange.   [2] *She, i.e.* Britomart.

43 "But wicked fortune mine, though mind be good,
   Can have no end nor hope of my desire,
   But feed on shadows whiles I die for food,
   And like a shadow wex,[1] whiles with entire
   Affection I do languish and expire.
   I, fonder then Cephisus' foolish child,[2]
   Who, having viewèd in a fountain shere[3]
   His face, was with the love thereof beguiled;
   I, fonder, love a shade, the body far exiled."

44 "Nought like," quoth she; "for that same wretched boy
   Was of himself the idle paramour,
   Both love and lover, without hope of joy;
   For which he faded to a wat'ry flower.
   But better fortune thine, and better hour,[4]
   Which lov'st the shadow of a warlike knight;
   No shadow, but a body hath in pow'r[5]:
   That body, wheresoever that it light,
   May learnèd be by cyphers,[6] or by magic might.

45 "But if thou may with reason yet repress
   The growing evil, ere it strength have got,
   And thee abandoned wholly do possess;
   Against it strongly strive, and yield thee not
   Till thou in open field adown be smott:

---

[1] *Wex*, wax, become.
[2] *Cephisus' foolish child*, i.e. Narcissus, who fell in love with his own image reflected in a pool, and pined away till he was changed into the flower that bears his name.
[3] *Shere*, clear.
[4] *Hour*, i.e. lot.
[5] *No shadow, but a body hath in pow'r*, i.e. there is no shadow that has not a body belonging to it.
[6] *Cyphers*, characters; here magic characters.

But if the passion mayster[1] thy frail might,
So that needs love or death must be thy lot,
Then I avow to thee, by wrong or right,
To compass thy desire, and find that lovèd knight."

46 Her cheerful words much cheered the feeble sprite[2]
Of the sick virgin, that her down she laid
In her warm bed to sleep, if that she might;
And the old woman carefully displayed[3]
The clothes about her round with busy aid;
So that at last a little creeping sleep
Surprised her sense. She,[4] therewith well apayed,[5]
The drunken lamp down in the oil did steep,
And sate her by to watch, and sate her by to weep.

47 Early, the morrow next, before that day
His joyous face did to the world reveal,
They both uprose and took their ready way
Unto the church, their prayers to appele,[6]
With great devotion, and with little zeal:
For the fair damsel from the holy herse[7]
Her love-sick heart to other thoughts did steal;
And that old dame said many an idle verse
Out of her daughter's heart fond[8] fancies to reverse.[9]

---

[1] *Mayster*, master.
[2] *Sprite*, spirit.
[3] *Displayed*, spread.
[4] *She, i.e.* Glaucè.
[5] *Apayed*, satisfied.
[6] *Appele, i.e.* to prefer, to make.
[7] *Herse*, rehearsal (of the service).
[8] *Fond*, foolish.
[9] *Reverse*, cause to depart.

48 Returnèd home, the royal infant[1] fell
　Into her former fit; for why? no pow'r
　Nor guidance of herself in her did dwell.
　But th' aged nurse,[2] her calling to her bow'r,[3]
　Had gathered rue, and savin, and the flow'r
　Of camphora,[4] and calamint,[5] and dill;
　All which she in an earthen pot did pour,
　And to the brim with coltwood[6] did it fill,
　And many drops of milk and blood through it did spill.

49 Then, taking thrice three hairs from off her head,
　Them trebly braided in a threefold lace,
　And round about the pot's mouth bound the thread;
　And, after having whisperèd a space
　Certain sad[7] words with hollow voice and base,[8]
　She to the virgin said, thrice said she it:
　"Come, daughter, come; come, spit upon my face;
　Spit thrice upon me, thrice upon me spit;
　Th' uneven number for this business is most fit."

50 That said, her round about she from her turned,
　She turnèd her contráry to the sun;
　Thrice she her turned contráry, and returned

---

[1] *Infant*, the same as infanta; a title given in Spain and Portugal to all the children of the king except the eldest.

[2] *But th' aged nurse*, etc. The classic poets, especially Theocritus and Virgil, have supplied Spenser with the various processes of Glaucè's incantation. Hillard.

[3] *Bower*, chamber.

[4] *Camphora*, camphor.

[5] *Calamint*, a book name for plants of the genus calamintha.

[6] *Coltwood*, an old name for dittany, a plant of the mint family.

[7] *Sad*, weighty, earnest.

[8] *Base*, low.

All cóntrary; for she the right did shun;
And ever what she did was straight¹ undone.
So thought she to undo her daughter's love:
But love, that is in gentle breast begun,
No idle charms so lightly may remove;
That well can witness, who by trial it does prove.

51 Ne aught it mote the noble maid avail,
Ne slake the fury of her cruel flame,
But that she still did waste, and still did wail,
That, through long languor and heart-burning brame²
She shortly like a pinèd³ ghost became
Which long hath waited by the Stygian strond.⁴
That when old Glaucè saw, for fear lest blame
Of her miscarriage⁵ should in her be fond,⁶
She wist⁷ not how t' amend, nor how it to withstand.

---

¹ *Straight*, immediately.
² *Brame*, desire.
³ *Pined*, tormented.
⁴ *Stygian Strond*, the strand or shore of the Styx, the principal river of the lower world, according to Greek mythology. Over this river the dead must go to reach their final habitation.
⁵ *Miscarriage*, *i.e.* sad condition.
⁶ *Fond*, found.
⁷ *Wist*, knew.

III.

Britomart and her nurse Glaucè visit Merlin who tells them of Artegall and of the future. They set out for Faeryland in the hope of meeting Artegall.

1 Most sacred fire, that burnest mightily
   In living breasts, ykindled first above
   Amongst th' eternal spheres and lamping[1] sky,
   And thence poured into men, which men call love;
   Not that same which doth base affections move,
   .   .   .   .
   But that sweet fit[2] that doth true beauty love,
   And chooseth virtue for his dearest dame,
   Whence spring all noble deeds and never-dying fame:

2 Well did antiquity a god thee deem,
   That over mortal minds hast so great might,
   To order them as best to thee doth seem,
   And all their actions to direct aright:
   The fatal[3] purpose of divine foresight
   Thou dost effect in destinèd descents,
   Through deep impression of thy secret might,
   And stirredst up th' heroës high intents,
   Which the late world[4] admires for wondrous moniments.[5]

[1] *Lamping*, shining.
[2] *Fit*, passion.
[3] *Fatal*, foreordained.
[4] *The late world*, i.e. men in late times.
[5] *Moniments*, monuments, reminders.

3 But thy dread darts in none do triumph more,
　Ne braver proof in any of thy pow'r
　Show'dst thou, than in this royal maid of yore,
　Making her seek an unknown paramour,[1]
　From the world's end, through many a bitter stowre.[2]

. . . .

4 Begin then, O my dearest sacred dame,
　Daughter of Phoebus and of Memory,
　That dost ennoble with immortal name
　The warlike worthies, from antiquity,
　In thy great volume of eternity;
　Begin, O Clio,[3] and recount from hence
　My glorious sovereign's goodly ancestry,
　Till that by due degrees, and long protense[4]
　Thou have it lastly brought unto her excellence.

5 Full many ways within her troubled mind
　Old Glaucè cast[5] to cure this lady's grief;
　Full many ways she sought, but none could find,
　Nor herbs, nor charms, nor counsel that is chief
　And choicest med'cine for sick heart's relief:
　Forthy[6] great care she took,[7] and greater fear,
　Lest that it should her turn to foul repriefe[8]
　And sore reproach, whenso her father dear
　Should of his dearest daughter's hard misfortune hear.

---

[1] *Paramour*, lover.
[2] *Stowre*, peril.
[3] *Clio*, the muse of history; more commonly spoken of as the daughter of Zeus and Mnemosyne.
[4] *Protense*, extension.
[5] *Cast*, planned.
[6] *Forthy*, therefore.
[7] *Great care she took*, *i.e.* she felt great concern.
[8] *Repriefe*, reproof.

6 At last she her avised,¹ that he which made
   That mirror, wherein the sick damosel
   So strangely viewèd her strange lover's shade,
   To weet, the learnèd Merlin, well could tell
   Under what coast of heaven the man did dwell,
   And by what means his love might best be wrought²:
   For, though beyond the Afric Ismaël³
   Or th' Indian Peru he were, she thought
   Him forth through infinite endeavour to have sought.

7 Forthwith themselves disguising both in strange
   And base attire, that none might them bewray,⁴
   To Maridunum, that is now by change
   Of name Cayr-Merdin⁵ called, they took their way:
   There the wise Merlin whilom⁶ wont (they say)
   To make his wonne,⁷ low underneath the ground
   In a deep delve,⁸ far from the view of day,
   That of no living wight he mote⁹ be found,
   Whenso he counselled with his sprites encompassed
       round.

8 And, if thou ever happen that same way
   To travel, go to see that dreadful place:
   It is an hideous hollow cave (they say)
   Under a rock that lies a little space

---

¹ *Avised*, bethought.
² *Wrought*, produced, effected; a peculiar use of the word.
³ *Afric Ismaël*, i.e. the northern part of Africa, inhabited by Moors and others, supposed to be the descendants of Ishmaël.
⁴ *Bewray*, discover.
⁵ *Cayr-Merdin*, i.e. the city of Merdin or Merlin, is Caermarthen, in South Wales. Prof. Child.
⁶ *Whilom*, formerly.
⁷ *Wonne*, dwelling.
⁸ *Delve*, dell.
⁹ *Mote*, might.

From the swift Barry, tumbling down apace
Amongst the woody hills of Dynevowre :
But dare thou not, I charge, in any case,
To enter into that same baleful bow'r,[1]
For fear the cruel fiends should thee unwares devour :

9 But, standing high aloft, low lay thine ear,
And there such ghastly noise of iron chains
And brazen caudrons[2] thou shalt rumbling hear,
Which thousand sprites with long enduring pains
Do toss, that it will stun thy feeble brains ;
And oftentimes great groans, and grievous stownds,[3]
When too huge toil and labour them constrains ;
And oftentimes loud strokes and ringing sounds
From under that deep rock most horribly rebounds.

10 The cause, some say, is this : a little while
Before that Merlin died, he did intend
A brazen wall in compass to compile[4]
About Cairmardin, and did it commend
Unto these sprites to bring to perfect end :
During which work the Lady of the Lake,
Whom long he loved, for him in haste did send ;
Who, thereby forced his workmen to forsake,
Them bound, till his return, their labour not to slake.[5]

[1] *Bower*, chamber.
[2] *Caudrons*, caldrons.
[3] *Stownds*, times ; here may be noises.
[4] *Compile*, construct.
[5] *Slake*, slacken.

11 In the meantime, through that false lady's traine [1]
    He was surprised, and buried under bier,
    Ne ever to his work returned again [2]:
    Natheless those fiends may not their work forbear,
    So greatly his commandèment they fear,
    But there do toil and travail day and night,
    Until that brazen wall they up do rear:
    For Merlin had in magic more insight
    Than ever him before or after living wight:

12 For he by words could call out of the sky
    Both sun and moon, and make them him obey;
    The land to sea, and sea to mainland dry,
    And darksome night he eke could turn to day;
    Huge hosts of men he could alone dismay,
    And hosts of men of meanest things could frame,
    Whenso him list his enemies to fray [3]:
    That to this day for terror of his fame,
    The fiends do quake when any him to them does name.

13 They, here arriving, stayed awhile without,
    Ne durst adventure rashly in to wend,
    But of their first intent gan make new doubt,
    For dread of danger, which it might portend:
    Until the hardy maid (with love to friend)
    First entering, the dreadful mage [4] there found
    Deep busièd 'bout work of wondrous end,

---

[1] *Traine*, artifice.
[2] *He was surprised, and buried under bier*, etc. See Malory's "Morte d'Arthur" and Tennyson's "Vivien" in the "Idylls of the King."
[3] *Fray*, terrify.
[4] *Mage*, magician.

And writing strange charácters in the ground,
With which the stubborn fiends he to his service
  bound.

14 He nought was movèd at their entrance bold,
For of their coming well he wist[1] afore;
Yet list them bid[2] their business to unfold,
As if ought in this world in secret store
Were from him hidden, or unknown of yore.
Then Glaucè thus: "Let not it thee offend,
That we thus rashly through thy darksome door
Unwares have pressed; for either fatal end,[3]
Or other mighty cause, us two did hether send."

15 He bade tell on; and then she thus began:
"Now have three moons with borrowed brother's
  light
Thrice shinèd fair, and thrice seemed dim and wan,
Sith[4] a sore evil, which this virgin bright
Tormenteth and doth plunge in doleful plight,
First rooting took; but what thing it mote[5] be,
Or whence it sprong, I cannot read[6] aright:
But this I read, that, but if[7] remedy
Thou her afford, full shortly I her dead shall see."

16 Therewith th' enchanter softly gan to smile
At her smooth speeches, weeting[8] inly well

---

[1] *Wist*, knew.
[2] *Yet list them bid, i.e.* Yet it pleased him to bid them.
[3] *Fatal end*, some purpose of the Fates.
[4] *Sith*, since.
[5] *Mote*, may.
[6] *Read*, declare.
[7] *But if*, unless.
[8] *Weeting*, knowing.

That she to him dissembled womanish guile,
And to her said: "Beldame, by that ye tell,
More need of leech-craft[1] hath your damosel,
Then of my skill: who help may have elsewhere,
In vain seeks wonders out of magic spell."
Th' old woman woxe[2] half blank those words to hear;
And yet was loath to let her purpose plain appear;

17 And to him said: "If any leech's skill,
Or other learnèd means, could have redressed
This my dear daughter's deep-engraffèd[3] ill,
Certes I should be loath thee to molest:
But this sad evil, which doth her infest,
Doth course of natural cause far exceed,
And housèd is within her hollow breast,
That either seems some cursèd witch's deed,
Or evil sprite,[4] that in her doth such torment breed."

18 The wizard could no longer bear her bord,[5]
But, bursting forth in laughter, to her said:
"Glaucè, what needs this colourable[6] word
To cloke the cause that hath itself bewrayed[7]?
Ne ye, fair Britomartis, thus arrayed,
More hidden are then sun in cloudy vele[8];
Whom thy good fortune, having fate obeyed,

---

[1] *Leech-craft*, physician's skill.
[2] *Woxe*, became.
[3] *Deep-engraffed*, deeply fixed.
[4] *Sprite*, spirit.
[5] *Bord*, trifling.
[6] *Colourable*, specious.
[7] *Bewrayed*, betrayed, revealed.
[8] *Vele*, veil.

BRITOMART.   53

    Hath hether brought for succour to appeal ;
    The which the pow'rs to thee are pleasèd to reveal."

19 The doubtful [1] maid, seeing herself descried,
    Was all abashed, and her pure ivory
    Into a clear carnation sudden dyed ;

    .   .   .   .

    But her old nurse was nought disheartenèd,
    But vantage made of that which Merlin had aread [2];

20 And said : "Sith then thou knowest all our grief,
    (For what dost not thou know?) of grace I pray,
    Pity our plaint, and yield us meet [3] relief !"
    With that the prophet still awhile did stay,
    And then his spirit thus gan forth display :
    " Most noble virgin, that by fatal lore
    Hast learned to love, let no whit thee dismay
    The hard begin that meets thee in the door,
    And with sharp fits thy tender heart oppresseth
        sore :

21 "For so must all things excellent begin ;
    And eke enrootèd deep must be that tree,
    Whose big embodied branches shall not lin [4]
    Till they to heaven's height forth stretchèd be.
    For from thy womb a famous progeny
    Shall spring out of the ancient Trojan blood,[5]

---

[1] *Doubtful*, fearful, apprehensive.

[2] *Aread*, declared.

[3] *Meet*, fit.

[4] *Lin*, stop.

[5] *Trojan blood ;* Brutus, the mythical founder of Britain, was the great-grandson of Æneas of Troy.

Which shall revive the sleeping memory
Of those same ántique peers, the heaven's brood,
Which Greek and Asian rivers stainèd with their blood.

22 "Renowmèd[1] kings, and sacred emperors,
Thy fruitful offspring, shall from thee descend;
Brave captains, and most mighty warriors,
That shall their conquests through all lands extend,
And their decayèd kingdoms shall amend:
The feeble Britons, broken with long war,
They shall uprear, and mightily defend
Against their foreign foe that comes from far,
Till universal peace compound all civil jar.

23 "It was not, Britomart, thy wand'ring eye
Glancing unwares in charmèd looking-glass,
But the straight course of heavenly destiny,
Led with eternal Providence, that has
Guided thy glance, to bring His will to pass:
Ne is thy fate, ne is thy fortune ill,
To love the prowest[2] knight that ever was:
Therefore submit thy ways unto His will,
And do, by all due means, thy destiny fulfill."

24 "But read,"[3] said Glaucè, "thou magician,[4]
What means shall she out-seek, or what ways take?
How shall she know, how shall she find the man?
Or what needs her to toil, sith Fates can make

---

[1] *Renowmed*, renowned.
[2] *Prowest*, most valiant.
[3] *Read*, declare.
[4] *Magician;* last syllable pronounced as two syllables.

Way for themselves, their purpose to pertake[1]?"
Then Merlin thus: "Indeed the Fates are firm,
And may not shrink, though all the world do shake:
Yet ought men's good endeavours them confirm,
And guide the heavenly causes to their constant term.[2]

25 "The man whom heavens have ordained to be
The spouse of Britomart, is Arthegall:
He wonneth[3] in the land of Faëry,
Yet is no faery born, ne sib[4] at all
To elfes, but sprong of seed terrestrial,
And whilom by false faeries stol'n away,
Whiles yet in infant cradle he did crawl;

. . . .

26 "But sooth[5] he is the son of Gorloïs,[6]
And brother unto Cador, Cornish king;
And for his warlike feats renowmèd is,
From where the day out of the sea doth spring,
Until the closure of the evening:
From thence him, firmly bound with faithful band,
To this his native soil thou back shalt bring,
Strongly to aid his country to withstand
The pow'r of foreign paynims[7] which invade thy land.

---

[1] *Pertake*, partake; a peculiar use of the word; seems here to signify *carry out*.

[2] *Constant term*, fixed conclusion.

[3] *Wonneth*, dwelleth.

[4] *Sib*, kinsman.

[5] *Sooth*, truly.

[6] *Gorloïs*, the Duke of Cornwall.

[7] *Paynims*, pagans, infidels.

Merlin then told Britomart something of the mythical history of the Britons and of their unsuccessful struggle against the Saxons; concluding as follows: —

27 "Then woe, and woe, and everlasting woe,
   Be to the Briton babe that shall be born
   To live in thraldom of his father's foe!
   Late king, now captive; late lord, now forlorn;
   The world's reproach; the cruel victor's scorn;
   Banished from princely bow'r to wasteful wood!
   O, who shall help me to lament and mourn
   The royal seed,[1] the ántique Trojan[2] blood,
   Whose empire lenger here than ever any stood!"

28 The damsel was full deep empassionèd
   Both for his grief and for her people's sake,
   Whose future woes so plain he fashionèd;
   And, sighing sore, at length him thus bespake:
   "Ah! but will heaven's fury never slake,
   Nor vengeance huge relent itself at last?
   Will not long misery late mercy make,
   But shall their name for ever be defaced,
   And quite from off the earth their memory be raste[3]?"

29 "Nay, but the term," said he, "is limited,
   That in this thraldom Britons shall abide;
   And the just revolution measurèd
   That they as strangers shall be notified[4]:
   For twice four hundred years shall be supplied,

---

[1] *Seed*, race.
[2] *Trojan*, refers to Trojan settlement of Britain.
[3] *Raste*, erased.
[4] *Notified*, marked.
[5] *Supplied*, fulfilled.

Ere they to former rule restored shall be,
And their impórtune¹ fates all satisfied :
Yet, during this their most obscurity,
Their beams shall oft break forth, that men them fair may see.

30 "For Rhodorick,² whose surname shall be Great,
Shall of himself a brave ensample show,
That Saxon kings his friendship shall intreat ;
And Howell Dha³ shall goodly well indew
The salvage⁴ minds with skill of just and true :
Then Griffyth Conan⁵ also shall uprear
His dreaded head, and the old sparks renew
Of native courage, that his foes shall fear
Lest back again the kingdom he from them should bear.

31 "Ne shall the Saxons selves all peaceably
Enjoy the crown, which they from Britons won
First ill, and after rulèd wickedly :
For, ere two hundred years be full outrun,
There shall a raven,⁶ far from rising sun,
With his wide wings upon them fiercely fly,
And bid his faithless chickens⁷ overrun
The fruitful plains, and with fell cruelty
In their avenge tread down the victor's surquedry.⁸

---

¹ *Importune*, troublesome.
² *Roderick the Great* began to reign in Wales in 843.
³ *Howell Dha* died about 948.
⁴ *Salvage*, wild, woodland.
⁵ *Griffyth Conan* died in 1136.
⁶ *Raven, i.e.* the leader of the Danes.
⁷ *Faithless chickens, i.e.* his heathen brood.
⁸ *Surquedry*, insolence.

32 "Yet shall a third both these and thine subdue:
There shall a lion[1] from the sea-board wood
Of Neustria[2] come roaring, with a crew
Of hungry whelps, his battailous[3] bold brood,
Whose claws were newly dipped in cruddy[4] blood,
That from the Daniske[5] tyrant's head shall rend
Th' usurpèd crown, as if that he were wood,[6]
And the spoil of the country conquerèd
Amongst his young ones shall divide with bounty-head.[7]

33 "Tho,[8] when the term is full accomplishid,
There shall a spark of fire, which hath longwhile
Been in his ashes rakèd up and hid,
Be freshly kindled in the fruitful isle
Of Mona,[9] where it lurkèd in exile[10];
Which shall break forth into bright burning flame,
And reach into the house that bears the style
Of royal majesty and sovereign name:
So shall the Briton blood their crown again reclaim.[11]

---

[1] *There shall a lion*, etc. This is William of Normandy.

[2] *Neustria* was the ancient name of the northwest part of France. Hillard.

[3] *Battailous*, eager for battle.

[4] *Cruddy*, curdled.

[5] *Daniske*, Danish.

[6] *Wood*, mad.

[7] *Bounty head*, generosity.

[8] *Tho*, then.

[9] *Mona*, the island now called Anglesey.

[10] *There shall a spark*, etc. Llewellyn, the last of the native Welsh princes, made an unsuccessful resistance to Edward I., and was defeated and slain. Edward soon after created his own infant son Prince of Wales. Hillard.

[11] *So shall the Briton blood their crown again reclaim.* By the accession of Henry of Richmond to the crown. Henry, descended from the Tudors, was born in Mona, now called Anglesey. Upton.

34 "Thenceforth eternal union shall be made
   Between the nations different afore,
   And sacred peace shall lovingly persuade
   The warlike minds to learn her goodly lore,
   And civil arms to exercise no more:
   Then shall a royal virgin reign, which shall
   Stretch her white rod over the Belgic shore,
   And the great Castle smite so sore withal,
   That it shall make him shake, and shortly learn
       to fall[1]:

35 "But yet the end is not —" There Merlin stayed,
   As overcomen of the spirit's pow'r,
   Or other ghastly spectacle dismayed,
   That secretly he saw, yet note discoure[2]:
   Which sudden fit and half ecstatic stoure[3]
   When the two fearful women saw, they grew
   Greatly confusèd in behaviour:
   At last, the fury past, to former hue
   He turned again, and cheerful looks as erst[4] did
       show.

36 Then, when themselves they well instructed had
   Of all that needed them to be inquired,
   They both, conceiving hope of comfort glad,
   With lighter hearts unto their home retired;

---

[1] *Then shall a royal virgin reign*, etc. This is Queen Elizabeth, who assisted the Belgian provinces, and shook the power of the king of Castile. Prof. Child.

[2] *Note discoure*, might not disclose.

[3] *Stoure*, paroxysm.

[4] *Erst*, at first.

Where they in secret counsel close[1] conspired,
How to effect so hard an enterprize,
And to possess the purpose they desired:
Now this, now that, twixt them they did devise,
And diverse plots did frame to mask in strange disguise.

37 At last the nurse in her fool-hardy wit
Conceived a bold device, and thus bespake:
"Daughter, I deem that counsel aye most fit,
That of the time doth due advantage take:
Ye see that good King Uther[2] now doth make
Strong war upon the paynim brethren, hight[3]
Octa and Oza, whom he lately brake
Beside Cayr Verolame[4] in victorious fight,
That now all Brittany doth burn in armës bright.

38 "That therefore nought our passage may impeach,[5]
Let us in feignèd arms ourselves disguise;
And our weak hands (need makes good scholars) teach
The dreadful spear and shield to exercise:
Ne certes,[6] daughter, that same warlike wise,
I ween,[7] would you mis-seem[8]; for ye been tall
And large of limb t' achieve an hard emprise[9];
Ne ought ye want but skill, which practice small
Will bring, and shortly make you a maid martial.

---

[1] *Close*, secretly.
[2] *Uther*, a Welsh king who lived just before Arthur.
[3] *Hight*, called.
[4] *Cayr Verolame, i.e.* the city of Verulam.
[5] *Impeach*, prevent.
[6] *Ne certes*, nor certainly.
[7] *Ween*, think.
[8] *Mis-seem*, misbecome.
[9] *Emprise*, undertaking.

39 "And, sooth,[1] it ought your courage much inflame
To hear so often, in that royal house,
From whence to none inferior ye came,
Bards tell of many women valorous,
Which have full many feats adventurous
Performed, in paragon[2] of proudest men:
The bold Bunduca,[3] whose victorious
Exploits made Rome to quake; stout Guendolen[4];
Renowmèd Martia[5]; and redoubted Emmilen[6];—

40 "And, that which more then all the rest may sway,
Late days' ensample, which these eyes beheld:
In this last field before Menevia,[7]
Which Uther with those foreign Pagans held,
I saw a Saxon virgin,[8] the which felled
Great Ulfin[9] thrice upon the bloody plain;
And, had not Carados[10] her hand withheld
From rash revenge, she had him surely slain;
Yet Carados himself from her escaped with pain."

41 "Ah! read,"[11] quoth Britomart, "how is she hight[12]?"
"Fair Angela," quoth she, "men do her call,

---

[1] *Sooth*, truly.
[2] *Paragon*, rivalry.
[3] *Bunduca*, Boadicea, who headed a revolt against the Romans. She died 62 A.D.
[4] *Guendolen*, wife of Locrine, a fabulous king of ancient Britain.
[5] *Martia*, the lawgiver mentioned in Geoffrey of Monmouth's history.
[6] *Emmilen*. Who Emmilen is, is uncertain. Prof. Child.
[7] *Menevia*, St. David's, a very old episcopal city in Wales.
[8] *A Saxon virgin*. This Saxon virgin is, I believe, entirely of Spenser's own feigning. Upton.
[9] *Ulfin*, } names taken from
[10] *Carados*, } old Welsh stories.
[11] *Read*, tell.
[12] *Hight*, called.

No whit less fair then terrible in fight :
She hath the leading of a martial
And mighty people, dreaded more then all
The other Saxons, which do, for her sake
And love, themselves of her name *Angles* call.
Therefore, fair infant, her ensample make
Unto thyself, and equal courage to thee take."

42 Her hearty words so deep into the mind
Of the young damsel sunk, that great desire
Of warlike arms in her forthwith they tined,[1]
And generous stout courage did inspire,
That she resolved, unweeting[2] to her sire,
Advent'rous knighthood on herself to don ;
And counselled with her nurse her maid's attire
To turn into a massy habergeon[3];
And bade her all things put in readiness anon.

43 Th' old woman nought that needed did omit ;
But all things did conveniently purvey.
It fortunèd (so time their turn did fit)
A band of Britons, riding on forray
Few days before, had gotten a great prey
Of Saxon goods ; amongst the which was seen
A goodly armour, and full rich array,
Which longed to Angela, the Saxon queen,
All fretted round with gold, and goodly well beseen.[4]

44 The same, with all the other ornaments,
King Ryence causèd to be hangèd high

---

[1] *Tined*, kindled.
[2] *Unweeting*, unknown.
[3] *Habergeon*, coat of mail.
[4] *Beseen*, appearing.

In his chief church, for endless moniments [1]
Of his success and gladful victory:
Of which herself avising [2] readily,
In th' evening late old Glaucè thether led
Fair Britomart, and, that same armoury
Down taking, her therein apparellèd
Well as she might, and with brave [3] baldric [4] gar-
   nishèd.

45 Beside those arms there stood a mighty spear,
Which Bladud [5] made by magic art of yore,
And used the same in battle aye to bear;
Sith [6] which it had been here preserved in store,
For his great virtues [7] provèd long afore:
For never wight so fast in sell [8] could sit,
But him perforce unto the ground it bore:
Both spear she took and shield which hung by it;
Both spear and shield of great pow'r, for her pur-
   pose fit.

46 Thus when she had the virgin all arrayed,
Another harness which did hang thereby
About herself she dight, [9] that the young maid
She might in equal arms accompany,

---

[1] *Moniments*, monuments, reminders.
[2] *Avising*, bethinking.
[3] *Brave*, handsome.
[4] *Baldric*, a broad belt worn over one shoulder.
[5] *Bladud*, a legendary king of England who was said to have built the city of Bath.
[6] *Sith*, since.
[7] *His great virtues*, its great powers, properties. Since Britomart is the knight of Chastity, the sword must represent the power of maidenly purity.
[8] *Sell*, saddle.
[9] *Dight*, disposed.

And as her squire attend her carefully:
Tho[1] to their ready steeds they clomb[2] full light;
And through back ways, that none might them espy,
Covered with secret cloud of silent night,
Themselves they forth conveyed, and passèd forward right.

47 Ne rested they, till that to Faery-lond
They came, as Merlin them directed late:
Where, meeting with this Redcross knight, she fond[3]
Of diverse things discourses to dilate,
But most of Arthegall and his estate.
At last their ways so fell that they mote part:
Then each to other, well affectionate,
Friendship professèd with unfeignèd heart:
The Redcross knight diverst[4]; but forth rode Britomart.

[1] *Tho*, then.
[2] *Clomb*, climbed.
[3] *Fond*, found.
[4] *Diverst*, turned off.

IV.

Britomart encounters Marinell. After his defeat, Marinell is carried by his mother to her chamber in the bottom of the sea.

1   WHERE is the ántique glory now become,
    That whilom wont in women to appear?
    Where be the brave achievements done by some?
    Where be the battles, where the shield and spear,
    And all the conquests which them high did rear,
    That matter made for famous poets' verse,
    And boastful men so oft abashed to hear?
    Been they all dead, and laid in doleful hearse [1]?
    Or doen [2] they only sleep, and shall again reverse [3]?

2   If they be dead, then woe is me therefore;
    But if they sleep, O let them soon awake!
    For all too long I burn with envy [4] sore
    To hear the warlike feats which Homer spake
    Of bold Penthesilee, [5] which made a lake
    Of Greekish blood so oft in Trojan plain;
    But when I read, how stout Deborah strake

---

[1] *Hearse*, tomb.
[2] *Doen*, do.
[3] *Reverse*, return.
[4] *Envy*, emulation.

[5] *Penthesilee*, Penthesilea, a queen of the Amazons who came to fight for Troy and was slain by Achilles. She is not mentioned by Homer.

Proud Sisera,[1] and how Camill'[2] hath slain
The huge Orsilochus, I swell with great disdain.[3]

3 Yet these, and all that else hath puissance,
Cannot with noble Britomart compare,
As well for glory of great valiance,[4]
As for pure chastity and virtue rare,
That all her goodly deeds do well declare.
Well worthy stock, from which the branches sprong
That in late years so fair a blossom bare,
As thee, O Queen, the matter of my song,
Whose lignage from this lady I derive along!

4 Who when, through speeches with the Redcross knight,
She learnèd had th' estate of Arthegall,
And in each point herself informed aright,
A friendly league of love perpetual
She with him bound, and congé[5] took withal.
Then he forth on his journey did proceed,
To seek adventures which mote him befall,
And win him worship through his warlike deed,
Which always of his pains he made the chiefest meed.

---

[1] *How stout Deborah strake proud Sisera.* Deborah prophesied that Sisera, a leader against the Israelites, should be slain by a woman. He was, however, killed by Jael, the wife of Heber, who drove a tent-peg into his temple.

[2] *Camilla*, in Virgil's Æneid; a virgin warrior who slew Orsilochus while fighting for Turnus against the Trojans.

[3] *Disdain*, scorn for the deeds of men (?).

[4] *Valiance*, valor.

[5] *Congé*, leave.

5   But Britomart kept on her former course,
    Ne ever doft her arms; but all the way
    Grew pensive through that amorous discourse,
    By which the Redcross knight did erst[1] display
    Her lover's shape and chivalrous array:
    A thousand thoughts she fashioned in her mind;
    And in her feigning fancy did portray
    Him, such as fittest she for love could find,
    Wise, warlike, personable,[2] courteous, and kind.

6   With such self-pleasing thoughts her wound she fed,
    And thought so to beguile her grievous smart;
    But so her smart was much more grievous bred,
    And the deep wound more deep engored her heart,
    That nought but death her dolour[3] mote depart.[4]
    So forth she rode, without repose or rest,
    Searching all lands and each remotest part,
    Following the guidance of her blinded guest,[5]
    Till that to the sea-coast at length she her addressed.

7   There she alighted from her light-foot beast,
    And, sitting down upon the rocky shore,
    Bade her old squire unlace her lofty crest:
    Tho,[6] having viewed a while the surges hoar
    That gainst the craggy clifts did loudly roar,
    And in their raging surquedry[7] disdained[8]
    That the fast earth affronted[9] them so sore,

---

[1] *Erst*, first.
[2] *Personable*, handsome.
[3] *Dolour*, grief.
[4] *Depart*, remove.
[5] *Blinded guest*, i.e. love.
[6] *Tho*, then.
[7] *Surquedry*, insolence.
[8] *Disdained*, felt contempt for the fact that the fast earth, etc. (?).
[9] *Affronted*, confronted.

And their devouring covetise[1] restrained;
Thereat she sighèd deep, and after thus complained:

8 "Huge sea of sorrow and tempestuous grief,
   Wherein my feeble bark is tossèd long,
   Far from the hopèd haven of relief,
   Why do thy cruel billows beat so strong,
   And thy moist mountains each on others throng,
   Threat'ning to swallow up my fearful life?
   O, do thy cruel wrath and spiteful wrong
   At length allay, and stint[2] thy stormy strife,
   Which in these troubled bowels[3] reigns and rageth rife!

9 "For else my feeble vessel, crazed and cracked
   Through thy strong buffets and outrageous blows,
   Cannot endure, but needs it must be wracked
   On the rough rocks, or on the sandy shallóws,
   The whiles that Love it steers, and Fortune rows:
   Love, my lewd[4] pilot, hath a restless mind;
   And Fortune, boatswain, no assurance[5] knows;
   But sail withouten stars gainst tide and wind:
   How can they other do, sith both are bold and blind!

10 "Thou god of winds, that reignest in the seas,
    That reignest also in the continent,[6]
    At last blow up some gentle gale of ease,
    The which may bring my ship, ere it be rent,

---

[1] *Covetise*, covetousness.
[2] *Stint*, stop.
[3] *Bowels*, used sometimes as heart, *i.e.* the seat of feeling.
[4] *Lewd*, ignorant.
[5] *Assurance*, steadiness.
[6] *In the continent*, *i.e.* on land.

Unto the gladsome port of her intent !
Then, when I shall myself in safety see,
A table, for eternal moniment
Of thy great grace and my great jeopardy,
Great Neptune, I avow to hallow unto thee [1] !"

11 Then sighing softly sore, and inly deep,
She shut up all her plaint in privy grief ;
(For her great courage would not let her weep ;)
Till that old Glaucè gan with sharp repriefe[2]
Her to restrain, and give her good relief
Through hope of those which Merlin had her told
Should of her name and nation[3] be chief,
And fetch their being from the sacred mould
Of her immortal womb, to be in heaven enrolled.

12 Thus as she her recomforted, she spied
Where far away one, all in armour bright,
With hasty gallop towards her did ride:
Her dolour soon she ceased, and on her dight[4]
Her helmet, to her courser mounting light:
Her former sorrow into sudden wrath
(Both cousin[5] passions of distroubled sprite[6])

---

[1] *A table*, etc. It was the custom among the Romans for any one who escaped shipwreck to express his gratitude by hanging up, in the temple of Neptune, a tablet or picture representing the circumstances of his danger and escape. Hillard.

[2] *Repriefe*, reproof.

[3] *Nation*, pronounced as a word of three syllables.

[4] *Dight*, put.

[5] *Cousin*, kindred.

[6] *Distroubled sprite*, disturbed mind.

Converting, forth she beats the dusty path:
Love and despite[1] at once her courage kindled hath.

13 As when a foggy mist hath overcast
The face of heaven and the clear air engroste,[2]
The world in darkness dwells; till that at last
The wat'ry southwind, from the seaboard coast
Upblowing, doth disperse the vapour lo'ste,[3]
And pours itself forth in a stormy show'r;
So the fair Britomart, having disclos'te[4]
Her cloudy care into a wrathful stowre,[5]
The mist of grief dissolved did into vengeance pour.

14 Eftsoones,[6] her goodly shield addressing[7] fair,
That mortal spear she in her hand did take,
And unto battle did herself prepare.
The knight, approaching, sternly her bespake:
"Sir knight, that dost thy voyage rashly make
By this forbidden way[8] in my despite,[9]
Ne dost by others' death ensample take,
I read[10] thee soon retire, whiles thou hast might,
Lest afterwards it be too late to take thy flight."

---

[1] *Despite*, contemptuous defiance.
[2] *Engroste*, made thick.
[3] *Lo'ste*, dissolved.
[4] *Disclo'ste*, developed, transmuted.
[5] *Stowre*, fury.
[6] *Eftsoones*, at once.
[7] *Addressing*, adjusting.
[8] *Forbidden way*, forbidden because the knight allows no one to pass.
[9] *In my despite*, in defiance or contempt of me.
[10] *Read*, advise.

15 Ythrilled with deep disdain of his proud threat,
   She shortly thus: "Fly they, that need to fly;
   Words fearen[1] babes: I mean not thee entreat
   To pass; but maugre[2] thee will pass or die:"
   Ne lenger stayed for th' other to reply,
   But with sharp spear the rest made dearly known.
   Strongly the strange knight ran, and sturdily
   Struck her full on the breast, that made her down
   Decline her head, and touch her crouper with her crown.

16 But she again him in the shield did smite
   With so fierce fury and great puissance,
   That, through his three-square scutcheon piercing quite
   And through his mailèd hauberk, by mischance
   The wicked steel through his left side did glance:
   Him so transfixèd she before her bore
   Beyond his croup, the length of all her lance;
   Till, sadly soucing[3] on the sandy shore,
   He tumbled on[4] an heap, and wallowed in his gore.

17 Like as the sacred ox that careless stands
   With gilden horns and flow'ry girlonds crowned,
   Proud of his dying honour and dear[5] bands,
   Whiles th' altars fume with frankincense around,
   All suddenly with mortal stroke astound
   Doth grovelling fall, and with his streaming gore

[1] *Fearen*, frighten.
[2] *Maugre*, in spite of.
[3] *Sadly soucing*, falling heavily.
[4] *On*, i.e. in.
[5] *Dear*, i.e. bands that are to cost him dear.

Distains[1] the pillars and the holy ground,
And the fair flow'rs that deckèd him afore:
So fell proud Marinell upon the precious shore.

18 The martial maid stayed not him to lament,
But forward rode, and kept her ready[2] way
Along the strond ; which, as she over-went,
She saw bestrowèd all with rich array
Of pearls and precious stones of great assay,[3]
And all the gravel mixed with golden ore:
Whereat she wond'red much, but would not stay
For gold, or pearls, or precious stones, an hour,
But them despisèd all, for[4] all was in her pow'r.

19 Whiles thus he lay in deadly 'stonishment,
Tidings hereof came to his mother's ear ;
His mother was the black-browed Cymoënt,
The daughter of great Nereus,[5] which did bear
This warlike son unto an earthly peer,
The famous Dumarin ; . . .
. . . .

20 . . . .
She, of his father, Marinell did name ;
And in a rocky cave as wight forlorn
Long time she fost'red up, till he became
A mighty man at arms, and mickle[6] fame
Did get through great adventures by him done:

---

[1] *Distains*, stains.
[2] *Ready*, speedy.
[3] *Assay*, value.
[4] *For*, notwithstanding.
[5] *Nereus*, an ancient sea-god.
[6] *Mickle*, much.

For never man he suffered by that same
Rich strond to travel, whereas he did wonne,[1]
But that he must do battle with the sea-nymph's
   son.

21 An hundred knights of honourable name
He had subdued, and them his vassals made:
That through all Faery-lond[2] his noble fame
Now blazèd was, and fear did all invade,
That none durst passen through that perilous glade:
And, to advance his name and glory more,
Her sea-god sire she dearly[3] did persuade
T' endow her son with treasure and rich store
'Bove all the sons that were of earthly wombs ybore.

22 The god did grant his daughter's dear demand,
To doen his nephew[4] in all riches flow[5]:
Eftsoones his heapèd waves he did command
Out of their hollow bosom forth to throw
All the huge treasure, which the sea below
Had in his greedy gulf devourèd deep,
And him enrichèd through the overthrow
And wrecks of many wretches, which did weep
And often wail their wealth which he from them
   did keep.

23 Shortly upon that shore there heapèd was
Exceeding riches and all precious things,

---

[1] *Wonne*, dwell.
[2] *Lond*, land.
[3] *Dearly*, with earnestness.
[4] *Nephew*, grandson.
[5] *To doen*, etc., to cause his grandson to abound in riches.

The spoil of all the world; that it did pass
The wealth of th' East, and pomp of Persian kings:
Gold, amber, ivory, pearls, owches,[1] rings,
And all that else was precious and dear,
The sea unto him voluntary brings;
That shortly he a great lord did appear,
As was in all the lond of Faery, or elsewhere.

24 Thereto[2] he was a doughty dreaded knight,
Tried often to the scath[3] of many dear,[4]
That none in equal arms him matchen might:
The which his mother seeing gan to fear
Lest his too haughty hardiness might rear[5]
Some hard mishap in hazard of his life:
Forthy[6] she oft him counselled to forbear
The bloody battle, and to stir up strife,[7]
But after all his war to rest his weary knife:

25 And, for his more assurance,[8] she inquired
One day of Proteus[9] by his mighty spell
(For Proteus was with prophesy inspired)
Her dear son's destiny to her to tell,
And the sad end of her sweet Marinell:
Who, through foresight of his eternal skill,
Bade her from womankind to keep him well;

---

[1] *Owches*, jewels.
[2] *Thereto*, besides.
[3] *Scath*, harm.
[4] *Dear*, dearly.
[5] *Rear*, raise, *i.e.* cause.
[6] *Forthy*, therefore.
[7] *And to stir up strife*, i.e. to forbear stirring up strife.
[8] *More assurance*, greater security.
[9] *Proteus*, a sea-god who assumed different shapes at will.

For of a woman he should have much ill;
A virgin strange and stout¹ him should dismay or
    kill.

26 Forthy she gave him warning every day
    The love of women not to entertain;
    A lesson too too² hard for living clay,
    From love in course of nature to refrain!
    Yet he his mother's lore did well retain,
    And ever from fair ladies' love did fly;
    Yet many ladies fair did oft complain,
    That they for love of him would algates³ die;
    Die whoso list for him, he was love's enemy.

27 But ah! who can deceive his destiny,
    Or ween⁴ by warning to avoid his fate?
    That, when he sleeps in most security
    And safest seems, him soonest doth amate,⁵
    And findeth due effect or soon or late;
    So feeble is the pow'r of fleshly arm!
    His mother bade him women's love to hate,
    For she of woman's force did fear no harm;
    So weening to have armed him, she did quite disarm

28 This was that woman, this the deadly wound,
    That Proteus prophesied should him dismay;
    The which his mother vainly did expound
    To be heart-wounding love, which should assay

---

¹ *Stout*, brave.
² *Too too*, exceedingly.
³ *Algates*, by all means, absolutely.
⁴ *Ween*, think, imagine.
⁵ *Amate*, confound.

To bring her son unto his last decay.[1]
So tickle[2] be the terms of mortal state
And full of subtile[3] sophisms, which do play
With double senses, and with false debate,
T' approve[4] the unknown purpose of eternal fate.

29 Too true the famous Marinell it found;
Who, through late trial, on that wealthy strond[5]
Inglorious now lies in senseless swownd,[6]
Through heavy stroke of Britomartis hond.[7]
Which when his mother dear did understond,
And heavy tidings heard, whereas[8] she played
Amongst her wat'ry sisters by a pond,
Gathering sweet daffadillies, to have made
Gay girlonds from the sun their foreheads fair to shade,

30 Eftsoones both flow'rs and girlonds far away
She flung, and her fair dewy locks yrent:
To sorrow huge she turned her former play,
And gamesome mirth to grievous dreriment[9]:
She threw herself down on the continent,[10]
Ne word did speak, but lay as in a swowne,
Whiles all her sisters did for her lament
With yelling outcries, and with shrieking sowne[11];
And every one did tear her girlond from her crown.

---

[1] *Decay*, ruin, destruction.
[2] *Tickle*, unstable.
[3] *Subtile*, subtle.
[4] *Approve*, prove.
[5] *Strond*, strand.
[6] *Swownd*, swoon.
[7] *Hond*, hand.
[8] *Whereas*, where.
[9] *Dreriment*, sorrow.
[10] *Continent*, land.
[11] *Sowne*, sound.

31 Soon as she up out of her deadly fit
　　Arose, she bade her charet to be brought;
　　And all her sisters, that with her did sit,
　　Bade eke[1] attonce[2] their charets to be sought:
　　Tho,[3] full of bitter grief and pensive thought,
　　She to her waggon clomb[4]; clomb all the rest,
　　And forth together went, with sorrow fraught[5]:
　　The waves obedient to their behest
　　Them yielded ready passage, and their rage sur-
　　　　ceased.[6]

32 Great Neptune stood amazèd at their sight,
　　While on his broad round back they softly slid,
　　And eke himself mourned at their mournful plight,
　　Yet wist[7] not what their wailing meant, yet did,
　　For great compassion of their sorrow, bid
　　His mighty waters to them buxom[8] be:
　　Eftsoones[9] the roaring billows still abid,[10]
　　And all the grisly[11] monsters of the sea
　　Stood gaping at their gate,[12] and wond'red them to
　　　　see.

33 A team of dolphins raungèd[13] in array
　　Drew the smooth charet of sad Cymoënt:
　　They were all taught by Triton to obey

---

[1] *Eke*, likewise.
[2] *Attonce*, at once.
[3] *Tho*, then.
[4] *Clomb*, climbed.
[5] *Fraught*, filled.
[6] *Surceased*, ended.
[7] *Wist*, knew.
[8] *Buxom*, yielding.
[9] *Eftsoones*, immediately.
[10] *Abid*, abode.
[11] *Grisly*, frightful.
[12] *Gate*, procedure.
[13] *Raunged in array*, arranged in proper order.

To the long reins at her commandëment:
As swift as swallows on the waves they went,
That their broad flaggy fins no foam did rear,
Ne bubbling rowndell[1] they behind them sent;
The rest of other fishes drawen were,
Which with their finny oars the swelling sea did shear.

34 Soon as they been arrived upon the brim
Of the rich strond, their charets they forlore,[2]
And let their teamèd[3] fishes softly swim
Along the margent[4] of the foamy shore,
Lest they their fins should bruise, and surbate[5] sore
Their tender feet upon the stony ground:
And coming to the place, where all in gore
And cruddy[6] blood enwallowèd[7] they found
The luckless Marinell lying in deadly swownd,

35 His mother swoonèd thrice, and the third time
Could scarce recovered be out of her pain;
Had she not been devoid of mortal slime,
She should not then have been re-lived[8] again:
But, soon as life recovered had the reign,
She made so piteous moan and dear wayment,[9]
That the hard rocks could scarce from tears refrain:

[1] *Rowndell*, globule.
[2] *Forlore*, left.
[3] *Teamed*, yoked as in a team.
[4] *Margent*, margin.
[5] *Surbate*, batter.
[6] *Cruddy*, curdled.
[7] *Enwallowed*, rolling in.
[8] *Re-lived*, revived.
[9] *Dear wayment*, heartfelt lamentation.

And all her sister nymphs with one consent
Supplied her sobbing breaches [1] with sad complement.[2]

36 "Dear image of myself," she said, "that is
The wretched son of wretched mother born,
Is this thine high advancement? O! is this
Th' immortal name, with which thee, yet unborn,
Thy grandsire Nereus promised to adorn?
Now liest thou of life and honour reft[3];
Now liest thou a lump of earth forlorn;
Ne of thy late life memory is left;
Ne can thy irrevocable destiny be wefte[4]!

37 "Fond[5] Proteus, father of false prophecies!
And they more fond that credit to thee give!
Not this the work of woman's hand ywis,[6]
That so deep wound through these dear members drive.
I fearèd love; but they that love do live;
But they that die do neither love nor hate:
Nathless to thee thy folly I forgive;
And to myself, and to accursèd fate,
The guilt I do ascribe: dear wisdom bought too late!

38 "O! what avails it of immortal seed [7]
To be ybred and never born to die?

---

[1] *Sobbing breaches*, i.e. the intervals of her sobbing.
[2] *Complement*, accessory, supplement.
[3] *Reft*, bereft.
[4] *Wefte*, avoided.
[5] *Fond*, foolish.
[6] *Ywis*, surely.
[7] *Seed*, race.

Far better I it deem to die with speed,
Then[1] waste in woe and wailful[2] misery:
Who dies, the utmost dolour doth abye[3];
But who that lives is left to wail his loss:
So life is loss, and death felicity:
Sad life worse than glad death; and greater cross
To see friend's grave, then dead the grave self to
    engross.[4]

39 "But if the heavens did his day envý,[5]
And my short bliss malign,[6] yet mote they well
Thus much afford me, ere that he did die,
That the dim eyes of my dear Marinell
I mote[7] have closèd, and him bed[8] farewell,
Sith other offices for mother meet
They would not grant——
Yet, maulgre[9] them, farewell, my sweetest sweet!
Farewell, my sweetest son, sith we no more shall
    meet!"

40 Thus when they all had sorrowèd their fill,
They softly gan to search his grisly[10] wound:
And, that they might him handle more at will,
They him disarmed; and, spreading on the ground
Their watchet[11] mantles fringed with silver round,
They softly wiped away the jelly blood

---

[1] *Then*, than.
[2] *Wailful*, mournful.
[3] *Abye*, endure.
[4] *Engross*, occupy.
[5] *Envy*, begrudge.
[6] *Malign*, begrudge.
[7] *Mote*, might.
[8] *Bed*, bade.
[9] *Maulgre*, in spite of.
[10] *Grisly*, dreadful.
[11] *Watchet*, pale blue.

From th' orifice ; which, having well upbound,
They poured in sovereign balm and nectar good,
Good both for earthly med'cine and for heavenly
  food.

41 Tho,[1] when the lily-handed Liagore
(This Liagore whilom[2] had learnèd skill
In leech's[3] craft, by great Apollo's lore,[4]
Sith her whilom upon high Pindus hill[5]
He lovèd,) .   .   .   .
  .   .   .   .
Did feel his pulse, she knew there stayèd still
Some little life his feeble sprites[6] among ;
Which to his mother told, despair she from her flung.

42 Tho, up him taking in their tender hands,
They easily unto her charett[7] bear:
Her team at her commandment quiet stands,
Whiles they the corse[8] into the waggon rear,
And strow with flow'rs the lamentable beare[9]:
Then all the rest into their coaches clim,[10]
And through the brackish waves their passage
  shear[11];
Upon great Neptune's neck they softly swim,
And to her wat'ry chamber swiftly carry him.

[1] *Tho*, then.
[2] *Whilom*, formerly.
[3] *Leech's*, physician's.
[4] *Apollo's lore ;* Apollo and his son Æsculapius were revered as the chief gods of healing.
[5] *Pindus hill*, a lofty mountain in Thessaly, the seat of the muses.
[6] *Sprites*, spirits.
[7] *Charett*, chariot.
[8] *Corse*, body.
[9] *Beare*, bier.
[10] *Clim*, climb.
[11] *Shear*, cut.

43 Deep in the bottom of the sea, her bow'r[1]
   Is built of hollow billows heapèd high,
   Like to thick clouds that threat a stormy show'r,
   And vauted[2] all within like to the sky,
   In which the gods do dwell eternally:
   There they him laid in easy couch well dight,[3]
   And sent in haste for Tryphon,[4] to apply
   Salve to his wounds, and medicines of might:
   For Tryphon of sea-gods the sovereign leech is hight.[5]

44 The whiles the nymphs sit all about him round,
   Lamenting his mishap and heavy plight;
   And oft his mother, viewing his wide wound,
   Cursèd the hand that did so deadly smite
   Her dearest son, her dearest heart's delight:
   But none of all those curses overtook
   The warlike maid, th' ensample of that might[6];
   But fairly well she thrived, and well did brook
   Her noble deeds,[7] ne her right course for ought forsook.

45 Yet did false Archimage[8] her still pursue,
   To bring to pass his mischievous intent,

---

[1] *Bower*, chamber, dwelling.
[2] *Vauted*, vaulted.
[3] *Dight*, arranged.
[4] *Tryphon.* There is no leech of the sea-gods in classical mythology. Hillard.
[5] *Hight*, called.
[6] *The warlike maid, th' ensample of that might, i.e.* Britomart, who had in the overthrow of Marinell given a specimen of her power.
[7] *And well did brook her noble deeds, i.e.* she did not suffer in consequence of her noble deeds.
[8] *Archimage*, or *Archimago*, a wicked enchanter described in the first book of the "Faery Queene," the chief enemy of the Redcross knight and Una.

Now that he had her singled from the crew
Of courteous knights, the prince and faery gent,[1]
Whom late in chase of beauty excellent
She left, pursuing that same foster[2] strong;
Of whose foul outrage they impatient,
And full of fiery zeal, him followed long,
To rescue her[3] from shame, and to revenge her wrong.

[1] *The prince and faery gent,* i.e. Prince Arthur and the noble faery, or faery knight, Sir Guyon, who left Britomart to go to the rescue of the lady "upon a milk-white palfrey."

[2] *Foster,* forester.

[3] *Her,* i.e. the lady pursued by the forester.

V.

The Night at Malbecco's Castle.

Satyrane and Paridell, two of Gloriana's champions, found themselves on a dark and stormy night outside the castle of a man known as Malbecco. As admittance was not readily granted, Paridell wished to force an entrance.

1 "Nay, let us first," said Satyrane, "entreat
 The man, by gentle means, to let us in ;
 And afterwards affray[1] with cruel threat,
 Ere that we to efforce[2] it do begin :
 Then, if all fail, we will by force it win,
 And eke[3] reward the wretch for his mesprise,[4]
 As may be worthy of his heinous sin."
 That counsel pleased : then Paridell did rise,
 And to the castle-gate approached in quiet wise :

2 Whereat soft knocking, entrance he desired.
 The good man self, which then the porter played,
 Him answerèd, that all were now retired
 Unto their rest, and all the keys conveyed
 Unto their master who in bed was laid,
 That none him durst awake out of his dream ;
 And therefore them of patience gently prayed.
 Then Paridell began to change his theme,
 And threat'ned him with force and punishment extreme.

[1] *Affray*, frighten. [3] *Eke*, also.
[2] *Efforce*, force.   [4] *Mesprise*, contempt.

3 But all in vain; for nought mote him relent[1]:
   And now so long before the wicket fast
   They waited, that the night was forward spent,
   And the fair welkin[2] foully overcast
   Gan blowen up a bitter stormy blast,
   With show'r and hail so horrible and dread,
   That this fair many[3] were compelled at last
   To fly for succour to a little shed,
   The which beside the gate for swine was orderèd.

4 It fortunèd,[4] soon after they were gone,
   Another knight, whom tempest thether brought,
   Came to that castle, and with earnest moan,
   Like as the rest, late entrance dear[5] besought;
   But, like so as the rest, he prayed for nought;
   For flatly he of entrance was refused:
   Sorely thereat he was displeased, and thought
   How to avenge himself so sore abused,
   And evermore the carle[6] of courtesy accused.[7]

5 But, to avoid th' intolerable stowre,[8]
   He was compelled to seek some refuge near,
   And to that shed, to shroud him from the show'r,
   He came, which full of guests he found whilere,[9]
   So as he was not let[10] to enter there;

---

[1] *Mote him relent*, could soften him.
[2] *Welkin*, sky.
[3] *Many*, company.
[4] *Fortuned*, happened.
[5] *Dear*, earnestly.
[6] *Carle*, churl.
[7] *Of courtesy accused*, i.e. accused of lack of courtesy.
[8] *Stowre*, storm.
[9] *Whilere*, before (him).
[10] *Let*, allowed.

Whereat he gan to wex[1] exceeding wroth,
And swore that he would lodge with them yfere,[2]
Or them dislodge, all were they lief or loath[3];
And so defied them each, and so defied them both.

6 Both were full loath to leave that needful tent,[4]
And both full loath in darkness to debate;
Yet both full lief him lodging to have lent,
And both full lief his boasting to abate:
But chiefly Paridell his heart did grate[5]
To hear him threaten so despitefully,
As if he did a dog in kennel rate
That durst not bark; and rather had he die
Then, when he was defied, in coward corner lie.

7 Tho,[6] hastily remounting to his steed,
He forth issued; like as a boistrous wind,
Which in th' earth's hollow caves hath long been hid
And shut up fast within her prisons blind,
Makes the huge element,[7] against her kind,[8]
To move and tremble as it were aghast,
Until that it an issue forth may find;
Then forth it breaks, and with his[9] furious blast
Confounds both land and seas, and skies doth overcast.

---

[1] *Wex*, wax, grow.
[2] *Yfere*, together.
[3] *All were they lief or loath, i.e.* whether they were willing or unwilling.
[4] *Tent*, shelter.
[5] *Grate*, fret.
[6] *Tho*, then.
[7] *The huge element, i.e.* the earth.
[8] *Kind*, nature.
[9] *His*. *Its* did not come into general use until after Spenser's time. Even Shakespeare uses *his* for *its* in many cases.

8 Their steel-head spears they strongly couched, and met
 Together with impetuous rage and force,
 That with the terror of their fierce affret [1]
 They rudely drove to ground both man and horse,
 That each awhile lay like a senseless corse.
 But Paridell, sore bruisèd with the blow,
 Could not arise, the counterchange to scorse [2];
 Till that young squire him rearèd from below;
 Then drew he his bright sword, and gan about him throw.

9 But Satyrane, forth stepping, did them stay,
 And with fair treaty pacified their ire:
 Then, when they were accorded [3] from the fray,
 Against that castle's lord they gan conspire,
 To heap on him due vengeance for his hire.
 They been agreed, and to the gates they go
 To burn the same with unquenchable fire,
 And that uncourteous carle, their common foe,
 To do foul death to die,[4] or wrap in grievous woe.

10 Malbecco seeing them resolved indeed
 To flame the gates, and hearing them to call
 For fire in earnest, ran with fearful speed,
 And, to them calling from the castle wall,
 Besought them humbly him to bear with all,
 As ignorant of servants' bad abuse
 And slack attendance unto strangers' call.

---

[1] *Affret*, encounter.
[2] *Scorse*, exchange, give back.
[3] *Accorded*, made to agree.
[4] *To do foul death to die, i.e.* to cause him to die a foul death.

The knights were willing all things to excuse,
Though nought believed, and entrance late did not
    refuse.

11 They been ybrought into a comely bow'r,[1]
And served of all things that mote needful be;
Yet secretly their host did on them low'r,
And welcomed more for fear than charitee;
But they dissembled what they did not see,[2]
And welcomèd themselves. Each gan undight[3]
Their garments wet, and weary armour free,
To dry themselves by Vulcan's[4] flaming light,
And eke[5] their lately bruisèd parts to bring in
    plight.[6]

12 And eke that stranger knight amongst the rest
Was for like need enforced to disarray:
Tho,[7] whenas vailèd was her lofty crest,[8]
Her golden locks, that were in trammels[9] gay
Upbounden, did themselves adown display,
And raught[10] unto her heels; like sunny beams,
That in a cloud their light did long time stay,
Their vapour vaded,[11] show their golden gleams,
And through the persant[12] air shoot forth their
    azure streams.

[1] *Bower*, room.
[2] *But they dissembled*, etc., *i.e.* they appeared as though they had been hospitably received.
[3] *Undight*, to put off.
[4] *Vulcan*, the god of fire.
[5] *Eke*, also.
[6] *Plight*, order.
[7] *Tho*, then.
[8] *Whenas vailed was her lofty crest*, *i.e.* when her helmet was doffed.
[9] *Trammels*, braids.
[10] *Raught*, reached.
[11] *Vaded*, dissipated.
[12] *Persant*, sharp, clear.

13 She also doft her heavy haberieon,[1]
    Which the fair feature of her limbs did hide;
    And her well-plighted[2] frock, which she did won[3]
    To tuck about her short when she did ride,
    She low let fall, that flowed from her lank side
    Down to her foot with careless modestee.
    Then of them all she plainly was espied
    To be a womanwight, unwist to be,
    The fairest womanwight that ever eye did see.

14 Like as Bellona,[4] being late returned
    From slaughter of the giants conquerèd, —
    Where proud Encelade,[5] whose wide nostrils burned
    With breathèd flames like to a furnace red,
    Transfixèd with her spear, down tumbled dead
    From top of Hemus[6] by him heapèd high, —
    Hath loosed her helmet from her lofty head,
    And her Gorgonian shield[7] gins to untie
    From her left arm, to rest in glorious victory.

15 Which whenas they beheld, they smitten were
    With great amazement at so wondrous sight;
    And each on other, and they all on her,
    Stood gazing; as if sudden great affright

---

[1] *Haberieon*, habergeon, coat of mail.
[2] *Well-plighted*, well-folded.
[3] *Did won*, did use.
[4] *Bellona*, the goddess of war; here stands for Minerva.
[5] *Encelade*, Enceladus, the giant buried under Mount Aetna.
[6] *Hemus*, Haemus; ancient name of the Balkan mountains.
[7] *Gorgonian shield*, Minerva's shield which bore the fatal Gorgon's head.

Had them surprised. At last avising[1] right
Her goodly personage and glorious hue,
Which they so much mistook, they took delight
In their first error, and yet still anew
With wonder of her beauty fed their hungry view:

16 Yet note[2] their hungry view be satisfied,
But, seeing, still the more desired to see,
And ever firmly fixèd did abide
In contemplation of divinitee:
But most they marvelled at her chivalree
And noble prowess, which they had approved,[3]
That much they fained[4] to know who she mote[5] be;
Yet none of all them her thereof amoved[6];
Yet every one her liked, and every one her loved.

The lady of the castle soon appeared and kindly welcomed the warriors.

17 Now, when of meats and drinks they had their fill,
Purpose was movèd by that gentle dame
Unto those knights adventurous, to tell
Of deeds of arms which unto them became,[7]
And every one his kindred and his name.

. . . .

18 So long these knights discoursèd diversely
Of strange affairs, and noble hardiment,[8]

---

[1] *Avising*, contemplating.
[2] *Note*, could not.
[3] *Approved*, proved.
[4] *Fained*, desired.
[5] *Mote*, might.
[6] *Amoved*, i.e. questioned.
[7] *Became*, happened.
[8] *Hardiment*, bold deeds.

Which they had passed with mickle jeopardy,
That now the humid night was far forth spent,
And heavenly lamps were halfendeale [1] ybrent [2]:
Which th' old man [3] seeing well, who too long thought
Every discourse, and every argument,
Which by the hours he measurèd, besought
Them go to rest. So all unto their bow'rs [4] were brought.

[1] *Halfendeale*, the half part.
[2] *Ybrent*, burned.
[3] *Th' old man*, i.e. Malbecco, the host.
[4] *Bowers*, chambers.

VI.

Amoret and the Garden of Venus.

Scudamour, whom Britomart was about to meet, was the husband of the beautiful Amoret. Amoret was the daughter of Chrysogonee and the twin sister of Belphœbe. Soon after the birth of these children, Chrysogonee fell asleep in a forest; and the goddesses Venus and Diana happening along just then, took each a child from the sleeping mother.

1 Up they them took, each one a babe uptook,
   And with them carried to be fosterèd:
   Dame Phœbe[1] to a nymph her babe betook
   To be upbrought in perfect maidenhead,[2]
   And, of herself, her name Belphœbe read[3]:
   But Venus hers thence far away conveyed,
   To be upbrought in goodly womanhead;
   And, in her little Love's stead which was strayed,[4]
   Her Amoretta called, to comfort her dismayed.[5]

2 She brought her to her joyous paradise
   Where most she wonnes,[6] when she on earth does
       dwell:
   So fair a place as nature can devise:

[1] *Phœbe*, Diana, the goddess of the moon; the maiden goddess devoted to the chase.
[2] *Maidenhead*, maidenhood.
[3] *And, of herself, her name Belphœbe read*, i.e. called her Belphœbe, after herself.
[4] *In her little Love's stead*, etc., i.e. in the place of Cupid who had run away from his mother.
[5] *Dismayed*, dejected.
[6] *Wonnes*, dwells.

Whether in Paphos,[1] or Cytheron hill,[2]
Or it in Gnidus[3] be, I wote[4] not well;
But well I wote by trial, that this same
All other pleasant places doth excel,
And callèd is, by her lost lover's name,
The garden of Adonis,[5] far renowmed by fame.

3 There is continual spring, and harvest there
Continual, both meeting at one time:
For both the boughs do laughing blossoms bear,
And with fresh colors deck the wanton prime,[6]
And eke attonce[7] the heavy trees they climb,
Which seem to labour under their fruits' load:
The whiles the joyous birds make their pastime
Among the shady leaves, their sweet abode,
And their true loves without suspicion tell abroad.

4 Right in the middest of that paradise
There stood a stately mount, on whose round top
A gloomy grove of myrtle trees did rise,
Whose shady boughs sharp steel did never lop,
Nor wicked beasts their tender buds did crop,
But like a garland compassèd the height,
And from their fruitful sides sweet gum did drop,

---

[1] *Paphos*, a city on the island of Cyprus, which contained a celebrated temple of Venus.

[2] *Cytheron hill*, refers to the town of Cythera in Crete, or to the island of Cythera, where Venus was said to have first landed.

[3] *Gnidus*, a Doric city in Caria celebrated for its statue of Venus, the work of Praxiteles.

[4] *Wote*, know.

[5] *Adonis*, a youth of extraordinary beauty beloved by Venus, and by her changed into an anemone.

[6] *Wanton prime*, luxuriant spring.

[7] *Eke attonce*, also together.

That all the ground, with precious dew bedight,¹
Threw forth most dainty odours and most sweet
  delight.

5 And in the thickest covert of that shade
There was a pleasant arbour, not by art
But of the trees' own inclination made,
Which knitting their rank ² branches part to part,
With wanton ivy-twine entrailed athwart,³
And eglantine ⁴ and caprifole ⁵ among,
Fashioned above within their inmost part,
That nether Phœbus' ⁶ beams could through them
  throng,
Nor Æolus' ⁷ sharp blast could work them any wrong.

6 And all about grew every sort of flow'r,
To which sad lovers were transformed of yore ;
Fresh Hyacinthus,⁸ Phœbus' paramour
And dearest love ;
Foolish Narcisse,⁹ that likes the wat'ry shore ;
Sad Amaranthus,¹⁰ made a flow'r but late,
Sad Amaranthus, in whose purple gore

¹ *Bedight*, covered.
² *Rank*, luxuriant.
³ *Entrailed athwart*, twisted across.
⁴ *Eglantine*, wild rose.
⁵ *Caprifole*, woodbine.
⁶ *Phœbus*, Apollo, the sun-god.
⁷ *Æolus*, the ruler of the winds.
⁸ *Hyacinthus*, a youth beloved by Apollo and accidentally killed by him. The hyacinth was fabled to have sprung from his blood.
⁹ *Narcisse*, Narcissus, a beautiful youth who fell in love with his own reflection as seen in a fountain. He was changed to the flower Narcissus.
¹⁰ *Amaranthus*, a m a r a n t h, which signifies unfading. Among the ancients this flower was the symbol of immortality.

Meseems I see Amintas' wretched fate,[1]
To whom sweet poets' verse hath given endless date.

7 Hether great Venus brought this infant fair,
   The younger daughter of Chrysogonee,
   And unto Psyche[2] with great trust and care
   Committed her, yfosterèd to be,
   And trainèd up in true feminitee[3]:
   Who no less carefully her tenderèd[4]
   Than her own daughter Pleasure, to whom she
   Made her companion, and her lessonèd[5]
   In all the lore of love and goodly womanhead.

8 In which when she to perfect ripeness grew,
   Of grace and beauty noble paragon,
   She brought her forth into the worldës view,
   To be th' ensample of true love alone,
   And loadstar of all chaste affection[6]
   To all fair ladies that do live on ground.
   To Faery court she came; where many one
   Admired her goodly 'haviour, and found
   His feeble heart wide launchèd[7] with love's cruel wound.

---

[1] *Amintas' wretched fate.* This is supposed to allude to the untimely fate of Sir Philip Sidney. Hillard.

[2] *Psyche* (breath or soul); a maiden beloved by Cupid and made immortal by Jupiter.

[3] *Feminitee*, womanhood.

[4] *Tendered*, cared for.

[5] *Lessoned*, taught.

[6] *Affection*, pronounced as word of four syllables.

[7] *Launched*, pierced.

9 But she to none of them her love did cast,
Save to the noble knight, Sir Scudamore,
To whom her loving heart she linkèd fast
In faithful love, t' abide for evermore;
And for his dearest sake endurèd sore,
Sore trouble of an heinous enemy,
Who her would forcèd have to have forlore [1]
Her former love and steadfast loyalty,
As ye may elsewhere read that rueful history.

[1] *Forlore*, abandoned.

VII.

After separating from Satyrane, Britomart meets Scudamour, the husband of Amoret. Together they proceed to the house of the enchanter Busyrane.

1   O HATEFUL hellish snake! what fury first
    Brought thee from baleful house of Prosperine,[1]
    Where in her bosom she thee long hath nurst,
    And fost'red up with bitter milk of tine[2];
    Foul Jealousy! that turnest love divine
    To joyless dread, and mak'st the loving heart
    With hateful thoughts to languish and to pine,
    And feed itself with self-consuming smart,
    Of all the passions in the mind thou vilest art!

2   O let him far be banishèd away,
    And in his stead let Love forever dwell!
    Sweet Love, that doth his golden wings embay[3]
    In blessèd nectar and pure pleasure's well,
    Untroubled of vile fear or bitter fell.[4]
    And ye, fair ladies, that your kingdoms make
    In th' hearts of men, them govern wisely well,
    And of fair Britomart ensample take,
    That was as true in love as turtle[5] to her make.[6]

[1] *Proserpine*, Proserpina, the daughter of Ceres, who was carried down to Hades by Pluto to be his bride.

[2] *Tine*, woe.
[3] *Embay*, bathe.
[4] *Fell*, gall.
[5] *Turtle*, turtle-dove.
[6] *Make*, mate.

3 Who, with Sir Satyrane, as erst[1] ye read,
   Forth riding from Malbecco's hostless[2] house,
   Far off espied a young man, the which fled
   From an huge giant, that with hideous
   And hateful outrage long him chasèd thus;
   It was that Ollyphant,[3] the brother dear
   Of that Argantè vile and vicious,[4]
   From whom the Squire of Dames was reft[5] whilere[6];
   This all as bad as she, and worse, if worse ought were.

4 . . . .
   Whom when as Britomart beheld behind
   The fearful boy so greedily pursue,
   She was emmovèd[7] in her noble mind
   T' employ her puissance to his rescue,
   And prickèd[8] fiercely forward where she did him view.

5 Ne[9] was Sir Satyrane her far behind,
   But with like fierceness did ensue[10] the chase;
   Whom when the giant saw, he soon resigned
   His former suit,[11] and from them fled apace:

---

[1] *Erst*, first, formerly.
[2] *Hostless*, inhospitable.
[3] *It was that Ollyphant*, etc. This refers to an incident related in Book III, Canto VII.
[4] *Vicious*, pronounced as a word of three syllables.
[5] *Reft*, torn away.
[6] *Whilere*, formerly.
[7] *Emmoved*, moved.
[8] *Pricked*, rode fast, using spurs.
[9] *Ne*, nor.
[10] *Ensue*, follow.
[11] *Resigned his former suit, i.e.* gave up his former pursuit.

They after both, and boldly bade him base,[1]
And each did strive the other to outgo;
But he them both outran a wondrous space,
For he was long, and swift as any roe,
And now made better speed t' escape his fearèd foe.

6 It was not Satyrane, whom he did fear,
But Britomart, the flow'r of chastity;
For he the pow'r of chaste hands might not bear,
But always did their dread encounter fly:
And now so fast his feet he did apply,
That he has gotten to a forest near,
Where he is shrouded in security.
The wood they enter, and search everywhere;
They searchèd diversely; so both divided were.

7 Fair Britomart so long him followèd,
That she at last came to a fountain sheer,[2]
By which there lay a knight all wallowèd[3]
Upon the grassy ground, and by him near
His haberieon,[4] his helmet, and his spear:
A little off, his shield was rudely thrown,
On which the wingèd boy[5] in colours clear
Depeincted[6] was, full easy to be known,
And he thereby, wherever it in field was shown.

8 His face upon the ground did grovelling lie,
As if he had been slumb'ring in the shade;

---

[1] *Bade him base*, *i.e.* began in their turn to pursue the giant.

[2] *Sheer*, clear.

[3] *Wallowed*, rolled about as in mire.

[4] *Haberieon*, habergeon, coat of mail,

[5] *Winged boy*, Cupid.

[6] *Depeincted*, depicted, portrayed.

That[1] the brave maid would not for courtesy
Out of his quiet slumber him abrade,[2]
Nor seem too suddenly him to invade :
Still as she stood, she heard with grievous throb
Him groan, as if his heart were pieces made,
And with most painful pangs to sigh and sob,
That pity did the virgin's heart of patience rob.

9 At last forth breaking into bitter plaints
He said : "O sovereign Lord, that sit'st on high
And reign'st in bliss amongst thy blessed saints,
How suff'rest thou such shameful cruelty,
So long unwreakèd[3] of thine enemy !
Or hast thou, Lord, of good men's cause no heed ?
Or doth thy justice sleep and silent lie ?
What booteth then the good and righteous deed,
If goodness find no grace, nor righteousness no meed !

10 "If good find grace, and righteousness reward,
Why then is Amoret in caytive[4] band,
Sith that more bounteous[5] creature never far'd[6]
On foot upon the face of living land !
Or if that heavenly justice may withstand
The wrongful outrage of unrighteous men,
Why then is Busyrane with wicked hand
Suff'red, these seven months day,[7] in secret den
My lady and my Love so cruelly to pen ?

[1] *That*, so that, for that reason.
[2] *Abrade*, rouse.
[3] *Unwreaked*, unavenged.
[4] *Caytive*, captive.
[5] *Bounteous*, virtuous.
[6] *Fared*, walked.
[7] *Day*, time.

11 "My lady and my love is cruelly penned
   In doleful darkness from the view of day,
   Whilst deadly torments do her chaste breast rend,
   And the sharp steel doth rive[1] her heart in tway,[2]—
   All for[3] she Scudamore[4] will not denay.[5]
   Yet thou, vile man, vile Scudamore, art sound,
   Ne canst her aid, ne canst her foe dismay;
   Unworthy wretch to tread upon the ground,
   For whom so fair a lady feels so sore a wound."

12 There an huge heap of singulfes[6] did oppress
   His struggling soul, and swelling throbs empeach[7]
   His falt'ring tongue with pangs of dreariness,[8]
   Choking the remnant of his plaintife speech,
   As if his days were come to their last reach.
   Which when she heard, and saw the ghastly fit
   Threat'ning into his life to make a breach,
   Both with great ruth[9] and terror she was smit,
   Fearing lest from her cage the weary soul would flit.

13 Tho, stooping down, she him amovèd light;
   Who, therewith somewhat starting, up gan look,
   And seeing him behind a stranger knight,

---

[1] *Rive*, rend.
[2] *In tway*, in two.
[3] *For*, because.
[4] *Scudamore*. It has seemed best to follow the original, and spell this name sometimes Scudamore, and at other times Scudamour. — The family of Scudamore derived this surname from their bearing the Shield of Divine Love (scudo d'amore) for their arms. Prof. Child.
[5] *Denay*, deny, *i.e.* to prove false to.
[6] *Singulfes*, for singults, sobs.
[7] *Empeach*, hinder.
[8] *Dreariness*, sorrow.
[9] *Ruth*, pity.

Whereas no living creature he mistook,[1]
With great indignance he that sight forsook,[2]
And, down again himself disdainfully
Abjecting,[3] th' earth with his fair forehead strook:
Which the bold virgin seeing, gan apply
Fit med'cine to his grief, and spake thus courtesly[4]:

14 "Ah! gentle knight, whose deep-conceivèd[5] grief
Well seems t' exceed the pow'r of patience,
Yet, if that heavenly grace some good relief
You send, submit you to high Providence;
And ever in your noble heart prepense,[6]
That all the sorrow in the world is less
Then virtue's might and value's[7] confidence:
For who nill[8] bide the burden of distress,
Must not here think to live; for life is wretchedness.

15 "Therefore, fair sir, do comfort to you take,
And freely read[9] what wicked felon so
Hath outraged you, and thralled[10] your gentle make.[11]
Perhaps this hand may help to ease your woe,
And wreak your sorrow on your cruel foe;
At least it fair endeavour will apply."
Those feeling words so near the quick did go,
That up his head he rearèd easily:
And, leaning on his elbow, these few words let fly:

[1] *Whereas no living creature*, etc., where he wrongly supposed that there was no living creature.
[2] *Forsook*, turned from.
[3] *Abjecting*, casting.
[4] *Courtesly*, courteously.
[5] *Deep-conceived*, deep-felt.
[6] *Prepense*, consider.
[7] *Value's*, valor's.
[8] *Nill*, will not.
[9] *Read*, explain.
[10] *Thralled*, enslaved.
[11] *Make*, mate.

16 "What boots it plain that cannot be redressed,[1]
    And sow vain sorrow in a fruitless ear[2];
    Sith pow'r of hand, nor skill of learnèd breast,
    Ne worldly price, cannot redeem my dear
    Out of her thraldom and continual fear!
    For he, the tyrant, which her hath in ward
    By strong enchantments and black magic lear,[3]
    Hath in a dungeon deep her close embarred,[4]
    And many dreadful fiends hath pointed[5] to her guard.

17 "There he tormenteth her most terribly,
    And day and night afflicts with mortal pain,
    Because to yield him love she doth deny,
    Once to me yold,[6] not to be yold again:
    But yet by torture he would her constrain
    Love to conceive in her disdainful breast;
    Till so she do, she must in doole[7] remain,
    Ne may by living means be thence relest[8]:
    What boots it then to plain that cannot be redressed!"

18 With this sad hersal[9] of his heavy stress[10]
    The warlike damsel was empassioned[11] sore,
    And said: "Sir knight, your cause is nothing less

---

[1] *What boots it plain of,* etc., *i.e.* What is the use of complaining of what cannot be helped.

[2] *And sow vain sorrow,* etc., *i.e.* and tell my sorrow to one who cannot help me.

[3] *Lear,* lore.

[4] *Embarred,* shut in.

[5] *Pointed,* appointed.

[6] *Yold,* yielded.

[7] *Doole,* grief.

[8] *Relest,* released.

[9] *Hersal,* rehearsal.

[10] *Stress,* distress.

[11] *Empassioned,* moved.

Then is your sorrow, certes,[1] if not more;
For nothing so much pity doth implore
As gentle lady's helpless misery:
But yet, if please ye listen to my lore,[2]
I will, with proof of last extremity,[3]
Deliver her fro thence, or with her for you die."

19 "Ah! gentlest knight alive," said Scudamore,
"What huge heroic magnanimity
Dwells in thy bounteous breast? what couldst thou more,
If she were thine, and thou as now am I?
O spare thy happy days, and them apply
To better boot[4]; but let me die that ought;
More is more loss; one is enough to die!"
"Life is not lost," said she, "for which is bought
Endless renowm, that more then death is to be sought."

20 Thus she at length persuaded him to rise,
And with her wend to see what new success
Mote[5] him befall upon new enterprize:
His arms, which he had vowed to disprofess,[6]
She gathered up and did about him dress,[7]
And his forwandred[8] steed unto him got:
So forth they both yfere[9] make their progréss,

---

[1] *Certes*, certainly.
[2] *Lore*, advice.
[3] *With proof of last extremity*, i.e. with a supreme effort.
[4] *Boot*, advantage.
[5] *Mote*, might.
[6] *Disprofess*, renounce.
[7] *Dress*, dispose.
[8] *Forwandred*, strayed away.
[9] *Yfere*, together.

And march, not past the mountenance of a shot,[1]
Till they arrived whereas[2] their purpose they did plot.

21 There they, dismounting, drew their weapons bold,
And stoutly came unto the castle gate,
Whereas no gate they found them to withhold,
Nor ward[3] to wait at morn and evening late;
But in the porch, that did them sore amate,[4]
A flaming fire ymixt with smouldry smoke
And stinking sulphur, that with grisly[5] hate
And dreadful horror did all entrance choke,
Enforcèd them their forward footing to revoke.[6]

22 Greatly thereat was Britomart dismayed,
Ne in that stownd[7] wist[8] how herself to bear;
For danger vain it were to have assayed
That cruel element, which all things fear,
Ne none can suffer to approachen near:
And, turning back to Scudamour, thus said:
"What monstrous enmity provoke we here?
Foolhardy as th' Earth's children,[9] the which made
Battle against the gods, so we a god invade.

23 "Danger without discretion to attempt,
Inglorious, beast-like, is: therefore, Sir Knight,

---

[1] *The mountenance of a shot*, i.e. the distance of a bow-shot.
[2] *Whereas*, where.
[3] *Ward*, guard.
[4] *Amate*, daunt.
[5] *Grisly*, terrible.
[6] *Revoke*, draw back.
[7] *Stownd*, exigency.
[8] *Wist*, knew.
[9] *Th' Earth's children*, i.e. the Giants and the Titans, the offspring of Uranus and Ge (earth).

Aread[1] what course of you is safest dempt,[2]
And how we with our foe may come to fight."
"This is," quoth he, "the dolorous despite,[3]
Which erst[4] to you I plained[5]: for neither may
This fire be quenched by any wit or might,
Ne yet by any means removed away;
So mighty be th' enchantments which the same do stay.[6]

24 "What is there else but cease these fruitless pains,
And leave me to my former languishing!
Fair Amoret must dwell in wicked chains,
And Scudamore here die with sorrowing!"
"Perdy,[7] not so," said she; "for shameful thing
It were t' abandon noble chevisance,[8]
For show of peril, without venturing:
Rather, let try extremities of chance
Then enterprisèd praise for dread to disavance."[9]

25 Therewith resolved to prove her utmost might,
Her ample shield she threw before her face,
And her sword's point directing forward right
Assailed the flame; the which eftsoons[10] gave place,
And did itself divide with equal space,
That through she passèd, as a thunderbolt
Pierceth the yielding air, and doth displace

---

[1] *Aread*, declare.
[2] *Dempt*, deemed.
[3] *Dolorous despite*, grievous vexation.
[4] *Erst*, first.
[5] *Plained*, lamented.
[6] *Stay*, maintain.
[7] *Perdy*, truly.
[8] *Chevisance*, enterprise.
[9] *Disavance*, retreat from.
[10] *Eftsoons*, immediately.

The soaring clouds into sad[1] show'rs ymolt[2];
So to her yold[3] the flames, and did their force
   revolt.[4]

26 Whom whenas Scudamour saw past the fire
Safe and untouched, he likewise gan assay
With greedy will and envious desire,
And bade the stubborn flames to yield him way:
But cruel Mulciber[5] would not obey
His threatful pride, but did the more augment
His mighty rage, and with imperious sway
Him forced, maulgre[6] his fierceness, to relent,
And back retire all scorched and pitifully brent.[7]

27 With huge impatience he inly swelt,[8]
More for great sorrow that he could not pass
Then for the burning torment which he felt;
That with fell woodness[9] he effiercèd[10] was,
And, wilfully him throwing on the grass,
Did beat and bounce his head and breast full sore:
The whiles the championess now entered has
The utmost[11] room, and passed the foremost door;
The utmost room abounding with all precious store:

28 For, round about, the walls yclothèd were
With goodly arras[12] of great majesty,

[1] *Sad*, heavy.
[2] *Ymolt*, melted.
[3] *Yold*, yielded.
[4] *Revolt*, turn back.
[5] *Mulciber*, a surname given to Vulcan, the god of fire who presided over the working of metals.
[6] *Maulgre*, in spite of.
[7] *Brent*, burned.
[8] *Swelt*, died.
[9] *Fell woodness*, fierce madness.
[10] *Effierced*, enraged.
[11] *Utmost*, outermost.
[12] *Arras*, tapestry.

Woven with gold and silk so close and near
That the rich metal lurkèd privily,
As feigning to be hid from envious [1] eye;
Yet here, and there, and everywhere, unwares,
It showed itself and shone unwillingly;
Like to a discoloured [2] snake, whose hidden snares [3]
Through the green grass his long bright burnished back declares.

29 And in those tapets [4] weren fashionèd
Many fair portraits, and many a fair feat;
And all of love, and all of lustyhed, [5]
As seemèd by their semblant,[6] did entreat [7]:
And eke [8] all Cupid's wars they did repeat,
And cruel battles, which he whilom [9] fought
Gainst all the gods to make his empire great;
Besides the huge massácres, which he wrought
On mighty kings and kesars [10] into thraldom brought.

30 Ne [11] did he spare (so cruel was the elf)
His own dear mother, (ah! why should he so?)
Ne did he spare sometime to prick himself,
That he might taste the sweet consuming woe,
Which he had wrought to many others moe.[12]

. . . .

[1] *Envious*, malignant, mischievous.
[2] *Discoloured*, party-colored.
[3] *Snares*, i.e. coils.
[4] *Tapets*, tapestries.
[5] *Lustyhed*, lustfulness.
[6] *Semblant*, appearance.
[7] *Entreat*, treat.
[8] *Eke*, also.
[9] *Whilom*, formerly.
[10] *Kesars*, emperors.
[11] *Ne*, nor.
[12] *Moe*, more.

31 Kings, queens, lords, ladies, knights, and damsels gent,[1]
 Were heaped together with the vulgar sort,
 And mingled with the rascal rabblement,[2]
 Without respect of person or of port,[3]
 To show Dan [4] Cupid's pow'r and great effórt:
 And round about a border was entrailed [5]
 Of broken bows and arrows shivered short;
 And a long bloody river through them railed,[6]
 So lively, and so like, that living sense it failed.[7]

32 And at the upper end of that fair rowme [8]
 There was an altar built of precious stone
 Of passing [9] value and of great renowme,[10]
 On which there stood an image all alone
 Of massy gold, which with his own light shone;
 And wings it had with sundry colours dight,[11]
 More sundry colours then the proud pavone [12]
 Bears in his boasted fan, or Iris [13] bright,
 When her discoloured bow she spreads through heaven's height.

33 Blindfold he was; and in his cruel fist
 A mortal [14] bow and arrows keen did hold,

[1] *Gent*, noble.
[2] *Rascal rabblement*, common rabble.
[3] *Port*, carriage, bearing.
[4] *Dan*, equivalent to master or sir.
[5] *Entrailed*, entwined.
[6] *Railed*, rolled.
[7] *Failed*, deceived.
[8] *Rowme*, room.
[9] *Passing*, surpassing.
[10] *Renowme*, renown.
[11] *Dight*, adorned.
[12] *Pavone*, peacock.
[13] *Iris*, the goddess of the rainbow.
[14] *Mortal*, death-giving.

With which he shot at random when him list,[1]
Some headed with sad[2] lead, some with pure gold;
(Ah! man, beware how thou those darts behold!)
A wounded dragon under him did lie,
Whose hideous tail his left foot did enfold,
And with a shaft was shot through either eye,
That no man forth might draw, ne no man remedy.

34 And underneath his feet was written thus:
Unto the victor of the gods this be;
And all the people in that ample house
Did to that image bow their humble knee,
And oft committed foul idolatree.
That wondrous sight fair Britomart amazed,
Ne seeing could her wonder satisfy,
But ever more and more upon it gazed,
The whiles the passing brightness her frail senses dazed.

35 Tho,[3] as she backward cast her busy eye
To search each secret of that goodly stead,[4]
Over the door thus written she did spy:
Be bold. She oft and oft it over read,
Yet could not find what sense it figurèd:
But whatso were therein or writ or meant,
She was no whit thereby discouragèd
From prosecuting of her first intent,
But forward with bold steps into the next room went.

---

[1] *When him list*, i.e. when he desired.
[2] *Sad*, heavy.
[3] *Tho*, then.
[4] *Stead*, place.

36 Much fairer then the former was that room.
    And richlier, by many parts[1] arrayed;
    For not with arras made in painful loom,
    But with pure gold, it all was overlaid,
    Wrought with wild antics[2] which their follies played
    In the rich metal, as they living were:
    A thousand monstrous forms therein were made,
    Such as false Love doth oft upon him wear;
    For Love in thousand monstrous forms doth oft appear.

37 And, all about, the glist'ring walls were hong
    With warlike spoils and with victorious praise
    Of mighty conquerors and captains strong,
    Which were whilóm captivèd in their days
    To cruel Love, and wrought their own decays[3]:
    Their swerds[4] and spears were broke, and hauberks[5] rent,
    And their proud girlonds of triumphant bays
    Trodden in dust with fury insolent,
    To show the victor's might and merciless intent.

38 The warlike maid, beholding earnestly
    The goodly ordinance[6] of this rich place,
    Did greatly wonder; ne could satisfy
    Her greedy eyes with gazing a long space:
    But more she marvelled that no footing's trace
    Nor wight appeared, but wasteful emptiness

---

[1] *By many parts*, i.e. by many times.
[2] *Antics*, fantastic figures.
[3] *Decays*, ruins.
[4] *Swerds*, swords.
[5] *Hauberks*, coats of mail.
[6] *Ordinance*, orderly arrangement.

And solemn silence over all that place:
Strange thing it seemed, that none was to possess
So rich purveyance,[1] ne them keep with carefulness.

39 And, as she looked about, she did behold
How over that same door was likewise writ,
Be bold, Be bold, and everywhere, *Be bold;*
That much she mused, yet could not construe it
By any riddling skill or common wit.
At last she spied at that room's upper end
Another iron door, on which was writ,
Be not too bold; whereto though she did bend
Her earnest mind, yet wist[2] not what it might intend.

40 Thus she there waited until eventide,
Yet living creature none she saw appear.
And now sad[3] shadows gan the world to hide
From mortal view, and wrap in darkness drear;
Yet nould she d'off[4] her weary arms, for fear
Of secret danger, ne let sleep oppress
Her heavy eyes with nature's burden dear,
But drew herself aside in sickerness,[5]
And her well pointed weapons did about her dress.[6]

[1] *Purveyance,* furniture.
[2] *Wist,* knew.
[3] *Sad,* heavy.
[4] *Nould she d'off, i.e.* she would not take off.
[5] *Sickerness,* safety.
[6] *Dress,* dispose.

VIII.

Britomart witnesses the Mask of Cupid and frees Amoret from the power of the enchanter.

1 Tho, whenas cheerless night ycovered had
　Fair heaven with an universal cloud,
　That[1] every wight dismayed with darkness sad[2]
　In silence and in sleep themselves did shroud,
　She heard a shrilling trumpet sound aloud,
　Sign of nigh battaill, or got victory:
　Nought therewith daunted was her courage proud,
　But rather stirred to cruel enmity,
　Expecting ever when some foe she might descry.

2 With that, an hideous storm of wind arose,
　With dreadful thunder and lightning atwixt,
　And an earthquake, as if it straight would lose[3]
　The world's foundations from his centre fixed:
　A direful stench of smoke and sulphur mixed
　Ensued,[4] whose noyance[5] filled the fearful stead[6]
　From the fourth hour of night until the sixt;
　Yet the bold Britoness was nought ydread,[7]
　Though much emmoved,[8] but steadfast still persé-
　　verèd.

[1] *That*, so that.
[2] *Sad*, heavy.
[3] *Lose*, loosen.
[4] *Ensued*, followed.
[5] *Noyance*, annoyance.
[6] *Stead*, place.
[7] *Ydread*, terrified.
[8] *Emmoved*, moved.

3   All suddenly a stormy whirlwind blew
    Throughout the house, that clappèd every door,
    With which that iron wicket open flew,
    As it with mighty levers had been tore;
    And forth issúed, as on the ready floor
    Of some theátre, a grave personage,
    That in his hand a branch of laurel bore,
    With comely haviour [1] and count'nance sage,
    Yclad in costly garments fit for tragic stage.

4   Proceeding to the midst he still did stand,
    As if in mind he somewhat had to say;
    And to the vulgar [2] beck'ning with his hand,
    In sign of silence, as to hear a play, [3]
    By lively actions [4] he gan bewray [5]
    Some argument [6] of matter passionèd [7];
    Which done, he back retirèd soft away,
    And, passing by, his name discoverèd,
    EASE, on his robe in golden letters ciphered. [8]

5   The noble maid, still standing, all this viewed,
    And marvelled at his strange intendiment [9]:
    With that a joyous fellowship issúed

---

[1] *Haviour*, behavior.

[2] *Vulgar*, common people.

[3] *As to hear a play*. In Elizabeth's time each act of a tragedy was usually preceded by a dumb show in which the argument of the act was given. The play acted before the king in Shakespeare's "Hamlet" is preceded by a dumb show.

[4] *Actions*, pronounced as a word of three syllables.

[5] *Bewray*, disclose.

[6] *Argument*, subject.

[7] *Passioned*, represented.

[8] *Ciphered*, written in occult characters.

[9] *Intendiment*, meaning.

Of minstrels making goodly merriment,
With wanton bards, and rhymers impudent;
All which together sang full cheerfully
A lay of love's delight with sweet concent[1]:
After whom marched a jolly company,
In manner of a mask,[2] enrangèd[3] orderly.

6   The whiles a most delicious harmony
In full strange notes was sweetly heard to sound,
That the rare sweetness of the melody
The feeble senses wholly did confound,
And the frail soul in deep delight nigh drowned:
And, when it ceased, shrill trumpets loud did bray,
That their report did far away rebound;
And, when they ceased, it gan again to play,
The whiles the maskers marchèd forth in trim array.

7   The first was Fancy,[4] like a lovely boy
Of rare aspect and beauty without peer,
Matchable either to that imp[5] of Troy,
Whom Jove did love and chose his cup to bear[6];
Or that same dainty lad, which was so dear
To great Alcides,[7] that, whenas he died,
He wailèd womanlike with many a tear,
And every wood and every valley wide
He filled with Hylas' name; the nymphs eke[8]
  "Hylas" cried.

[1] *Concent*, harmony.
[2] *Mask*, a dramatic and musical production, such as Milton's "Comus."
[3] *Enranged*, arranged.
[4] *Fancy*, capricious love.
[5] *Imp*, child, youth.
[6] *That imp of Troy*, etc., Ganymede.
[7] *Alcides*, Hercules.
[8] *Eke*, likewise.

8 His garment nether was of silk nor say,[1]
   But painted plumes in goodly order dight,[2]
   Like as the sunburnt Indians do array
   Their tawny bodies, in their proudest plight:
   As those same plumes, so seemed he vain and light,
   That by his gait might easily appear;
   For still he fared[3] as dancing in delight,
   And in his hand a windy fan did bear,
   That in the idle air he moved, still here and there.

9 And him beside marched amorous Desire,
   Who seemed of riper years than th' other swain,
   Yet was that other swain this elder's sire,
   And gave him being, common to them twain;
   His garment was disguisèd very vain,
   And his embrodered bonnet[4] sat awry:
   Twixt both his hands few sparks he close[5] did strain,
   Which still he blew and kindled busily,
   That soon they life conceived, and forth in flames did fly.

10 Next after him went Doubt, who was yclad
   In a discoloured[6] coat of strange disguise,
   That at his back a broad capuccio[7] had,
   And sleeves dependant[8] Albanese-wise[9];
   He looked askew with his mistrustful eyes,

---

[1] *Say*, satin.
[2] *Dight*, disposed.
[3] *Fared*, passed along.
[4] *Bonnet*, cap.
[5] *Close*, secretly.
[6] *Discoloured*, party-colored.
[7] *Capuccio*, hood.
[8] *Dependant*, hanging down.
[9] *Albanesè-wise*, Albanian fashion.

And nicely¹ trod, as thorns lay in his way,
Or that the floor to shrink he did avise²;
And on a broken reed he still did stay
His feeble steps, which shrunk when hard thereon
    he lay.

11 With him went Danger, clothed in ragged weed³
Made of bear's skin, that him more dreadful made;
Yet his own face was dreadful, ne did need
Strange⁴ horror to deform his grisly⁵ shade:
A net in th' one hand, and a rusty blade
In th' other was; this mischief, that mishap;
With th' one his foes he threatened to invade,
With th' other he his friends meant to enwrap⁶:
For whom he could not kill he practised⁷ to entrap.

12 Next him was Fear, all armed from top to toe,
Yet thought himself not safe enough thereby,
But feared each shadow moving to or fro;
And, his own arms when glittering he did spy
Or clashing heard, he fast away did fly,
As ashes pale of hue, and wingèd heeled;
And evermore on Danger fixed his eye,
Gainst whom he always bent a brazen shield,
Which his right hand unarmèd fearfully⁸ did wield.

13 With him went Hope in rank, a handsome maid,
Of cheerful look and lovely to behold;

---

¹ *Nicely*, carefully.   ⁵ *Grisly*, dreadful.
² *Avise*, perceive.   ⁶ *Enwrap*, involve in difficulty.
³ *Weed*, garment.   ⁷ *Practised*, plotted.
⁴ *Strange*, foreign, or borrowed.   ⁸ *Fearfully*, with fear.

In silken samite[1] she was light arrayed,
And her fair locks were woven up in gold:
She always smiled, and in her hand did hold
An holy-water-sprinkle, dipt in deowe,[2]
With which she sprinkled favours manifold
On whom she list, and did great liking sheowe,[3]
Great liking unto many, but true love to feowe.[4]

14 And after them Dissemblance[5] and Suspect[6]
Marched in one rank, yet an unequal pair;
For she was gentle and of mild aspéct,
Courteous to all and seeming debonair,[7]
Goodly adornèd and exceeding fair;
Yet was that all but painted and purloined,
And her bright brows were decked with borrowed hair;
Her deeds were forgèd, and her words false coined,
And always in her hand two clews[8] of silk she twined:

15 But he was foul, ill favourèd, and grim,
Under his eyebrows looking still[9] askance;
And ever, as Dissemblance laughed on him,
He low'red on her with dangerous eye-glance,
Showing his nature in his countenance;
His rolling eyes did never rest in place,

---

[1] *Samite*, silk stuff sometimes inwrought with gold.
[2] *Deowe*, dew.
[3] *Sheowe*, show.
[4] *Feowe*, few.
[5] *Dissemblance*, dissimulation.
[6] *Suspect*, suspicion.
[7] *Debonair*, gracious.
[8] *Clews*, balls.
[9] *Still*, always.

But walked[1] each where for fear of hid mischance,
Holding a lattice still before his face,
Through which he still did peep as forward he did pace.

16 Next him went Grief and Fury matched yfere[2];
Grief all in sable sorrowfully clad,
Down hanging his dull head with heavy cheer,[3]
Yet inly being more then seeming sad:
A pair of pincers in his hand he had,
With which he pinchèd people to the heart,
That from thenceforth a wretched life they lad,[4]
In wilful languor and consuming smart,
Dying each day with inward wounds of dolour's dart.

17 But Fury was full ill apparallèd
In rags, that naked nigh she did appear,
With ghastly looks and dreadful drearihead[5];
For from her back her garments she did tear,
And from her head oft rent her snarlèd hair:
In her right hand a firebrand she did toss
About her head, still roaming here and there;
As a dismayèd deer in chase embossed,[6]
Forgetful of his safety, hath his right way lost.

18 After them went Displeasure and Pleasance[7];
He looking lumpish[8] and full sullen sad,

---

[1] *Walked*, rolled.
[2] *Yfere*, together.
[3] *Cheer*, coutenance.
[4] *Lad*, led.
[5] *Drearihead*, sorrow.
[6] *Embossed*, hard pressed.
[7] *Pleasance*, pleasure.
[8] *Lumpish*, heavy, melancholy.

. And hanging down his heavy countenance;
  She cheerful, fresh, and full of joyance glad,
  As if no sorrow she ne felt ne drad[1];
  That evil matchèd pair they seemed to be:
  An angry wasp th' one in a vial had,
  Th' other in hers an honey-laden bee.
  Thus marchèd these six couples forth in fair degree.[2]

19 After all these there marched a most fair dame,[3]
  Led of two grysie[4] villeins[5]; th' one Despite,[6]
  The other clepèd[7] Cruelty by name:
  She doleful lady, like a dreary sprite
  Called by strong charms out of eternal night,
  Had death's own image figured in her face,
  Full of sad signs, fearful to living sight;
  Yet in that horror showed a seemly grace,
  And with her feeble feet did move a comely pace.

20 Her breast all naked, as net[8] ivory
  Without adorn of gold or silver bright
  Wherewith the craftsman wonts it beautify,[9]
  Of her due-honour was despoilèd quite;
  And a wide wound therein (O rueful sight!)
  Entrenchèd deep with knife accursèd keen,
  Yet freshly bleeding forth her fainting sprite,[10]

---

[1] *Drad*, dreaded.
[2] *Degree*, step.
[3] *A most fair dame*, i.e. Amoret, the wife of Scudamore.
[4] *Grysie*, squalid.
[5] *Villeins*, base-born or inferior persons.
[6] *Despite*, malice, spite.
[7] *Cleped*, called.
[8] *Net*, pure.
[9] *Wonts it beautify*, i.e. is accustomed to beautify it.
[10] *Sprite*, spirit.

(The work of cruel hand) was to be seen,
That dyed in sanguine¹ red her skin all snowy clean:

21 At that wide orifice her trembling heart
Was drawn forth, and in silver basin laid,
Quite through transfixèd with a deadly dart,
And in her blood yet steaming fresh embayed.²
And those two villeins which her steps upstayed,
When her weak feet could scarcely her sustain,
And fading vital powers gan to fade,
Her forward still with torture did constrain,
And evermore increasèd her consuming pain.

22 Next after her, the wingèd god³ himself
Came riding on a lion ravenous,
Taught to obey the menage⁴ of that elf
That man and beast with pow'r imperious
Subdueth to his kingdom tyrannous:
His blindfold eyes he bade awhile unbind,
That his proud spoil of that same dolorous
Fair dame he might behold in perfect kind⁵;
Which seen, he much rejoicèd in his cruel mind.

23 Of which full proud, himself uprearing high,
He lookèd round about with stern disdain,
And did survey his goodly company;
And, marshalling the evil-ordered train,
With that the darts which his right hand did strain

---

¹ *Sanguine*, the color of blood.
² *Embayed*, bathed.
³ *Wingèd god*, Cupid.
⁴ *Menage*, manege, horsemanship.
⁵ *In perfect kind, i.e.* with perfect distinctness.

Full dreadfully he shook, that all did quake,
And clapped on high his coloured wingës twain,
That all his many[1] it afraid did make:
Tho, blinding him again, his way he forth did take.

24 Behind him was Reproach, Repentance, Shame;
Reproach the first, Shame next, Repent behind:
Repentance feeble, sorrowful, and lame;
Reproach despiteful, careless, and unkind;
Shame most ill-favoured, bestial, and blind:
Shame low'red, Repentance sighed, Reproach did scold;
Reproach sharp stings, Repentance whips entwined,
Shame burning brond-irons in her hands did hold:
All three to each unlike, yet all made in one mould.

25 And after them a rude confusèd rout
Of persons flocked, whose names is hard to read[2]:
Amongst them was stern Strife; and Anger stout[3];
Unquiet Care; and fond Unthriftyhead[4];
Lewd Loss of Time; and Sorrow seeming dead;
Inconstant Change; and false Disloyality;
Consuming Riotise[5]; and guilty Dread
Of heavenly vengeance; faint Infirmity;
Vile Poverty; and, lastly, Death with infamy.

---

[1] *Many*, company.
[2] *Read*, tell.
[3] *Stout*, dauntless.
[4] *Fond Unthriftyhead*, foolish thriftlessness.
[5] *Riotise*, riotousness.

26 There were full many moe¹ like maladies,
   Whose names and natures I note readen² well;
   So many moe, as there be fantasies
   In wavering women's wit, that none can tell,
   Or pains in love, or punishments in hell:
   All which, disguisèd, marched in masking-wise
   About the chamber by the damosel;
   And then returnèd, having marchèd thrise,
   Into the inner room from whence they first did rise.³

27 So soon as they were in, the door straightway
   Fast lockèd, driven with that stormy blast
   Which first it opened, and bore all away.
   Then the brave maid, which all this while was plast⁴
   In secret shade, and saw both first and last,
   Issuèd forth and went unto the door
   To enter in, but found it lockèd fast:
   In vain she thought with rigorous uproar
   For to efforce,⁵ when charms had closèd it afore.

28 Where force might not avail, there sleights and art
   She cast⁶ to use, both fit for hard emprise⁷:
   Forthy⁸ from that same room not to depart
   Till morrow next she did herself avise,⁹
   When that same mask again should forth arise.
   The morrow next appeared with joyous cheer,
   Calling men to their daily exercise:

¹ *Moe*, more.
² *Note readen*, cannot tell.
³ *Rise*, come forth.
⁴ *Plast*, placed.
⁵ *Efforce*, force.
⁶ *Cast*, planned.
⁷ *Emprise*, undertaking.
⁸ *Forthy*, therefore.
⁹ *Avise*, bethink.

Then she, as morrow fresh, herself did rear
Out of her secret stand that day for to outwear.[1]

29 All that day she outwore in wandering
    And gazing on that chamber's ornament,
    Till that again the second evening
    Her covered with her sable vestiment,
    Wherewith the world's fair beauty she hath blent[2]:
    Then, when the second watch[3] was almost past,
    That brazen door flew open, and in went
    Bold Britomart, as she had late forecast,[4]
    Neither of idle shows nor of false charms aghast.

30 So soon as she was entered, round about
    She cast her eyes to see what was become
    Of all those persons which she saw without.
    But lo! they straight were vanished all and some[5];
    Ne living wight she saw in all that room,
    Save that same woful lady; both whose hands
    Were bounden fast, that did her ill become,[6]
    And her small waist girt round with iron bands
    Unto a brazen pillar, by the which she stands.

31 And, her before, the vile enchanter sate,
    Figuring strange charácters of his art;
    With living blood he those charácters wrate,[7]

---

[1] *Outwear*, pass.
[2] *Blent*, obscured.
[3] *The second watch* began at nine and ended at twelve.
[4] *Forecast*, previously determined.
[5] *All and some*, i.e. one and all.
[6] *That did her ill become*, i.e. such treatment was unworthy of her.
[7] *Wrate*, wrote.

Dreadfully dropping from her dying heart,
Seeming transfixèd with a cruel dart;
And all perforce to make her him to love.
Ah! who can love the worker of her smart!
A thousand charms he formerly did prove[1];
Yet thousand charms could not her steadfast heart remove.

32 Soon as that virgin knight he saw in place,
His wicked books in haste he overthrew,
Not caring his long labours to deface[2];
And, fiercely running to that lady true,
A murd'rous knife out of his pocket drew,
The which he thought, for villainous despite,
In her tormented body to imbrue[3]:
But the stout[4] damsel, to him leaping light,
His cursèd hand witheld, and maisterèd his might.

33 From her, to whom his fury first he meant,
The wicked weapon rashly he did wrest,[5]
And, turning to herself[6] his fell intent,
Unwares it strooke into her snowy chest,
That little drops empurpled her fair breast.
Exceeding wroth therewith the virgin grew,
Albe[7] the wound were nothing deep impressed,
And fiercely forth her mortal blade she drew,
To give him the reward for such vile outrage due.

---

[1] *Did prove*, made trial of.
[2] *Not caring*, etc., *i.e.* not caring for the fact that he might destroy the result of his long labors.
[3] *Imbrue*, moisten.
[4] *Stout*, valiant, undaunted.
[5] *Rashly he did wrest*, quickly he turned aside.
[6] *Herself*, *i.e.* Britomart.
[7] *Albe*, although.

34 So mightily she smote him, that to ground
    He fell half dead; next stroke him should have slain,
    Had not the lady, which by him stood bound,
    Dernly[1] unto her callèd to abstain
    From doing him to die[2]; for else her pain
    Should be remèdiless; sith[3] none but he
    Which wrought it could the same recure again.
    Therewith she stayed her hand, loath stayed to be;
    For life she him enviéd,[4] and longed revenge to see:

35 And to him said: "Thou wicked man, whose meed
    For so huge mischief and vile villainy
    Is death, or if that ought do death exceed;
    Be sure that nought may save thee from to die
    But if[5] that thou this dame do presently
    Restore unto her health and former state;
    This do, and live; else die undoubtedly."
    He, glad of life, that looked for death but late,
    Did yield himself right willing to prolong his date:

36 And, rising up, gan straight to overlook[6]
    Those cursèd leaves, his charms back to reverse.
    Full dreadful things out of that baleful book
    He read, and measured many a sad[7] verse,
    That horror gan the virgin's heart to perse,[8]
    And her fair locks up starèd[9] stiff on end,
    Hearing him those same bloody lines rehearse;

[1] *Dernly*, sadly.
[2] *Doing him to die*, causing him to die.
[3] *Sith*, since.
[4] *Envied*, grudged.
[5] *But if*, unless.
[6] *Overlook*, look over.
[7] *Sad*, i.e. of great import.
[8] *Perse*, pierce.
[9] *Up stared*, stood up.

And, all the while he read, she did extend
Her swordhigh over him, if ought he did offend.[1]

37 Anon she gan perceive the house to quake,
And all the doors to rattle round about;
Yet all that did not her dismayèd make,
Nor slack her threatful hand for danger's doubt,[2]
But still with steadfast eye and courage stout
Abode, to weet[3] what end would come of all:
At last that mighty chain, which round about
Her[4] tender waist was wound, adown gan fall,
And that great brazen pillar broke in pieces small.

38 The cruel steel, which thrilled[5] her dying heart,
Fell softly forth, as of his own accord;
And the wide wound, which lately did dispart[6]
Her bleeding breast and riven bowels gored,
Was closèd up, as it had not been bored;
And every part to safëty full sound,
As she were never hurt, was soon restored:
Tho,[7] when she felt herself to be unbound
And perfect whole, prostrate she fell unto the ground;

39 Before fair Britomart she fell prostráte,
Saying: "Ah! noble knight, what worthy meed
Can wretched lady, quit from woful state,
Yield you in lieu of this your gracious deed?

---

[1] *If ought he did offend, i.e.* in case he should do any harm.

[2] *Danger's doubt*, apprehension of danger.

[3] *Weet*, know.

[4] *Her;* this refers, of course, to the lady, Amoret.

[5] *Thrilled*, pierced.

[6] *Dispart*, divide.

[7] *Tho*, then.

Your virtue self her own reward shall breed,
Even immortal praise and glory wide,
Which I, your vassal, by your prowess freed,
Shall through the world make to be notified,[1]
And goodly well advance that goodly well was tried."[2]

40 But Britomart uprearing her from ground,
Said: "Gentle dame, reward enough I ween,[3]
For many labours more then I have found,
This, that in safety now I have you seen,
And mean[4] of your deliverance have been:
Henceforth, fair lady, comfort to you take,
And put away remembrance of late teen[5];
Instead thereof, know that your loving make[6]
Hath no less grief endurèd for your gentle sake."

41 She much was cheered to hear him mentioned,[7]
Whom of all living wights she lovèd best.
Then laid the noble championess strong hond[8]
Upon th' enchanter which had her distressed
So sore, and with foul outrages oppressed:
With that great chain, wherewith not long ygoe
He bound that piteous lady prisoner now relest,
Himself she bound, more worthy to be so,
And captive with her led to wretchedness and woe.

[1] *Notified*, proclaimed.
[2] *And goodly well advance*, etc., i.e. and do my best to extol the valor which was so well tried.
[8] *Ween*, think.
[4] *Mean*, means.
[5] *Teen*, sorrow.
[6] *Make*, mate.
[7] *Mentioned*; the second syllable pronounced as two syllables.
[8] *Hond*, hand.

42 Returning back, those goodly rooms, which erst [1]
    She saw so rich and royally arrayed,
    Now vanished utterly and clean subversed [2]
    She found, and all their glory quite decayèd,[3]
    That sight of such a change her much dismayed.
    Thenceforth, descending to that perlous [4] porch,
    Those dreadful flames she also found delayed [5]
    And quenchèd quite, like a consumèd torch,
    That erst all ent'rers wont so cruelly to scorch.

43 More easy issue now then entrance late
    She found; for now that feignèd [6] dreadful flame,
    Which choked the porch of that enchanted gate
    And passage barred to all that thither came,
    Was vanished quite, as it were not the same,
    And gave her leave at pleasure forth to pass.
    Th' enchanter self, which all that fraud did frame
    To have efforced [7] the love of that fair lass,
    Seeing his work now wasted, deep engrievèd was.

44 But when the victoress arrivèd there
    Where late she left the pensife Scudamore
    With her own trusty squire, both full of fear,
    Neither of them she found where she them lore [8]:
    Thereat her noble heart was 'stonished sore;
    But most fair Amoret, whose gentle sprite [9]
    Now gan to feed on hope, which she before

---

[1] *Erst*, first.
[2] *Subversed*, overturned.
[3] *Decayed*, destroyed.
[4] *Perlous*, perilous.
[5] *Delayed*, abated.
[6] *Feigned*, i.e. not real, but produced by magic.
[7] *Efforced*, forced.
[8] *Lore*, left.
[9] *Sprite*, spirit.

Conceivèd had, to see her own dear knight,
Being thereof beguiled, was filled with new affright.

45   But he, sad man, when he had long in dread
Awaited there for Britomart's return,
Yet saw her not, nor sign of her good speed,
His expectation to despair did turn,
Misdeeming[1] sure that her those flames did burn;
And therefore gan advise with her old squire,
Who her dear nursling's loss no less did mourn,
Thence to depart for further aid t' enquire:
Where let them wend at will, whilst here I do respire.

---

[1] *Misdeeming*, mistakenly judging.

IX.

During an adventure at a castle, Amoret learns that her deliverer is a woman. The maidens soon after meet Paridell and Blandamour, and their companions, Duessa and Atè. Later, Scudamour and Glaucè come upon the scene.

1. Of lovers' sad calamities of old
   Full many piteous stories do remain,
   But none more piteous ever was ytold
   Then that of Amoret's heart-binding chain,
   And this of Florimell's unworthy pain :
   The dear compassion of whose bitter fit [1]
   My softened heart so sorely doth constrain,
   That I with tears full oft do pity it,
   And oftentimes do wish it never had been writ.

2. For, from the time that Scudamour her bought [2]
   In perilous fight, she never joyèd day ;
   A perilous fight! when he with force her brought
   From twenty knights that did him all assay [3] ;
   Yet fairly well he did them all dismay, [4]
   And with great glory both the shield of love
   And eke the lady self he brought away [5] ;
   Whom having wedded, as did him behoove,
   A new unknowen mischief did from him remove.

[1] *Fit*, stroke, misfortune.
[2] *Bought*, ransomed.
[3] *Assay*, assail.
[4] *Dismay*, overpower.

[5] *And with great glory*, etc. In Book IV, Canto X, the poet describes the shield of love and tells how Scudamore won Amoret.

3 For that same vile enchanter Busyran,
   The very self same day that she was wedded,
   Amidst the bridal feast, whilst every man
   Surcharged with wine were heedless and ill-headed,
   . . . .
   Brought in that Mask of Love which late was showen;
   And there the lady ill of friends bestedded,[1]
   By way of sport, as oft in masks is knowen,
   Conveyèd quite away to living wight unknowen.

4 Seven months he so her kept in bitter smart,
   . . . .
   Until such time as noble Britomart
   Releasèd her, that else was like to sterve [2]
   Through cruel knife that her dear heart did kerve [3];
   And now she is with her upon the way
   Marching in lovely [4] wise, that could deserve
   No spot of blame, though spite did oft assay
   To blot her [5] with dishonour of so fair a prey.

5 Yet should it be a pleasant tale, to tell
   The diverse usage, and demeanour daint,[6]
   That each to other made, as oft befell:
   For Amoret right fearful was and faint,[7]
   . . . .

---

[1] *Bestedded*, assisted.
[2] *Sterve*, die.
[3] *Kerve*, carve, cut.
[4] *Lovely*, affectionate.
[5] *Her*, i.e. Britomart.
[6] *Demeanour daint*, delicate conduct.

[7] *For Amoret right fearful*, etc. Amoret knew that she owed everything to Britomart whom she supposed, of course, to be a man. She feared that her deliverer might desire her love.

That every word did tremble as she spake,
And every look was coy and wondrous quaint,[1]
And every limb that touchèd her [2] did quake;
Yet could she not but courteous countenance to her make.

6 For well she [3] wist, as true it was indeed,
That her life's lord and patron of her health [4]
Right well deservèd, as his dueful meed,
Her love, her service, and her utmost wealth:
All is his justly that all freely deal'th.[5]

. . . .

7 Thereto her fear was made so much the greater,
Through fine abusion [6] of that Briton maid [7];
Who, for to hide her feignèd sex the better
And mask her wounded mind,[8] both did and said
Full many things so doubtful to be weighed,
That well she wist not what by them to guess:

. . . .

8 It so befell one evening that they came
Unto a castle, lodgèd there to be,
Where many a knight, and many a lovely dame,
Was then assembled deeds of arms to see:

---

[1] *Quaint*, nice, reserved.
[2] *Her*, i.e. Britomart.
[3] *She*, i.e. Amoret.
[4] *Patron of her health*, defender of her safety.
[5] *Deal'th, dealeth;* distributes, gives.
[6] *Abusion*, deception.
[7] *Briton maid*, i.e. Britomart.
[8] *Her wounded mind*, i.e. wounded from love of Artegall.

Amongst all which was none more fair then she,[1]
That many of them moved to eye her sore.

. . . .

It was the custom at this castle to allow those knights only to enter who were accompanied by ladies.

9 Amongst the rest there was a jolly[2] knight,
Who, being askèd for his love, avowed
That fairest Amoret was his by right,
And off'red that to justify[3] aloud.
The warlike virgin, seeing his so proud
And boastful challenge,[4] wexèd[5] inly wroth,
But for the present did her anger shroud;
And said, her love to lose she was full loath,
But either he should neither of them have, or both.

10 So forth they went, and both together jousted;
But that same younker[6] soon was overthown,
And made repent that he had rashly lusted
For thing unlawful that was not his own:
Yet since he seemèd valiant, though unknown,
She, that no less was courteous then stout,[7]
Cast how to salve,[8] that both the custom shown[9]

---

[1] *She*, i.e. Amoret.
[2] *Jolly*, handsome.
[3] *Justify*, prove.
[4] *Challenge*, claim.
[5] *Wexed*, waxed, became.
[6] *Younker*, stripling.
[7] *Stout*, brave.
[8] *Cast how to salve*, planned how to secure, to arrange.
[9] *Shown*, published; i.e. the custom that no knight might enter the castle unless he had a lady-love.

Were kept, and yet that knight not lockèd out;
That seemed full hard t'accord two things so far in
   doubt.¹

11 The seneschal² was called to deem³ the right;
Whom she required, that first fair Amoret
Might be to her allowed, as to a knight
That did her win and free from challenge set:
Which straight to her was yielded without let⁴:
Then, since that strange knight's love from him
   was quitted,⁵
She claimed that to herself, as lady's debt,
He as a knight might justly be admitted;
So none should be out shut, sith all of loves were
   fitted.

12 With that, her glist'ring helmet she unlaced;
Which doft, her golden locks, that were upbound
Still⁶ in a knot, unto her heels down traced,⁷
And like a silken veil in compass⁸ round
About her back and all her body wound:
Like as the shining sky in summer's night,
What time the days with scorching heat abound,
Is crested all with lines of fi'ry light,
That it prodigious seems in common people's sight.

---

¹ *So far in doubt;* a peculiar expression which seems to mean, *so difficult to reconcile.*

² *Seneschal,* an officer who had the superintendence of feasts and domestic ceremonies; a steward.

³ *Deem,* judge.

⁴ *Let,* hindrance, opposition.

⁵ *Quitted,* taken.

⁶ *Still,* always.

⁷ *Down traced, i.e.* fell down.

⁸ *In compass,* in a circle.

13 Such, when those knights and ladies all about
    Beheld her, all were with amazement smit,
    And every one gan grow in secret doubt
    Of this and that, according to each wit[1]:
    Some thought that some enchantment feignèd it[2];
    Some, that Bellona[3] in that warlike wise
    To them appeared, with shield and armour fit;
    Some, that it was a mask of strange disguise:
    So diversely each one did sundry doubts devise.

14 But that young knight, which through her gentle deed
    Was to that goodly fellowship restored,
    Ten thousand thanks did yield her for her meed,
    And, doubly overcommen, her adored:
    So did they all their former strife accord;

    .   .   .   .

    When the time for rest came, the two girls sought their couch, —

15 Where all that night they of their loves did treat,
    And hard adventures, twixt themselves alone,
    That each the other gan with passion[4] great
    And grieful pity privately bemoan.
    The morrow next, so soon as Titan[5] shone,
    They both uprose and to their ways them dight[6]:
    Long wand'red they, yet never met with none

---

[1] *According to each wit, i.e.* each had his own way of interpreting the wonder.

[2] *Feigned it, i.e.* produced it as an illusion.

[3] *Bellona*, the goddess of war.

[4] *Passion*, suffering, sorrow.

[5] *Titan*, Hyperion, the sun-god.

[6] *To their ways them dight*, made ready to start on their way.

That to their wills could them direct aright,
Or to them tidings tell that mote their hearts delight.

16 Lo! thus they rode, till at the last they spied
Two armèd knights, that toward them did pace,[1]
And each of them had riding by his side
A lady, seeming in so far a space[2];
But ladies none they were, albe in face
And outward show fair semblance they did bear;
For under mask of beauty and good grace
Vile treason and foul falsehood hidden were,
That mote[3] to none but to the wary wise appear.

17 The one of them the false Duessa[4] hight,[5]
That now had changed her former wonted hue[6];
For she could don so many shapes in sight,
As ever could chameleon colours new;
So could she forge all colours, save the true:
The other no whit better was then she,
But that, such as she was, she plain did shew;
Yet otherwise much worse, if worse might be,
And daily more offensive unto each degree.[7]

18 Her name was Atè,[8] mother of debate
And all dissension which doth daily grow

---

[1] *Pace*, step.
[2] *A lady seeming*, etc., *i.e.* at that distance she seemed to be a lady.
[3] *Mote*, might.
[4] *Duessa*, a character portrayed in the first book of the Faery Queene, representing falsehood.
[5] *Hight*, was called.
[6] *Hue*, form, appearance.
[7] *Unto each degree*, *i.e.* to people of all kinds, high and low.
[8] *Atè*, goddess of discord.

Amongst frail men, that many a public state
And many a private oft doth overthrow.
Her false Duessa, who full well did know
To be most fit to trouble noble knights
Which hunt for honour, raisèd from below
Out of the dwellings of the damnèd sprites,
Where she in darkness wastes her cursèd days and
    nights.

19 Hard by the gates of hell her dwelling is;
There, whereas [1] all the plagues and harms abound
Which punish wicked men that walk amiss:
It is a darksome delve [2] far under ground,
With thorns and barren brakes environed round,
That none the same may easily out-win [3];
Yet many ways to enter may be found,
But none to issue forth when one is in:
For discord harder is to end then to begin.

20 And all within, the riven [4] walls were hung
With ragged monuments of times forepast,[5]
All which the sad effects of discord sung:
There were rent robes and broken sceptres plast [6];
Altars defiled, and holy things defast [7];
Disshivered [8] spears and shields ytorn in twain;
Great cities ransacked, and strong castles rast [9];
Nations captivèd, and huge armies slain:
Of all which ruins there some relics did remain.

[1] *Whereas*, where.
[2] *Delve*, dell.
[3] *Out-win*, get out of.
[4] *Riven*, rent, broken.
[5] *Forepast*, bygone.
[6] *Plast*, placed.
[7] *Defast*, defaced.
[8] *Disshivered*, shivered in pieces.
[9] *Rast*, rased, razed, levelled with the ground.

21 Her mate, he was a jolly[1] youthful knight,
    That bore great sway in arms and chivalry,
    And was indeed a man of mickle[2] might;
    His name was Blandamour,[3] that did descry[4]
    His fickle mind full of inconstancy:
    And now himself he fitted had right well
    With two companions of like quality,
    Faithless Duessa, and false Paridell,
    That whether[5] were more false, full hard it is to tell.

22 Now when this gallant with his goodly crew
    From far espied the famous Britomart,
    Like knight adventurous in outward view,
    With his fair paragon,[6] his conquest's part,[7]
    Approaching nigh; eftsoones[8] his wanton heart
    Was tickled with delight, and jesting said:
    "Lo! there, Sir Paridell, for your desart,[9]
    Good luck presents you with yon lovely maid,
    For pity that ye want a fellow for your aid."

23 By that the lovely pair drew nigh to hond[10]:
    Whom whenas Paridell more plain beheld,
    Albe[11] in heart he like affection fond,[12]

---

[1] *Jolly*, handsome.
[2] *Mickle*, great.
[3] *Blandamour, i.e.* flattering, deceitful love.
[4] *Descry*, denote.
[5] *Whether*, which of the two.
[6] *Paragon*, companion.
[7] *His conquest's part, i.e.* the prize gained by conquest.
[8] *Eftsoones*, immediately.
[9] *Desart*, desert, reward.
[10] *Hond*, hand.
[11] *Albe*, although.
[12] *Fond*, found.

Yet mindful how he late by one was felled [1]
That did those arms and that same scutcheon weld,[2]
He had small lust [3] to buy his love so dear,
But answered: " Sir, him wise I never held,
That, having once escapèd peril near,
Would afterwards afresh the sleeping evil rear.[4]

24 " This knight too late his manhood and his might
I did assay, that me right dearly cost;
Ne list I [5] for revenge provoke new fight,
Ne for light lady's love, that soon is lost."
The hot-spur [6] youth [7] so scorning to be crossed,
" Take then to you this dame of mine," quoth he,
" And I, without your peril or your cost,
Will challenge [8] yond same other for my fee." [9]
So forth he fiercely pricked,[10] that one him scarce
    could see.

25 The warlike Britoness her soon addressed,[11]
And with such uncouth [12] welcome did receive
Her fainèd paramour,[13] her forcèd guest,
That, being forced his saddle soon to leave,

[1] *Yet mindful how he late by one was felled.* Paridell was overcome by Britomart when they struggled together before Malbecco's Castle. The poet seems to have forgotten the fact that Paridell discovered later, when Britomart doffed her helmet, that the dauntless knight was a woman.
[2] *Weld*, wield.
[3] *Lust*, desire.
[4] *Rear*, rouse.

[5] *Ne list I, i.e.* nor do I desire.
[6] *Hot-spur*, headstrong.
[7] *The hot-spur youth, i.e.* Blandamour.
[8] *Challenge*, claim.
[9] *Fee*, property.
[10] *Pricked*, rode, using spurs.
[11] *Her soon addressed*, soon made ready.
[12] *Uncouth*, strange, unexpected.
[13] *Her fained paramour, i.e.* the would-be lover.

Himself he did of his new love deceive [1];
And made himself th' ensample of his folly.
Which done, she passèd forth, not taking leave,
And left him now as sad as whilom [2] jolly,
Well warnèd to beware with whom he dared to dally.

26 Which when his other company beheld,
They to his succour ran with ready aid;
And, finding him unable once to weld,[3]
They rearèd him on horse-back and upstayed,
Till on his way they had him forth conveyed:
And all the way, with wondrous grief of mind
And shame, he showed himself to be dismayed
More for the love which he had left behind,
Then that which he had to Sir Paridell resigned.

27 Nathless[4] he forth did march, well as he might,
And made good semblance to his company,
Dissembling his disease and evil plight;
Till that ere long they chancèd to espy
Two other knights, that towards them did ply
With speedy course, as bent to charge them new:
Whom when as Blandamour approaching nigh
Perceived to be such as they seemed in view,
He was full woe,[5] and gan his former grief renew.

28 For th' one of them he perfectly descried
To be Sir Scudamour, (by that he bore
The god of love with wings displayèd wide,)

---

[1] *Deceive*, deprive.   [3] *Weld*, turn, move.
[2] *Whilom*, formerly.   [4] *Nathless*, nevertheless.
[5] *Woe*, sad.

Whom mortally he hated evermore,
Both for his worth, that all men did adore,
And eke [1] because his love he won by right:
Which when he thought, it grievèd him full sore,
That, through the bruises of his former fight,
He now unable was to wreak [2] his old despite.[3]

29 Forthy [4] he thus to Paridell bespake:
"Fair Sir, of friendship let me now you pray,
That as I late adventured [5] for your sake,
The hurts whereof me now from battle stay,
Ye will me now with like good turn repay,
And justify [6] my cause on yonder knight."
"Ah! Sir," said Paridell, "do not dismay
Yourself for this; myself will for you fight,
As ye have done for me: The left hand rubs the right." [7]

30 With that he put his spurs unto his steed,
With spear in rest, and toward him did fare,
Like shaft out of a bow preventing [8] speed.
But Scudamour was shortly well aware
Of his approach, and gan himself prepare
Him to receive with entertainment meet.
So furiously they met, that either bare

---

[1] *Eke*, also.
[2] *Wreak*, revenge.
[3] *Despite*, malice.
[4] *Forthy*, therefore.
[5] *Adventured*, ran the risk of.
[6] *Justify*, vindicate.
[7] *The left hand*, etc., *i.e.* one good turn deserves another.
[8] *Preventing*, coming before, surpassing.

The other down under their horses' feet,
That what of them became themselves did scarsly weet.[1]

31 As when two billows in the Irish sounds,
Forcibly driven with contráry tides,
Do meet together, each aback rebounds
With roaring rage; and dashing on all sides,
That filleth all the sea with foam, divides
The doubtful current into divers[2] ways:
So fell those two in spite of both their prides;
But Scudamour himself did soon upraise,
And, mounting light, his foe for lying long upbrays[3]:

32 Who, rollèd on an heap, lay still in swound,[4]
All careless of his taunt and bitter rail[5];
Till that the rest, him seeing lie on ground,
Ran hastily, to weet what did him ail:
Where finding that the breath gan him to fail,
With busy care they strove him to awake,
And doft his helmet, and undid his mail:
So much they did, that at the last they brake
His slumber, yet so mazèd that he nothing spake.

33 Which whenas Blandamour beheld, he said:
"False faitour[6] Scudamour, that hast by sleight
And foul advantage this good knight dismayed,
A knight much better then thyself behight,[7]

---

[1] *Weet*, know.
[2] *Divers*, diverse, opposite.
[3] *Upbrays*, upbraids.
[4] *Swound*, swoon.
[5] *Rail*, railing.
[6] *False faitour*, false doer, traitor.
[7] *Behight*, reputed.

Well falls it thee that I am not in plight,[1]
This day, to wreak the damage by thee done!
Such is thy wont, that still when any knight
Is weak'ned, then thou dost him overrun:
So hast thou to thyself false honour often won."

34 He little answered, but in manly heart
His mighty indignation did forbear;
Which was not yet so secret, but some part
Thereof did in his frowning face appear:
Like as a gloomy cloud, the which doth bear
An hideous storm, is by the northern blast
Quite overblown, yet doth not pass so clear
But that it all the sky doth overcast
With darkness dread, and threatens all the world to waste.

35 "Ah! gentle knight," then false Duessa said,
"Why do ye strive for ladies' love so sore,
Whose chief desire is love and friendly aid
Mongst gentle knights to nourish ever more!
Ne[2] be ye wroth Sir Scudamour, therefóre,
That she your love list[3] love another knight,
Ne do yourself dislike a whit the more;
For love is free, and led with self-delight,
Ne will enforcèd be with maisterdome[4] or might."

36 So false Duessa: but vile Atè thus:
"Both foolish knights, I can but laugh at both,

---

[1] *Well falls it thee*, etc., *i.e.* it is well for you that I am not in condition.
[2] *Ne*, nor.
[3] *List*, likes to, chooses to.
[4] *Maisterdome*, rule, mastery.

That strive and storm with stir outrageous,
For her, that each of you alike doth loth,[1]
And loves another, with whom now she goth
In lovely wise, ...
Whilst both you here with many a cursèd oath
Swear she is yours, and stir up bloody frays,
To win a willow bough, whilst other wears the bays."[2]

37 "Vile hag," said Scudamour, "why dost thou lie,
And falsely seekst a virtuous wight to shame?"
"Fond[3] knight," said she, "the thing that with this eye
I saw, why should I doubt[4] to tell the same?"
"Then tell," quoth Blandamour, "and fear no blame;
Tell what thou saw'st, maulgre whoso it hears."[5]

. . . .

Atè then told how she had seen a strange knight making love to Amoret. She did not know his name, but in his shield he bore the heads of many broken spears. "And," the hag went on, "I saw him kiss; I saw him her embrace."

38 . . . .
Which when as Scudamour did hear, his heart
Was thrilled with inward grief; as when in chase
The Parthian strikes a stag with shivering dart,
The beast astonished stands in middest of his smart[6];

---

[1] *Loth*, loathe.
[2] *To win a willow bough*, etc. The willow was the sign of the forsaken lover; the bay was worn by victors. Britomart, of course, appears to be Amoret's lover and her true knight.
[3] *Fond*, foolish.
[4] *Doubt*, fear.
[5] *Maulgre whoso it hears*, i.e. no matter who hears it.
[6] *In middest of*, etc., i.e. in the midst of his pain.

39 So stood Sir Scudamour when this he heard,
 Ne word he had to speak for great dismay,
 But looked on Glaucè grim,[1] who woxe [2] afeared
 Of outrage for the words which she heard say,
 Albe [3] untrue she wist [4] them by assay.[5]
 But Blandamour, whenas he did espy
 His change of cheer [6] that anguish did bewray,[7]
 He woxe full blithe, as he had got thereby,[8]
 And gan thereat to triumph without victory.

40 "Lo! recreant," said he, "the fruitless end
 Of thy vain boast, and spoil of love misgotten,
 Whereby the name of knighthood thou dost shend,[9]
 And all true lovers with dishonour blotten [10]:
 All things not rooted well will soon be rotten."
 "Fie, fie, false knight," then false Duessa cried,
 "Unworthy life, that love with guile hast gotten;
 Be thou, wherever thou do go [11] or ride,
 Loathèd of ladies all, and of all knights defied!"

41 But Scudamour, for passing [12] great despite,
 Stayed not to answer; scarcely did refrain
 But that in all those knights' and ladies' sight
 He for revenge had guiltless Glaucè slain:

[1] *But looked on Glaucè grim* (*grim* refers of course to Scudamour). For some reason, Glaucè does not choose to reveal the truth about Britomart.
[2] *Woxe*, grew, became.
[3] *Albe*, although.
[4] *Wist*, knew.
[5] *Assay*, experience, knowledge.
[6] *Cheer*, appearance, countenance.
[7] *Bewray*, betray.
[8] *As he had got thereby*, as though he had gained by this.
[9] *Shend*, disgrace.
[10] *Blotten*, stain.
[11] *Go*, walk.
[12] *Passing*, surpassing.

But, being past, he thus began amain[1];
"False traitor squire,[2] false squire of falsest knight,
Why doth mine hand from thine avenge[3] abstain,
Whose lord hath done my love this foul despite!
Why do I not it wreak[4] on thee now in my might!

42 "Discourteous, disloyal Britomart,
Untrue to God, and unto man unjust!
What vengeance due can equal thy desart,[5]

. . . .

Let ugly shame and endless infamy
Colour thy name with foul reproaches' rust:
Yet thou, false squire, his fault shalt dear aby,[6]
And with thy punishment his penance shalt supply."

43 The agèd dame, him seeing so enraged,
Was dead with fear; nathless[7] as need required
His flaming fury sought to have assuaged
With sober words, that sufferance[8] desired
Till time the trial of her truth expired[9];
And evermore sought Britomart to clear:
But he the more with furious rage was fired,
And thrice his hand to kill her did uprear,
And thrice he drew it back: so did at last forbear.

---

[1] *Amain*, violently.
[2] *False traitor squire*, i.e. Glaucè.
[3] *From thine avenge*, i.e. from taking vengeance upon thee.
[4] *Wreak*, avenge.
[5] *Desart*, desert.
[6] *Aby*, pay for.
[7] *Nathless*, nevertheless.
[8] *Sufferance*, patience.
[9] *Expired*, discovered.

X.

Satyrane institutes a tournament. Artegall appears on the scene. Britomart is declared victor in the jousts.

Sir Satyrane, the knight whom Britomart met at the castle of Malbecco in company with Paridell, had by some means come into possesion of the magic girdle belonging to fair Florimell, a lady noted for her beauty. The knight appointed a time and place for a tournament, declaring that the victor should be rewarded by the hand of the fairest lady present, and that she, as the queen of beauty, should receive the magic girdle. Among others, Paridell and Blandamour with their companions — among whom was the cowardly Braggadochio — decided to enter the lists.

1 . . . .
. . . at length upon th' appointed day
Unto the place of tournament they came;
Where they before them found in fresh array
Many a brave knight and many a dainty dame
Assembled for to get the honor of that game.

2 There this fair crew arriving did divide
Themselves asunder: Blandamour with those
Of his on th' one, the rest on th' other side.
But boastful Braggadochio rather chose,
For glory vain, their fellowship to lose,
That men on him the more might gaze alone.
The rest themselves in troops did else dispose,
Like as it seemèd best to every one;
The knights in couples marched with ladies linked attone.[1]

[1] *Attone*, together.

3 Then first of all forth came Sir Satyrane,
  Bearing that precious relic in an ark
  Of gold, that bad eyes might it not profane;
  Which drawing softly forth out of the dark,
  He open showed, that all men it mote mark;
  A gorgeous girdle, curiously embossed
  With pearl and precious stone, worth many a mark [1];
  Yet did the workmanship far pass the cost:
  It was the same which lately Florimell had lost.

4 That same aloft he hong in open view,
  To be the prize of beauty and of might;
  The which, eftsoones,[2] discovered, to it drew
  The eyes of all, allured with close [3] delight,
  And hearts quite robbèd with so glorious sight,
  That all men threw out vows and wishes vain.
  Thrice happy lady, and thrice happy knight,
  Them seemed, that could so goodly riches gain,
  So worthy of the peril, worthy of the pain.

5 Then took the bold Sir Satyrane in hand
  An huge great spear, such as he wont to wield,
  And vauncing [4] forth from all the other band
  Of knights, addressed his maiden-headed shield,
  Showing himself all ready for the field:
  Gainst whom there singled from the other side
  A paynim [5] knight that well in arms was skilled,

---

[1] *Mark*, a coin formerly current in England and Scotland, equal to thirteen shillings and four pence.
[2] *Eftsoones*, immediately.
[3] *Close*, secret.
[4] *Vauncing*, advancing.
[5] *Paynim*, pagan, infidel.

And had in many a battle oft been tried,
Hight[1] Bruncheval the bold, who fiercely forth did ride.

6 So furiously they both together met,
That neither could the other's force sustain:
As two fierce bulls, that strive the rule to get
Of all the herd, meet with so hideous main,[2]
That both rebutted tumble on the plain;
So these two champions to the ground were felled;
Where in a maze they both did long remain,
And in their hands their idle truncheons held,
Which neither able were to wag,[3] or once to weld.[4]

7 Which when the noble Ferramont espied,
He prickèd[5] forth in aid of Satyran;
And him against Sir Blandamour did ride
With all the strength and stiffness that he can;
But the more strong and stiffly that he ran,
So much more sorely to the ground he fell,
That on an heap were tumbled horse and man:
Unto whose rescue forth rode Paridell;
But him likewise with that same spear he eke[6] did quell.

8 Which Braggadochio seeing had no will
To hasten greatly to his party's aid,
Albe[7] his turn were next; but stood there still,

[1] *Hight*, called.
[2] *Main*, force.
[3] *Wag*, move.
[4] *Weld*, wield.
[5] *Pricked*, rode, using spurs.
[6] *Eke*, also.
[7] *Albe*, although.

As one that seemèd doubtful or dismayed :
But Triamond, half wroth to see him stayed,
Sternly stept forth and raught [1] away his spear,
With which so sore he Ferramont assayed,[2]
That horse and man to ground he quite did bear,
That neither could in haste themselves again uprear.

9   Which to avenge Sir Devon him did dight,[3]
But with no better fortune then the rest ;
For him likewise he quickly down did smite :
And after him Sir Douglas him addressed [4] ;
And after him Sir Palimord forth pressed ;
But none of them against his strokes could stand ;
But, all the more,[5] the more his praise increst [6] :
For either they were left upon the land,[7]
Or went away sore wounded of his hapless hand.

10 And now by this Sir Satyran abraid [8]
Out of the swoon, in which too long he lay ;
And looking round about, like one dismayed,
Whenas he saw the merciless affray [9]
Which doughty Triamond had wrought that day
Unto the noble knights of Maidenhead,
His mighty heart did almost rend in tway [10]
For very gall,[11] that rather wholly dead
Himself he wished have been then in so bad a stead.[12]

---

[1] *Raught*, snatched.
[2] *Assayed*, i.e. attacked.
[3] *Him did dight*, i.e. prepared himself.
[4] *Him addressed*, i.e. made himself ready.
[5] *But, all the more*, i.e. the more there were of them,
[6] *Increst*, increased.
[7] *Land*, ground.
[8] *Abraid*, awoke.
[9] *Affray*, assault.
[10] *In tway*, in two.
[11] *Gall*, bitterness, impatient anger.
[12] *Stead*, situation.

11 Eftsoones he gan to gather up around
    His weapons which lay scattered all abrode,[1]
    And, as it fell,[2] his steed he ready found:
    On whom remounting, fiercely forth he rode,
    Like spark of fire that from the anvil glode,[3]
    There where he saw the valiant Triamond
    Chasing, and laying on them heavy load,
    That none his force were able to withstand;
    So dreadful were his strokes, so deadly was his
        hond.

12 With that, at him his beamlike spear he aimed,
    And thereto all his power and might applied:
    The wicked steel for mischief first ordained,
    And having now misfortune got for guide,
    Stayed not till it arrivèd in his side,
    And therein made a very grisly[4] wound,
    That streams of blood his armour all bedyed.
    Much was he daunted with that direful stound,[5]
    That scarce he him upheld from falling in a swound.

13 Yet, as he might, himself he soft withdrew
    Out of the field, that none perceived it plain:
    Then gan the part[6] of challengers anew
    To range the field, and victorlike to reign,
    That none against them battle durst maintain.
    By that the gloomy evening on them fell,
    That forcèd them from fighting to refrain,

---

[1] *Abrode*, abroad.
[2] *As it fell*, as it happened.
[3] *Glode*, glanced.
[4] *Grisly*, horrible.
[5] *Stound;* here means stunning blow.
[6] *Part*, party.

And trumpets' sound to cease did them compel:
So Satyrane that day was judged to bear the bell.[1]

14 The morrow next the tourney gan anew;
And with the first the hardy Satyrane
Appeared in place, with all his noble crew:
On th' other side full many a warlike swain
Assembled were, that glorious prize to gain.
But 'mongst them all was not Sir Triamond;
Unable he new battle to darrain,[2]
Through grievance of his late receivèd wound,
That doubly did him grieve when so himself he found:

15 Which Cambell seeing, though he could not salve,[3]
Ne done undo,[4] yet, for to salve his name
And purchase honour in his friend's behalve,
This goodly counterfesance[5] he did frame:
The shield and arms, well known to be the same
Which Triamond had worn, unwares to wight[6]
And to his friend unwist,[7] for doubt[8] of blame
If he misdid,[9] he on himself did dight,[10]
That none could him discern; and so went forth to fight.

---

[1] *Bear the bell;* this meant to bear away the bell as a prize in a race; and hence to win in anything, to be superior.

[2] *Darrain,* wage.

[3] *Salve,* save, help.

[4] *Ne done undo, i.e.* nor undo what had been done.

[5] *Counterfesance,* here, disguise

[6] *Unwares to wight,* unbeknown to any one.

[7] *Unwist,* unbeknown.

[8] *Doubt,* fear.

[9] *Misdid,* did amiss.

[10] *Dight, i.e.* put on.

16 There Satyrane lord of the field he found,
　　Triumphing in great joy and jollity;
　　Gainst whom none able was to stand on ground:
　　That much he gan his glory to envý,[1]
　　And cast[2] t'avenge his friend's indignity:
　　A mighty spear eftsoones at him he bent;
　　Who, seeing him come on so furiously,
　　Met him mid-way with equal hardiment,[3]
　　That forcibly to ground they both together went.

17 They up again themselves can[4] lightly rear,
　　And to their trièd swords themselves betake;
　　With which they wrought such wondrous marvels there,
　　That all the rest it did amazèd make,
　　Ne any dared their peril to partake;
　　Now cuffing close, now chasing to and fro,
　　Now hurtling[5] round advantage for to take:
　　As two wild boars together grappling go,
　　Chaufing and foaming choler each against his foe.

18 So as they coursed, and tourneyed here and there,
　　It chanced Sir Satyrane his steed at last,
　　Whether through found'ring or through sudden fear,
　　To stumble,[6] that his rider nigh he cast;
　　Which vantage Cambell did pursue so fast,
　　That, ere himself he had recovered well,

[1] *His glory to envy*, i.e. he felt a grudge against him on account of his glory.
[2] *Cast*, planned.
[3] *Hardiment*, boldness.
[4] *Can*, gan, i.e. did.
[5] *Hurtling*, skirmishing.
[6] *It chanced Sir Satyrane his steed*, etc., i.e. it chanced that Sir Satyrane's steed at last stumbled.

So sore he soused him [1] on the compassed [2] crest,
That forcèd him to leave his lofty sell,[3]
And rudely tumbling down under his horse' feet fell.

19 Lightly Cambello leapt down from his steed,
For to have rent his shield and arms away,
That whilom wont to be the victor's meed ;
When all unwares he felt an hideous sway
Of many swords that load on him did lay :
An hundred knights had him enclosèd round,
To rescue Satyrane out of his prey [4];
All which at once huge strokes on him did pound,
In hope to take him prisoner, where he stood on ground.

20 He with their multitude was nought dismayed,
But with stout courage turned upon them all,
And with his brond-iron [5] round about him laid ;
Of which he dealt large alms, as did befall :
Like as a lion, that by chance doth fall
Into the hunters' toil, doth rage and roar,
In royal heart disdaining to be thrall :
But all in vain : for what might one do more ?
They have him taken captive, though it grieve him sore.

---

[1] *He soused him, i.e.* Cambell struck Satyrane.
[2] *Compassed,* rounded.
[3] *Sell,* saddle.
[4] *Out of his prey, i.e.* out of his power.
[5] *Brond-iron,* brand-iron, sword.

21 Whereof when news to Triamond was brought
    There as he lay, his wound he soon forgot,
    And starting up straight for his armour sought:
    In vain he sought; for there he found it not;
    Cambello it away before had got:
    Cambello's arms therefore he on him threw,
    And lightly issued forth to take his lot.[1]
    There he in troop found all that warlike crew
    Leading his friend away, full sorry to his view.[2]

22 Into the thickest of that knightly preasse[3]
    He thrust, and smote down all that was between,
    Carried with fervent zeal; ne did he cease,
    Till that he came where he had Cambell seen
    Like captive thrall two other knights atween:
    There he amongst them cruel havoc makes,
    That they which led him soon enforcèd been
    To let him loose to save their proper stakes[4];
    Who, being freed, from one a weapon fiercely takes.

23 With that he drives at them with dreadful might,
    Both in remembrance of his friend's late harm,
    And in revengement of his own despite:
    So both together give a new alarm,
    As if but now the battle waxèd warm.
    As when two greedy wolves do break by force
    Into an herd, far from the husband farm,[5]

---

[1] *To take his lot*, i.e. to try his fortune.

[2] *Full sorry to his view*, i.e. a sorry sight to him.

[3] *Preasse*, press.

[4] *To save their proper stakes*, i.e. to secure their own safety.

[5] *Husband farm*, i.e. the husbandman's farm.

They spoil and ravine[1] without all remorse;
So did these two through all the field their foes
   enforce.[2]

24 Fiercely they followed on their bold emprise,[3]
   Till trumpet's sound did warn them all to rest:
   Then all with one consent did yield the prize
   To Triamond and Cambell as the best:
   But Triamond to Cambell it relest,[4]
   And Cambell it to Triamond transferred;
   Each labouring t' advance the other's gest,[5]
   And make his praise before his own preferred:
   So that the doom[6] was to another day deferred.

25 The last day came; when all those knights again
   Assembled were their deeds of arms to show.
   Full many deeds that day were showèd plain:
   But Satyrane, bove all the other crew,
   His wondrous worth declared in all men's view;
   For from the first he to the last endured:
   And though some while fortune from him withdrew,
   Yet evermore his honour he recured,[7]
   And with unwearied pow'r his party still assured.[8]

26 Ne was there knight that ever thought of arms,
   But that his utmost prowess there made knowen:
   That, by their many wounds and careless harms,[9]

---

[1] *Ravine*, plunder.
[2] *Enforce*, i.e. drive before them.
[3] *Emprise*, enterprise.
[4] *Relest*, released, let go.
[5] *Gest*, achievement.
[6] *Doom*, decision.
[7] *Recured*, recovered.
[8] *Assured*, secured.
[9] *Careless harms*, uncared for hurts.

By shivered spears and swords all under[1] strowen,
By scattered shields, was easy to be showen.
There might ye see loose steeds at random run,
Whose luckless riders late were overthrown;
And squires make haste to help their lords fordone[2]:
But still the knights of Maidenhead[3] the better won.[4]

27 Till that there ent'red on the other side
A stranger knight, from whence no man could read,[5]
In quaint[6] disguise, full hard to be descried[7]:
For all his armour was like salvage[8] weed
With woody moss bedight,[9] and all his steed
With oaken leaves attrapped,[10] that seemèd fit
For salvage wight, and thereto well agreed
His word,[11] which on his ragged shield was writ,
Salvagesse sans finesse,[12] showing secret wit.

28 He, at the first incoming, charged his spear
At him that first appearèd in his sight;
That was to weet the stout[13] Sir Sangliere,
Who well was known to be a valiant knight,
Approvèd oft in many a perlous[14] fight:

---

[1] *Under*, i.e. on the ground.
[2] *Fordone*, defeated.
[3] *The knights of Maidenhead*, i.e. the knights owing allegiance to Gloriana, the Faery Queen.
[4] *The better won*, i.e. came off victors.
[5] *Read*, tell.
[6] *Quaint*, ingenious.
[7] *Descried*, made out.
[8] *Salvage weed*, wild dress. Salvage has the meaning of the French *sauvage* rather than of our savage. Salvage knight means wild knight, knight of the woods.
[9] *Bedight*, bedecked.
[10] *Attrapped*, adorned.
[11] *Word*, motto.
[12] *Salvagesse sans finesse*, wildness without art.
[13] *Stout*, brave, dauntless.
[14] *Perlous*, perilous.

Him at the first encounter down he smote,
And overbore beyond his crouper quite;
And after him another knight, that hote[1]
Sir Brianor, so sore, that none him life behote.[2]

29 Then, ere his hand he reared, he overthrew
Seven knights, one after other, as they came:
And, when his spear was brust,[3] his sword he drew,
The instrument of wrath, and with the same
Fared[4] like a lion in his bloody game,
Hewing and slashing shields and helmets bright,
And beating down whatever nigh him came,
That every one gan shun his dreadful sight
No less than death itself, in dangerous affright.

30 Much wond'red all men what or whence he came,
That did amongst the troops so tyrannise;
And each of other gan inquire his name:
But, when they could not learn it by no wise,
Most answerable to his wild disguise
It seemèd, him to term the salvage knight
But certes[5] his right name was otherwise,
Though known to few that Arthegall[6] he hight,[7]
The doughtiest knight that lived that day, and most of might.

---

[1] *Hote*, was named.
[2] *Behote*, promised.
[3] *Brust*, broken.
[4] *Fared*, went.
[5] *Certes*, truly.
[6] *Arthegall*, or *Artegall*, the knight whose image Britomart had seen in the magic mirror.
[7] *Hight*, was called.

31 Thus was Sir Satyrane with all his band
By his sole manhood and achievement stout
Dismayed, that none of them in field durst stand,
But beaten were and chasèd all about.
So he continued all that day throughout,
Till evening that the sun gan downward bend :
Then rushèd forth out of the thickest rout
A stranger knight, that did his glory shend[1]:
So nought may be esteemèd happy till the end !

32 He at his entrance charged his pow'rful spear
At Artegall, in middest of his pride,
And therewith smote him on his umbriere[2]
So sore, that, tumbling back, he down did slide
Over his horse's tail above a stride ;
Whence little lust[3] he had to rise again.
Which Cambell seeing, much the same envièd.[4]
And ran at him[5] with all his might and main ;
But shortly was likewise seen lying on the plain.

33 Whereat full inly wroth was Triamond,
And cast[6] t' avenge the shame done to his friend :
But by his friend himself eke soon he fond[7]
In no less need of help then him he weened.[8]
All which when Blandamour from end to end[9]

---

[1] *Shend*, shame.
[2] *Umbriere*, visor.
[3] *Lust*, desire.
[4] *The same envied*, i.e. was sorely vexed on account of the circumstance.
[5] *Him*, i.e. the stranger knight.
[6] *Cast*, planned.
[7] *Fond*, found.
[8] *Then him he weened*, than he whom he thought in need of it.
[9] *From end to end*, i.e. from begining to end.

Beheld, he woxe[1] therewith displeasèd sore,
And thought in mind it shortly to amend :
His spear he feutered,[2] and at him it bore ;
But with no better fortune then the rest afore.

34 Full many others at him likewise ran ;
But all of them likewise dismounted were :
Ne certes wonder[3]; for no pow'r of man
Could bide the force of that enchanted spear,
The which this famous Britomart did bear ;
With which she wondrous deeds of arms achieved,
And overthrew whatever came her near,
That all those stranger knights full sore agrieved,
And that late weaker band of challengers relieved.

35 Like as in summer's day, when raging heat
Doth burn the earth and boilèd rivers dry,
That all brute beasts, forced to refrain fro meat,[4]
Do hunt for shade where shrouded they may lie,
And, missing it, fain from themselves to fly[5] ;
All travellers tormented are with pain :
A wat'ry cloud doth overcast the sky,
And poureth forth a sudden show'r of rain,
That all the wretched world recomforteth again :

36 So did the warlike Britomart restore
The prize to knights of Maidenhead that day,

---

[1] *Woxe*, became.
[2] *Feutered*, put in rest.
[3] *Ne certes wonder*, *i.e.* and certainly, no wonder.
[4] *Meat*, food.
[5] *Fain from themselves to fly;* meaning doubtful. Prof. Child suggests, — act as if they would (?).

Which else was like to have been lost,[1] and bore
The praise of prowess from them all away.
Then shrilling trumpets loudly gan to bray,
And bade them leave their labours and long toil
To joyous feast and other gentle play,[2]
Where beauty's prize should win that precious spoil[3]:
Where I with sound of trump will also rest awhile.

[1] *Like to have been lost.* Artegall was disguised so that no one recognized him as one of the knights of Maidenhead.

[2] *Play*, amusement.

[3] *That precious spoil, i.e.* Florimell's girdle.

XI.

The girdle is given to the false Florimell. Scudamour spends the night in the house of Care.

1 It hath been through all ages ever seen,
   That with the praise of arms and chivalry
   The prize of beauty still hath joinèd been;
   And that for reason's special privity [1];
   For either doth on other much rely:
   For he me seems most fit the fair to serve,
   That can her best defend from villainy;
   And she most fit his service doth deserve,
   That fairest is, and from her faith will never swerve.

2 So fitly now here cometh next in place,
   After the proof of prowess ended well,
   The controverse [2] of beauty's sovereign grace;
   In which, to her that doth the most excel,
   Shall fall the girdle of fair Florimell;
   That many wish to win for glory vain,
   And not for virtuous use, which some do tell
   That glorious belt, did in itself contain,
   Which ladies ought to love, and seek for to obtain.

[1] *For reason's special privity;* means for a special and particular a peculiar phrase which probably reason.
[2] *Controverse,* controversy.

After telling how Vulcan made this precious ornament for his wife, Venus, "When first he lovèd her with heart entire," the poet goes on:—

3 That goodly belt was Cestus hight by name,
   And as her life by her[1] esteemèd dear:
   No wonder then, if that to win the same
   So many ladies sought, as shall appear;
   For peerless she was thought that it did bear.
   And now by this their feast all being ended,
   The judges, which thereto selected were,
   Into the Martian field[2] adown descended
   To deem[3] this doubtful case, for which they all contended.

4 But first was question made, which of those knights
   That lately tourneyed had the wager won:
   There was it judgèd, by those worthy wights,
   That Satyrane the first day best had done:
   For he last ended, having first begun.
   The second was to Triamond behight,[4]
   For that he saved the victor from fordonne[5]:
   For Cambell victor was, in all men's sight,
   Till by mishap he in his foemen's hand did light.

5 The third day's prize unto that stranger knight,
   Whom all men termed knight of the hebene[6] spear,

---

[1] *Her*, i.e. Florimell, the rightful owner of the belt.

[2] *Martian field*, the Campus Martius, field of battle.

[3] *Deem*, judge.

[4] *Behight*, adjudged.

[5] *Saved the victor from fordonne*, i.e. saved the victor from ruin.

[6] *Hebene*, yew. It has been supposed that *hebene* meant *ebony*. Dr. Brinsley Nicholson has, however, proved conclusively that this word stands for *yew*. *Hebenon*, supposed to signify *henbane*, has the same meaning.

To Britomart, was given by good right;
For that with puissant stroke she down did bear
The salvage[1] knight that victor was whilere,[2]
And all the rest which had the best afore,
And, to the last, unconquered did appear;
For last is deemèd best: to her therefore
The fairest lady was adjudged for paramour.[3]

6 But thereat greatly grudgèd[4] Arthegall,
And much repined, that both of victor's meed
And eke of honor she did him forestall:
Yet mote he not withstand what was decreed;
But inly thought of that despiteful[5] deed
Fit time t' await avengèd for to be.
This being ended thus, and all agreed,
Then next ensued the paragon to see
Of beauty's praise, and yield the fairest her due fee.

7 Then first Cambello brought into their view
His fair Cambina covered with a veale[6];
Which, being once withdrawn, most perfect hue
And passing[7] beauty did eftsoones reveal,
That able was weak hearts away to steal.
Next did Sir Triamond unto their sight
The face of his dear Canacee unheale[8];
Whose beauty's beam eftsoones did shine so bright,
That dazed the eyes of all, as with exceeding light.

---

[1] *Salvage*, wild, woodland.
[2] *Whilere*, before.
[3] *Paramour*, sweetheart.
[4] *Grudged*, felt great vexation.
[5] *Despiteful*, vexatious, hateful.
[6] *Veale*, veil.
[7] *Passing*, surpassing.
[8] *Unheale*, uncover.

8 And after her did Paridell produce
   His false Duessa, that she might be seen;
   Who with her forgèd beauty did seduce
   The hearts of some that fairest did her ween;
   As diverse wits affected divers been.[1]
   Then did Sir Ferramont unto them show
   His Lucida, that was full fair and sheen[2]:
   And after these an hundred ladies moe[3]
   Appeared in place, the which each other did outgo.[4]

9 All which whoso dare think for to enchase,[5]
   Him needeth sure a golden pen I ween
   To tell the feature[6] of each goodly face.
   For, since the day that they created been,
   So many heavenly faces were not seen
   Assembled in one place: ne he that thought[7]
   For Chian[8] folk to pourtraict[9] beauty's queen,
   By view of all the fairest to him brought,
   So many fair did see, as here he might have sought.

10 At last, the most redoubted Britoness
   Her lovely Amoret did open show;
   Whose face, discovered, plainly did express

---

[1] *As diverse wits*, etc., *i.e.* as different minds are affected in different ways.

[2] *Sheen*, radiant.

[3] *Moe*, more.

[4] *The which each other did outgo*, *i.e.* each of whom seemed to surpass the others.

[5] *Enchase*, set forth, describe.

[6] *Feature*, appearance.

[7] *Ne he that thought*, etc. An allusion to the well-known picture of Apelles of Cos. Prof. Child. The Venus Anadyomene was Apelles' best picture.

[8] *Chian*, of or pertaining to the island of Chios (now Scio) in the Ægean sea.

[9] *Pourtraict*, portray.

The heavenly portraict of bright angel's hue.
Well weenèd all, which her that time did view,
That she should surely bear the bell away [1];
Till Blandamour, who thought he had the true
And very Florimell,[2] did her display :
The sight of whom once seen did all the rest
    dismay.[3]

11 For all afore that seemèd fair and bright,
Now base and cóntemptible did appear,
Compared to her that shone as Phœbe's [4] light
Amongst the lesser stars in evening clear.
All that her saw with wonder ravished were,
And weened no mortal creature she should be,
But some celestial shape that flesh did bear :
Yet all were glad there Florimell to see ;
Yet thought that Florimell was not so fair as she.

12 As guileful goldsmith that by secret skill
With golden foil doth finely over-spread
Some baser metal, which commend he will
Unto the vulgar for good gold instead,
He much more goodly gloss thereon doth shed
To hide his falsehood, then if it were true :
So hard this idol [5] was to be aread,[6]

---

[1] *Bear the bell away, i.e.* take the prize.
[2] *The true and very Florimell.* Blandamour's lady was the creation of a witch. Being the exact counterpart of Florimell, the rightful owner of the girdle, she was called the false Florimell.
[3] *Dismay*, overpower.
[4] *Phœbe*, the same as Diana, the moon goddess.
[5] *Idol*, image.
[6] *Aread*, detected.

That Florimell herself in all men's view
She seemed to pass: so forgèd things do fairest shew.

13 Then was that golden belt by doom[1] of all
Granted to her, as to the fairest dame :
Which being brought, about her middle[2] small
They thought to gird, as best it her became ;
But by no means they could it thereto frame :
For, ever as they fast'ned it, it loosed
And fell away, as feeling secret blame.[3]
Full oft about her waist she it enclosed ;
And it as oft was from about her waist disclosed[4] :

14 That all men wond'red at the uncouth[5] sight,
And each one thought as to their fancies came :
But she herself did think it done for spite,
And touchèd was with secret wrath and shame
Therewith, as thing devised her to defame.
Then many other ladies likewise tried
About their tender loins to knit the same ;
But it would not on none of them abide,
But when they thought it fast, eftsoones[6] it was
    untied.

15 .   .   .   .
Till that at last the gentle Amoret
Likewise assayed to prove that girdle's pow'r ;

---

[1] *Doom*, judgment.
[2] *Middle*, waist.
[3] *And fell away, as feeling secret blame*. This magic girdle could be worn only by the purest and best of women.
[4] *Disclosed*, unfastened.
[5] *Uncouth*, strange.
[6] *Eftsoones*, immediately.

And, having it about her middle set,
Did find it fit withouten breach or let [1];
Whereat the rest gan greatly to envý [2]:
But Florimell exceedingly did fret,
And, snatching from her hand half angrily
The belt again, about her body gan it tie:

16 Yet nathëmore [3] would it her body fit;
Yet nathëless [4] to her, as her due right,
It yielded was by them that judgèd it;
And she herself adjudgèd to the knight
That bore the heben [5] spear, as won in fight.
But Britomart would not thereto assent,
Ne her own Amoret forego so light
For that strange dame, whose beauty's wonderment [6]
She less esteemed than th' other's virtuous government. [7]

17 Whom when the rest did see her to refuse,
They were full glad, in hope themselves to get her:
Yet at her choice they all did greatly muse. [8]
But, after that, the judges did arret [9] her
Unto the second best that loved her better;
That was the salvage knight: but he was gone
In great displeasure, that he could not get her.

---

[1] *Withouten breach or let*, i.e. without gap or obstacle.
[2] *Gan greatly to envy*, i.e. were greatly vexed.
[3] *Nathëmore*, not the more.
[4] *Nathëless*, nevertheless.
[5] *Heben*, yew.
[6] *Whose beauty's wonderment*, i.e. whose wonderful beauty.
[7] *Government*, i.e. mode of life, behavior.
[8] *Muse*, wonder.
[9] *Arret*, adjudge.

Then was she judgèd Triamond his one[1];
But Triamond loved Canacee and other none.

18 Tho[2] unto Satyran she was adjudged,
Who was right glad to gain so goodly meed:
But Blandamour thereat full greatly grudged,[3]
And little praised his labour's evil speed,[4]
That, for to win the saddle, lost the steed.[5]
Ne less thereat did Paridell complain,
And thought t' appeal, from that which was decreed,
To single combat with Sir Satyrane:
Thereto him Atè stirred, new discord to maintain.

19 And eke,[6] with these, full many other knights
She through her wicked working did incense
Her to demand and challenge[7] as their rights,
Deservèd for their perils' recompense.
Amongst the rest, with boastful vain pretence
Stepped Braggadochio forth, and as his thrall[8]
Her claimed, by him in battle won long sens[9]:
Whereto herself he did to witness call;
Who, being asked, accordingly confessèd all.

20 Thereat exceeding wroth was Satyran;
And wroth with Satyran was Blandamour;
And wroth with Blandamour was Erivan;

---

[1] *Judged Triamond his one, i.e.* she was adjudged to Triamond.
[2] *Tho,* then.
[3] *Grudged,* complained.
[4] *Speed,* issue.
[5] *That, for to win,* etc. The false Florimell had come to the tournament in company with Blandamour.
[6] *Eke,* also.
[7] *Challenge,* claim.
[8] *Thrall,* captive.
[9] *Sens,* since.

And at them both Sir Paridell did lower.
So altogether stirred up strifull stoure,[1]
And ready were new battle to darrain [2]:
Each one professed to be her paramour,[3]
And vowed with spear and shield it to maintain ;
Ne judge's pow'r, ne reason's rule, mote [4] them restrain.

21 Which troublous stir when Satyrane avised,[5]
He gan to cast [6] how to appease the same,
And, to accord them all, this means devised :
First in the midst to set that fairest dame,
To whom each one his challenge [7] should disclaim,
And he himself his right would eke releasse :
Then, look to whom she voluntary came,
He should without disturbance her possess :
Sweet is the love that comes alone with willingness.

22 They all agreed ; and then that snowy maid
Was in the middest placed among them all :
All on her gazing wished, and vowed, and prayed,
And to the queen of beauty [8] close [9] did call,
That she unto their portion might befall.
Then when she long had looked upon each one,
As though she wishèd to have pleased them all,
At last to Braggadochio self alone,
She came of her accord, in spite of all his fone.[10]

[1] *Stoure*, tumult.
[2] *Darrain*, wage.
[3] *Professed to be her paramour*, i.e. asserted that he was her rightful lover.
[4] *Mote*, might.
[5] *Avised*, perceived.
[6] *Cast*, plan.
[7] *Challenge*, claim.
[8] *Queen of beauty*, i.e. Venus.
[9] *Close*, secretly.
[10] *Fone*, foes.

23 Which when they all beheld, they chafed, and raged,
    And woxe[1] nigh mad for very heart's despite,[2]
    That from revenge their wills they scarce assuaged[3]:
    Some thought from him her to have reft[4] by might;
    Some proffer made with him for her to fight:
    But he nought cared for all that they could say;
    For he their words as wind esteemèd light:
    Yet not fit place he thought it there to stay,
    But secretly from thence that night her bore away.

24 They which remained, so soon as they perceived
    That she was gone, departed thence with speed,
    And followed them, in mind her to have reaved[5]
    From wight unworthy of so noble meed.
    In which pursuit how each one did succeed,
    Shall else[6] be told in order, as it fell.
    But now of Britomart it here doth need
    The hard adventures and strange haps to tell;
    Since with the rest she went not after Florimell.

25 For soon as she them saw to discord set,
    Her list[7] no longer in that place abide;
    But, taking with her lovely Amoret,
    Upon her first adventure[8] forth did ride,
    To seek her loved, making blind Love her guide.
    Unlucky maid, to seek her enemy!
    Unlucky maid, to seek him far and wide,

---

[1] *Woxe*, grew, became.
[2] *Despite*, vexation.
[3] *Assuaged*, pacified, appeased.
[4] *Reft*, taken away.
[5] *Reaved*, taken away.
[6] *Else*, elsewhere.
[7] *Her list*, she desired.
[8] *Her first adventure*, i.e. the object for which she left her home.

Whom, when he was unto herself most nigh,
She through his late disguisement could him not descry!

26 So much the more her grief, the more her toil:
Yet neither toil nor grief she once did spare,
In seeking him that should her pain assoil[1];
Whereto great comfort in her sad misfare[2]
Was Amoret, companion of her care:
Who likewise sought her lover long miswent,[3]
The gentle Scudamour,[4] whose heart whileare[5]
That stryfull hag, with jealous discontent
Had filled, that he to fell[6] revenge was fully bent;

27 Bent to revenge on blameless Britomart
The crime which cursèd Atè kindled erst,[7]
The which like thorns did prick his jealous heart,
And through his soul like poisoned arrow persed,[8]
That by no reason it might be reversed,[9]
For ought that Glaucé could or do or say:
For, aye the more that she the same rehearsed,
The more it galled and grieved him night and day,
That nought but dire revenge his anger mote defray.[10]

---

[1] *Assoil*, remove.
[2] *Misfare*, misfortune.
[3] *Miswent*, gone astray.
[4] *The gentle Scudamour*, etc. The poet makes a sudden transition here, taking us back to Scudamour whom we left full of wrath against the supposed knight, Britomart.
[5] *Whileare*, whilere, recently.
[6] *Fell*, fierce.
[7] *Erst*, first.
[8] *Persed*, pierced.
[9] *Reversed*, drawn out.
[10] *Mote defray*, might appease.

28 So as they travellèd, the drooping night
    Covered with cloudy storm and bitter shower,
    That dreadful seemed to every living wight,
    Upon them fell, before her timely hour;
    That forcèd them to seek some covert bower,
    Where they might hide their heads in quiet rest,
    And shroud their persons from that stormy stowre.[1]
    Not far away, not meet for any guest,
    They spied a little cottage, like some poor man's nest.

29 Under a steep hill's side it placèd was,
    There where the mould'red earth had caved[2] the bank;
    And fast beside a little brook did pass
    Of muddy water, that like puddle stank,
    By which few crooked sallows[3] grew in rank:
    Whereto approaching nigh, they heard the sound
    Of many iron hammers beating rank,[4]
    And answering their weary turns around,
    That seemèd some blacksmith dwelt in that desert ground.

30 There ent'ring in, they found the goodman[5] self
    Full busily unto his work ybent;
    Who was to weet a wretched wearish[6] elf,
    With hollow eyes and rawbone cheeks forspent,[7]

[1] *Stowre*, tumult.
[2] *Caved*, made hollow.
[3] *Sallows*, willows.
[4] *Rank*, fiercely.
[5] *Goodman*, i.e. the master of the house; often used in speaking familiarly.
[6] *Wearish*, withered.
[7] *Forspent*, wasted.

As if he had in prison long been pent :
Full black and grisly¹ did his face appear,
Besmeared with smoke that nigh his eyesight blent²;
With rugged beard, and hoary shaggèd hair,
The which he never wont to comb, or comely sheare.

31 Rude was his garment, and to rags all rent,
Ne better had he, ne for better cared :
With blist'red hands amongst the cinders brent,³
And fingers filthy with long nails unpared,
Right fit to rend the food on which he fared.
His name was Care ; a blacksmith by his trade,
That neither day nor night from working spared,
But to small purpose iron wedgès made :
Those be unquiet thoughts, that careful⁴ minds invade.

32 In which his work he had six servants⁵ prest,⁶
About the andvile standing evermore,
With huge great hammers, that did never rest
From heaping strokes which thereon sousèd⁷ sore :
All six strong grooms, but one then other more ;
For by degrees they all were disagreed⁸ ;
So likewise did the hammers which they bore
Like bells in greatness orderly succeed,
That he which was the last the first did far exceed.

¹ *Grisly*, horrible.
² *Blent*, blinded.
³ *Brent*, burnt.
⁴ *Careful*, full of care.
⁵ *Six servants*. Upton says that Care and his six servants represent the seven days of the week.
⁶ *Prest*, ready.
⁷ *Soused*, pounced upon, fell upon.
⁸ *Disagreed*, made to differ.

33 He like a monstrous giant seemed in sight,
    Far passing Bronteus or Pyracmon¹ great,
    The which in Lipari² do day and night
    Frame thunderbolts for Jove's avengeful threat.
    So dreadfully he did the andvile beat,
    That seemed to dust he shortly would it drive :
    So huge his hammer, and so fierce his heat,
    That seemed a rock of diamond it could rive³
    And rend asunder quite, if he thereto list⁴ strive.

34 Sir Scudamour there ent'ring much admired⁵
    The manner of their work and weary pain ;
    And, having long beheld, at last enquired
    The cause and end thereof ; but all in vain ;
    For they for nought would from their work refrain,
    Ne let his speeches come unto their ear ;
    And eke the breathful bellows blew amain,
    Like to the northern wind, that none could hear ;
    Those pensifeness did move ; and sighs the bellows
        weare.⁶

35 Which when that warrior saw, he said no more,
    But in his armour laid him down to rest :
    To rest he laid him down upon the floor,
    (Whilom⁷ for ventrous⁸ knights the bedding best,)
    And thought his weary limbs to have redressed.⁹

---

¹ *Bronteus or Pyracmon*, Cyclopes, servants of Vulcan.

² *Lipari*, one of the Æolian isles, north of Sicily.

³ *Rive*, rend.

⁴ *List*, desired to.

⁵ *Admired*, wondered at.

⁶ *Weare*, were.

⁷ *Whilom*, formerly.

⁸ *Ventrous*, adventurous.

⁹ *Redressed*, refreshed.

And that old, agèd dame, his faithful squire,
Her feeble joints laid eke adown to rest ;
That needed much her weak age to desire,[1]
After so long a travel which them both did tire.

36 There lay Sir Scudamour long while expecting
When gentle sleep his heavy eyes would close ;
Oft changing sides, and oft new place electing,
Where better seemed he mote himself repose ;
And oft in wrath he thence again uprose ;
And oft in wrath he laid him down again.
But, wheresoever he did himself dispose,
He by no means could wishèd ease obtain :
So every place seemed painful, and each changing vain.

37 And evermore, when he to sleep did think,
The hammers' sound his senses did molest ;
And evermore, when he began to wink,[2]
The bellows' noise disturbed his quiet rest,
Ne suff'red sleep to settle in his breast.
And all the night the dogs did bark and howl
About the house, at scent of stranger guest :
And now the crowing cock, and now the owl
Loud shrieking, him afflicted to the very sowle.[3]

38 And, if by fortune any little nap
Upon his heavy eye-lids chanced to fall,
Eftsoones one of those villeins [4] him did rap

---

[1] *That needed much*, etc., *i.e.* that her weak age must necessarily desire.

[2] *Wink*, close his eyes.

[3] *Sowle*, soul.

[4] *Villeins*, men of low birth, menials.

THE FAERY QUEENE.

Upon his head-piece with his iron mall[1];
That he was soon awakèd therewithal,
And lightly started up as one afraid,
Or as if one him suddenly did call:
So oftentimes he out of sleep abrayed,[2]
And then lay musing long on that him ill apayed.[3]

39 So long he musèd, and so long he lay,
That at the last his weary sprite[4] oppressed
With fleshly weakness, which no creature may
Long time resist, gave place to kindly rest,
That all his senses did full soon arrest:
Yet, in his soundest sleep, his daily[5] fear
His idle brain gan busily molest,
And made him dream those two disloyal were[6]:
The things that day most minds, at night do most appear.

40 With that the wicked carle,[7] the maister smith,
A pair of red-hot iron tongs did take
Out of the burning cinders, and therewith
Under his side him nipped; that, forced to wake,
He felt his heart for very pain to quake,
And started up avengèd for to be
On him the which his quiet slumber brake:

---

[1] *Mall*, hammer.
[2] *Abrayed*, awoke.
[3] *On that him ill apayed, i.e.* on that which disturbed him or made him dissatisfied.
[4] *Sprite*, spirit.
[5] *Daily*, i.e. of the day.
[6] *And made him dream*, etc., *i.e.* made him dream that Amoret had accepted as her lover the supposed knight, Britomart.
[7] *Carle*, churl.

Yet, looking round about him, none could see ;
Yet did the smart remain, though he himself[1] did flee.

41 In such disquiet and heart-fretting pain
He all that night, that too long night, did pass.
And now the day out of the ocean main[2]
Began to peep above this earthly mass,
With pearly dew sprinkling the morning grass :
Then up he rose like heavy lump of lead,
That in his face, as in a looking-glass,
The signs of anguish one mote plainly read,
And guess the man to be dismayed[3] with jealous[4] dread.

42 Unto his lofty steed he clomb[5] anone,[6]
And forth upon his former voyage fared,[7]
And with him eke that agèd squire attone[8] ;
Who, whatsoever peril was prepared,
Both equal pains and equal peril shared :
The end whereof and dangerous event
Shall for another canticle[9] be spared :
But here my weary team, nigh over-spent,[10]
Shall breathe itself awhile after so long a went.[11]

---

[1] *He himself, i.e.* Care who had tormented Scudamour.

[2] *Ocean main*, that is, the great sea as distinguished from an arm or bay.

[3] *Dismayed*, overpowered.

[4] *Jealous*, suspicious, apprehensive.

[5] *Clomb*, climbed.

[6] *Anone*, anon.

[7] *Fared*, went.

[8] *Attone*, together.

[9] *Canticle*, canto.

[10] *Over-spent*, over-exhausted.

[11] *Went*, journey.

XII.

Britomart encounters Artegall and Scudamour. Artegall wins her love. Scudamour learns of the disappearance of Amoret.

1 WHAT equal torment to the grief of mind
  And pining anguish hid in gentle heart,
  That inly feeds itself with thoughts unkind,
  And nourisheth her own consuming smart!
  What medicine can any leech's [1] art
  Yield such a sore, that doth her grievance hide,
  And will to none her malady impart!
  Such was the wound that Scudamour did gride [2]:
  For which Dan Phœbus self cannot a salve provide.[3]

2 Who having left that restless house of Care,
  The next day, as he on his way did ride,
  Full of melancholy and sad misfare [4]
  Through misconceit,[5] all unawares espied
  An armèd knight under a forest side
  Sitting in shade beside his grazing steed;
  Who, soon as them approaching he descried,
  Gan towards them to prick [6] with eager speed,
  That seemed he was full bent to some mischiévous deed.

[1] *Leech's*, physician's.
[2] *Gride*, pierce.
[3] *For which Dan Phœbus self*, etc. *Dan*, a title of respect placed before personal nouns. *Phœbus Apollo* and his son *Æsculapius* were revered as the chief gods of healing.
[4] *Misfare*, unhappiness.
[5] *Misconceit*, misconception.
[6] *Prick*, ride, using spurs.

3 Which Scudamour perceiving forth issued
   To have rencount'red him in equal race[1];
   But, soon as th' other nigh approaching viewed
   The arms he bore, his spear he gan abase
   And void his course[2]; at which so sudden case
   He wond'red much: but th' other thus can[3] say:
   "Ah! gentle Scudamour, unto your grace
   I me submit, and you of pardon pray,
   That almost had against you trespassèd this day."

4 Whereto thus Scudamour: "Small harm it were
   For any knight upon a ventrous[4] knight
   Without displeasance[5] for to prove his spear.
   But read[6] you, sir, sith[7] ye my name have hight,[8]
   What is your own, that I mote you requite?"
   "Certes,"[9] said he, "ye mote as now excuse
   Me from discovering you my name aright[10]:
   For time yet serves that I the same refuse[11];
   But call ye me the salvage[12] knight, as others
        use."

5 "Then this, Sir Salvage Knight," quoth he, "aread;
   Or do you here within this forest wonne,[13]

[1] *To have rencountered him*, etc., *i.e.* that he might encounter him at equal speed.
[2] *His spear he gan abase*, etc., *i.e.* he lowered his spear and turned from his course.
[3] *Can say*, gan say, did say.
[4] *Ventrous*, adventurous.
[5] *Displeasance*, displeasure.
[6] *Read*, declare.
[7] *Sith*, since.
[8] *Hight*, called.
[9] *Certes*, truly.
[10] *From discovering you*, etc., *i.e.* from telling you my real name.
[11] *For time yet serves*, etc., *i.e.* at the present time I have a reason for refusing to make myself known.
[12] *Salvage*, wild, woodland.
[13] *Wonne*, dwell.

That seemeth well to answer to your weed,[1]
Or have ye it for some occasion done?
That rather seems, sith knowen arms ye shun."[2]
"This other day," said he, "a stranger knight
Shame and dishonour hath unto me done;
On whom I wait to wreak[3] that foul despite,
Whenever he this way shall pass by day or night."

6 "Shame be his meed," quoth he, "that meaneth shame[4]!
But what is he by whom ye shamèd were?"
"A stranger knight," said he, "unknown by name,
But known by fame, and by an heben[5] spear
With which he all that met him down did bear.
He, in an open tourney lately held,
Fro me the honour of that game did rear[6];
And having me, all weary erst,[7] down felled,
The fairest lady reft,[8] and ever since withheld."[9]

7 When Scudamour heard mention of that spear,
He wist[10] right well that it was Britomart,
The which from him his fairest love did bear.
Tho gan he swell in every inner part

---

[1] *Weed*, dress.
[2] *That rather seems*, etc., i.e. that seems to be the case since you shun the encounter with me whose arms you recognize.
[3] *Wreak*, revenge.
[4] *Shame be his meed*, etc. Upton says that "Honi soit qui mal y pense" was the motto of the knights of Maidenhead.
[5] *Heben*, yew.
[6] *Rear*, lift, take away (a peculiar use of the word).
[7] *Erst*, before.
[8] *Reft*, took away.
[9] *The fairest lady reft*, etc. Artegall does not know that "the false Florimell," the acknowledged "queen of beauty," left the tournament with Braggadochio — not with Britomart.
[10] *Wist*, knew.

For fell despite,¹ and gnaw his jealous heart,
That thus he sharply said : "Now by my head,
Yet is not this the first unknightly part,
Which that same knight, whom by his lance I read,²
Hath done to noble knights, that many makes him dread ³:

8 "For lately he my love hath fro me reft,
. . . .
In shame of knighthood and fidelity ;
The which ere long full dear he shall aby⁴ ;
And if to that avenge by you decreed
This hand may help or succour ought supply,
It shall not fail whenso ye shall it need."
So both to wreak their wraths on Britomart agreed.

9 Whiles thus they commúnèd, lo ! far away
A knight soft riding towards them they spied,
Attired in foreign arms and straunge array :
Whom when they nigh approached, they plain descried
To be the same for whom they did abide.
Said then Sir Scudamour, "Sir Salvage Knight,
Let me this crave, sith first I was defied,
That first I may that wrong to him requite :
And, if I hap to fail, you shall recure⁵ my right."

10 Which being yielded, he his threatful spear
Gan feuter,⁶ and against her fiercely ran.

¹ *Fell despite*, fierce vexation.
² *Read*, declare; here, recognize.
³ *That many*, etc., *i.e.* his actions make many knights dread him.
⁴ *Aby*, pay for.
⁵ *Recure*, recover, retrieve.
⁶ *Feuter*, put in rest.

Who soon as she him saw approaching near
With so fell rage, herself she lightly gan
To dight,[1] to welcome him well as she can ;
But entertained him in so rude a wise,
That to the ground she smote both horse and man ;
Whence neither greatly hasted to arise,
But on their common harms together did devise.

11 But Artegall, beholding his mischance,
New matter added to his former fire ;
And, eft[2] avent'ring[3] his steel-headed lance,
Against her rode, full of despiteous[4] ire,
That nought but spoil and vengeance did require[5] :
But to himself his felonous intent
Returning disappointed his desire,
Whiles unawares his saddle he forwent,[6]
And found himself on ground in great amazëment.

12 Lightly he started up out of that stound,[7]
And, snatching forth his direful deadly blade,
Did leap to her, as doth an eager hound
Thrust to an hind within some covert glade,
Whom without peril he cannot invade :
With such fell greediness he her assailed,
That though she mounted were, yet he her made
To give him ground, (so much his force prevailed,)
And shun his mighty strokes, gainst which no arms availed.

[1] *Gan to dight*, i.e. did prepare.
[2] *Eft*, again (in his turn).
[3] *Aventering*, pushing forward.
[4] *Despiteous*, cruel.
[5] *Require*, seek.
[6] *Forwent*, forsook.
[7] *Stound*, situation.

13 So, as they coursèd here and there, it chanced
    That, in her wheeling round, behind her crest
    So sorely he her strooke, that thence it glanced
    Adown her back, the which it fairly blessed [1]
    From foul mischance ; ne did it ever rest,
    Till on her horse's hinder parts it fell ;
    Where, biting deep, so deadly it impressed,
    That quite it chined [2] his back behind the sell,[3]
    And to alight on foot her algates [4] did compel :

14 Like as the lightning-brond from riven sky,
    Thrown out by angry Jove in his vengeánce,
    With dreadful force falls on some steeple high ;
    Which batt'ring, down it on the church doth glance,
    And tears it all with terrible mischance.
    Yet she no whit dismayed her steed forsook ;
    And, casting from her that enchanted lance,
    Unto her sword and shield her soon betook ;
    And therewithal at him right furiously she strook.

15 So furiously she strooke in her first heat,
    Whiles with long fight on foot he breathless was,
    That she him forcèd backward to retreat,
    And yield unto her weapon way to pass :
    Whose raging rigour neither steel nor brass
    Could stay, but to the tender flesh it went,
    And poured the purple blood forth on the grass ;

---

[1] *Blessed*, preserved. [3] *Sell*, saddle.
[2] *Chined*, split. [4] *Algates*, at all events.

That all his mail yrived,[1] and plates yrent,[2]
Showed all his body bare unto the cruel dent.[3]

16 At length, whenas he saw her hasty heat
Abate, and panting breath begin to fail,
He through long sufferance[4] growing now more great,
Rose in his strength, and gan her fresh assail,
Heaping huge strokes as thick as show'r of hail,
And lashing dreadfully at every part,
As if he thought her soul to disentrail.[5]
Ah! cruel hand, and thrice more cruel heart,
That workst such wreck on her to whom thou dearest art!

17 What iron courage[6] ever could endure
To work such outrage on so fair a creature!
And in his madness think with hands impure
To spoil so goodly workmanship of nature,
The Maker self resembling in her feature[7]!
Certes[8] some hellish fury or some fiend
This mischief framed, for their first love's defeature,[9]
To bathe their hands in blood of dearest friend,
Thereby to make their love's beginning their lives' end.

18 Thus long they traced[10] and traversed to and fro,
Sometimes pursuing, and sometimes pursued,

---

[1] *Yrived*, torn apart.
[2] *Yrent*, rent.
[3] *Dent*, dint, blow.
[4] *Sufferance*, endurance.
[5] *Disentrail, i.e.* dislodge.
[6] *Courage*, heart.
[7] *Feature*, general appearance.
[8] *Certes*, surely.
[9] *Defeature*, defeat.
[10] *Traced*, went.

Still as advantage they espied thereto:
But toward th' end Sir Arthegall renewed
His strength still more, but she still more decrewed.[1]
At last his luckless hand he heaved on high,
Having his forces all in one accrued,[2]
And therewith stroke at her so hideously,
That seemèd nought but death mote be her destiny.

19 The wicked stroke upon her helmet chanced,
And with the force, which in itself it bore,
Her vèntail[3] shard[4] away, and thence forth glanced
Adown in vain, ne harmed her any more.
With that, her angel's face, unseen afore,
Like to the ruddy morn appeared in sight,
Dewèd with silver drops through sweating sore;
But somewhat redder then beseemed aright,
Through toilsome heat and labour of her weary fight:

20 And round about the same her yellow hair,
Having through stirring loosed their wonted band,
Like to a golden border did appear,
Framèd in goldsmith's forge with cunning hand:
Yet goldsmith's cunning could not understand
To frame such subtile[5] wire, so shiny clear;
For it did glister like the golden sand,

---

[1] *Decrewed*, decreased.
[2] *Accrued*, collected.
[3] *Ventail*, beaver, the piece of armor that protected the lower part of the face.
[4] *Shard*, cut.
[5] *Subtile*, fine, delicate.

> The which Pactolus[1] with his waters sheer[2]
> Throws forth upon the rivage[3] round about him near.

21 And as his hand he up again did rear,
   Thinking to work on her his utmost wrack,[4]
   His pow'rless arm benumbed with secret fear
   From his revengeful purpose shronke aback,
   And cruel sword out of his fingers slack
   Fell down to ground, as if the steel had sense
   And felt some ruth,[5] or sense his hand did lack,
   Or both of them did think obedience
   To do to so divine a beauty's excellence.

22 And he himself, long gazing thereupon,
   At last fell humbly down upon his knee,
   And of his wonder made religion,[6]
   Weening[7] some heavenly goddess he did see,
   Or else unweeting[8] what it else might be;
   And pardon her besought his error frail,
   That had done outrage in so high degree:
   Whilst trembling horror did his sense assail,
   And made each member quake, and manly heart to quail.

---

[1] *Pactolus*, a river in Smyrna, Asia Minor, said to have golden sands.
[2] *Sheer*, clear, pure.
[3] *Rivage*, bank.
[4] *Wrack*, ruin.
[5] *Ruth*, pity
[6] *Religion*, pronounced as four syllables. *And of his wonder*, etc., *i.e.* he first wondered, and then adored.
[7] *Weening*, thinking.
[8] *Unweeting*, not knowing.

23 Natheless[1] she, full of wrath for that late stroke,
   All that long while upheld her wrathful hand,
   With fell[2] intent on him to bene ywroke[3];
   And, looking stern, still over him did stand,
   Threat'ning to strike unless he would withstand[4];
   And bade him rise, or surely he should die.
   But, die or live, for nought he would upstand;
   But her of pardon prayed more earnestly,
   Or wreak on him her will for so great injury.

24 Which whenas Scudamour, who now abrayed,[5]
   Beheld, whereas he stood not far aside,
   He was therewith right wondrously dismayed;
   And drawing nigh, whenas he plain descried
   That peerless pattern of Dame Nature's pride
   And heavenly image of perfection,[6]
   He blest himself as one sore terrified;
   And, turning fear to faint devotion,
   Did worship her as some celestial vision.

25 But Glaucè, seeing all that chancèd there,
   Well weeting how their error to assoil,[7]
   Full glad of so good end, to them drew near,
   And her salued[8] with seemly bel-accoyle,[9]
   Joyous to see her safe after long toil:
   Then her besought, as she to her was dear,

---

[1] *Natheless*, nevertheless.
[2] *Fell*, cruel.
[3] *Ywroke*, avenged.
[4] *Withstand*, resist.
[5] *Abrayed*, awoke.
[6] *Perfection*; last syllable pronounced as two syllables; the same is true of *devotion* and *vision*.
[7] *Assoil*, dispel.
[8] *Salued*, saluted.
[9] *Bel-accoyle* (*bel-accueil*), greeting.

To grant unto those warriors truce awhile ;
Which yielded, they their beavers up did rear,
And showed themselves to her such as indeed they
    were.

26 When Britomart with sharp aviseful[1] eye
Beheld the lovely face of Artegall
Temp'red with sternness and stout[2] majesty,
She gan eftsoones[3] it to her mind to call[4]
To be the same which, in her father's hall
Long since in that enchanted glass she saw :
Therewith her wrathful courage gan appall,[5]
And haughty spirits meekly to adaw,[6]
That her enhauncèd[7] hand she down can[8] soft
    withdraw.

27 Yet she it forced to have again upheld,
As feigning choler which was turned to cold :
But ever, when his visage she beheld,
Her hand fell down, and would no longer hold
The wrathful weapon gainst his count'nance bold :
But, when in vain to fight she oft assayed,
She armèd her tongue, and thought at him to scold :
Natheless her tongue not to her will obeyed,
But brought forth speeches mild when she would
    have missaid.[9]

28 But Scudamour, now woxen[10] inly glad
That all his jealous fear he false had found,

---

[1] *Aviseful*, observant.
[2] *Stout*, brave, dauntless.
[3] *Eftsoones*, immediately.
[4] *Call*, recall.
[5] *Gan appall*, began to weaken.
[6] *Adaw*, abate.
[7] *Enhaunced*, raised.
[8] *Can*, gan, i.e. did.
[9] *Missaid*, abused, berated.
[10] *Woxen*, grown.

And how that hag[1] his love abusèd had
With breach of faith and loyalty unsound,
The which long time his grievèd heart did wound,
He thus bespake : "Certes, Sir Artegall,
I joy to see you lout[2] so low on ground,
And now become to live a lady's thrall,
That whilom[3] in your mind wont to despise them
    all."

29 Soon as she heard the name of Artegall,
Her heart did leap, and all her heart-strings tremble,
For sudden joy and secret fear withal ;
And all her vital pow'rs, with motion nimble
To succour it, themselves gan there assemble ;
That by the swift recourse[4] of flushing blood
Right plain appeared, though she it would dissemble,
And feignèd still her former angry mood,
Thinking to hide the depth by troubling of the flood.

30 When Glaucè thus gan wisely all upknit :
" Ye gentle knights, whom fortune here hath brought
To be spectators of this úncouth fit,[5]
Which secret fate hath in this lady wrought
Against the course of kind,[6] ne marvel nought ;
Ne thenceforth fear the thing that hitherto
Hath troubled both your minds with idle thought,
Fearing lest she your loves away should woo ;

  .   .   .   .

---

[1] *That hag, i.e.* Atè, the goddess of discord.
[2] *Lout*, bow.
[3] *Whilom*, formerly.
[4] *Recourse*, frequent passage.
[5] *Uncouth fit*, strange fact or effect.
[6] *Kind*, nature.

31 "And you, Sir Artegall, the salvage knight,[1]
    Henceforth may not disdain that woman's hand
    Hath conquered you anew in second fight:
    For whilom they have conquered sea and land,
    And heaven itself, that nought may them withstand:
    Ne henceforth be rebellious unto love,
    That is the crown of knighthood and the band
    Of noble minds derivèd from above,
    Which, being knit with virtue, never will remove.

32 "And you, fair lady knight, my dearest dame,
    Relent the rigour of your wrathful will,
    Whose fire were better turned to other flame;
    And, wiping out remembrance of all ill,
    Grant him your grace; but so that he fulfil
    The penance which ye shall to him empart[2];
    For lover's heaven must pass by sorrow's hell."
    Thereat full inly blushèd Britomart;
    But Artegall, close-smiling,[3] joyed in secret heart.

33 Yet durst he not make love so suddenly,
    Ne think th' affection of her heart to draw
    From one to other so quite contrary:
    Besides her modest countenance he saw
    So goodly grave, and full of princely awe,
    That it his ranging fancy did refrain,
    And looser thoughts to lawful bounds withdraw:
    . . . .

---

[1] *Salvage knight*, wild knight, knight of the woods.
[2] *Empart*, make known.
[3] *Close-smiling*, secretly smiling.

34 But Scudamour, whose heart twixt doubtful fear
    And feeble hope hung all this while suspense,[1]
    Desiring of his Amoret to hear
    Some gladful news and sure intelligence,
    Her thus bespake : " But, sir, without offence,
    Mote I request you tidings of my love,
    My Amoret, sith you her freed fro thence
    Where she, captívèd long, great woes did prove[2] ;
    That where ye left I may her seek, as doth behove."

35 To whom thus Britomart : " Certes,[3] sir knight,
    What is of her become, or whither reft,[4]
    I cannot unto you aread[5] aright.
    For from that time I from enchanter's theft
    Her freed, in which ye her all hopeless left,
    I her preserved from peril and from fear,
    And evermore from villainy her kept :
    Ne ever was there wight to me more dear
    Then she, ne unto whom I more true love did bear :

36 " Till on a day, as through a desert wild
    We travellèd, both weary of the way,
    We did alight, and sate in shadow mild ;
    Where fearless I to sleep me down did lay :
    But, whenas I did out of sleep abray,[6]
    I found her not where I her left whilere,[7]
    But thought she wand'red was, or gone astray :
    I called her loud, I sought her far and near ;
    But nowhere could her find, nor tidings of her hear."

[1] *Suspense*, suspended.
[2] *Prove*, experience.
[3] *Certes*, truly.
[4] *Reft*, taken away by violence.
[5] *Aread*, declare.
[6] *Abray*, awake.
[7] *Whilere*, a little while before.

37 When Scudamour those heavy tidings heard,
   His heart was thrilled [1] with point of deadly fear,
   Ne in his face or blood or life appeared ;
   But senseless stood, like to a mazèd [2] steer
   That yet of mortal stroke the stound [3] doth bear :
   Till Glaucè thus : "Fair sir, be nought dismayed
   With needless dread, till certainty ye hear ;
   For yet she may be safe though somewhat strayed :
   It's best to hope the best, though of the worst afraid."

38 Nathless he hardly of her cheerful speech
   Did comfort take, or in his troubled sight
   Showed change of better cheer, so sore a breach
   That sudden news had made into his sprite,[4]
   Till Britomart him fairly thus behight [5] :
   "Great cause of sorrow certes,[6] sir, ye have ;
   But comfort take ; for, by this heaven's light,
   I vow you dead or living not to leave,
   Till I her find, and wreak on [7] him that her did reave." [8]

39 Therewith he rested, and well pleasèd was,
   So, peace being confirmed amongst them all,
   They took their steeds, and forward thence did pass
   Unto some resting-place, which mote befall,[9]

---

[1] *Thrilled*, pierced.
[2] *Mazed*, dazed.
[3] *Stound*, sudden pain or alarm.
[4] *So sore a breach*, etc., *i.e.* such a dreadful effect had been made upon his mind by the sudden news.
[5] *Behight*, promised.
[6] *Certes*, certainly.
[7] *Wreak on*, take vengeance on.
[8] *Reave*, carry off.
[9] *Which mote befall*, *i.e.* that they might happen upon.

All being guided by Sir Artegall :
Where goodly solace was unto them made,
And daily feasting both in bow'r and hall,
Until that they their wounds well healèd had,
And weary limbs recured [1] after late usage bad.

40 In all which time Sir Artegall made way
Unto the love of noble Britomart.
And with meek service and much suit did lay
Continual siege unto her gentle heart ;
Which, being whilom launcht [2] with lovely dart,[3]
More eath [4] was new impression to receive ;
However she her pained [5] with womanish art
To hide her wound, that none might it perceive :
Vain is the art that seeks itself for to deceive.

41 So well he wooed her, and so well he wrought her,[6]
With fair entreaty and sweet blandishment,
That at the length unto a bay [7] he brought her,
So as she to his speeches was content
To lend an ear, and softly to relent.
At last, through many vows which forth he poured
And many oaths, she yielded her consent
To be his love, and take him for her lord,
Till they with marriage meet might finish that accord.[8]

---

[1] *Recured*, restored.
[2] *Launcht*, pierced.
[3] *Lovely dart*, i.e. dart of love.
[4] *Eath*, easy.
[5] *She her pained*, i.e. she made an effort.
[6] *Wrought her*, i.e. worked upon her feelings.
[7] *Unto a bay*, i.e. to bay, to a position from which she could not escape.
[8] *Accord*, agreement.

42 Tho, when they had long time there taken rest,
   Sir Artegall, who all this while was bound
   Upon an hard adventure yet in quest,[1]
   Fit time for him thence to depart it found,
   To follow that which he did long propound[2];
   And unto her his congé[3] came to take:
   But her therewith full sore displeased he found,
   And loath to leave her late betrothèd make[4];
   Her dearest love full loath so shortly to forsake.

43 Yet he with strong persuasions her assuaged,[5]
   And won her will to suffer him depart;
   For which his faith with her he fast engaged,
   And thousand vows from bottom of his heart,
   That, all so soon as he by wit or art
   Could that achieve whereto he did aspire,
   He unto her would speedily revert[6]:
   No longer space thereto he did desire,
   But till the hornèd moon three courses did expire.[7]

44 With which she for the present was appeased,
   And yielded leave, however malcontent
   She inly were and in her mind displeased.
   So, early on the morrow next, he went
   Forth on his way to which he was ybent;
   Ne wight him to attend, or way to guide,
   As whilom was the custom ancient

---

[1] *Yet in quest*, i.e. upon which he was still bent.
[2] *Propound*, purpose.
[3] *Congé*, farewell.
[4] *Make*, mate.
[5] *Assuaged*, appeased.
[6] *Revert*, return.
[7] *Expire*, wear out.

Mongst knights when on adventures they did ride,
Save that she algates[1] him awhile accompanied.

45 And by the way she sundry purpose[2] found
Of this or that, the time for to delay,
And of the perils whereto he was bound,
The fear whereof seemed much her to affray:
But all she did was but to wear out day.[3]
Full oftentimes she leave of him did take;
And eft[4] again devised somewhat to say,
Which she forgot, whereby excuse to make:
So loath she was his company for to forsake.

46 At last, when all her speeches she had spent,
And new occasion failed her more to find,
She left him to his fortune's government,
And back returnèd with right heavy mind
To Scudamour, who she had left behind;
With whom she went to seek fair Amoret,
Her second care, though in another kind:
For virtue's only sake, which doth beget
True love and faithful friendship, she by her did set.[5]

47 Back to that desert forest they retired,
Where sorry Britomart had lost her late:
There they her sought, and everywhere inquired
Where they might tidings get of her estate;
Yet found they none.   But, by what hapless fate

---

[1] *Algates*, to be sure.
[2] *Purpose*, matter of discourse.
[3] *Day*, time.
[4] *Eft*, soon.
[5] *By her did set*, i.e. valued her.

Or hard misfortune she was thence conveyed,
And stol'n away from her belovèd mate,
Were long to tell; therefore I here will stay
Until another tide,[1] that I it finish may.

[1] *Tide*, time.

XIII.

Prince Arthur, having rescued Amoret, leaves her and goes to the assistance of Britomart and Scudamour.

The poet tells how Amoret was stolen by a monstrous creature, —
    . . . a wild and salvage man, —
    Yet was no man, but only like in shape, —
and how she was carried by him to his cave. After much suffering she managed to make her escape, and later fell in with Prince Arthur, the perfect knight. He cared for her most tenderly. As they were journeying together in the hope of meeting Scudamour, Amoret's husband, they saw in the distance a group of knights, among them, — Druon, Claribell, Blandamour, and Paridell.

1 BUT those two other, which beside them stood,
   Were Britomart and gentle Scudamour;
   Who all the while beheld their wrathful mood,
   And wond'red at their implacable stoure,[1]
   Whose like they never saw till that same hour:
   So dreadful strokes each did at other drive,
   And laid on load with all their might and pow'r,
   As if that every dint[2] the ghost[3] would rive[4]
   Out of their wretched corses,[5] and their lives deprive[6]:

2 As when Dan Æolus,[7] in great displeasure
   For loss of his dear love by Neptune hent,[8]

[1] *Stoure*, assault.
[2] *Dint*, blow.
[3] *Ghost*, spirit.
[4] *Rive*, rend, tear.
[5] *Corses*, bodies.
[6] *Deprive*, destroy.
[7] *Æolus*, the ruler of the winds.
[8] *Hent*, seized, taken away.

Sends forth the winds out of his hidden treasure
Upon the sea to wreak his full intent;
They, breaking forth with rude unruliment[1]
From all four parts of heaven, do rage full sore,
And toss the deeps, and tear the firmament,
And all the world confound with wide uproar;
As if instead thereof they chaos would restore.

3 Cause of their discord and so fell debate[2]
Was for the love of that same snowy maid,[3]
Whom they had lost in tournament of late;
And, seeking long to weet[4] which way she strayed,
Met here together; where, through lewd upbraid[5]
Of Atè and Duessa, they fell out;
And each one taking part in other's aid,
This cruel conflict raisèd thereabout,
Whose dangerous success depended yet in doubt[6]:

4 For sometimes Paridell and Blandamour
The better had, and bet the others back;
Eftsoones[7] the others did the field recoure,[8]
And on their foes did work full cruel wrack[9]:
Yet neither would their fiend-like fury slack,
But evermore their malice did augment;

---

[1] *Unruliment*, unruliness.

[2] *Fell debate*, fierce contest.

[3] *That same snowy maid, i.e.* the false Florimell, the lady that received the magic girdle. It will be remembered that she left the tournament with Braggadochio.

[4] *Weet*, know.

[5] *Lewd upbraid*, wicked contumely.

[6] *Whose dangerous success*, etc., *i.e.* the issue of this dangerous conflict was still doubtful.

[7] *Eftsoones*, immediately.

[8] *Recoure*, recover.

[9] *Wrack*, ruin.

Till that unneath [1] they forcèd were, for lack
Of breath, their raging rigour to relent,
And rest themselves for to recover spirits spent.

5 There gan they change their sides, and new parts take;
For Paridell did take to Druon's side,
For old despite which now forth newly brake
Gainst Blandamour, whom always he enviéd [2];
And Blandamour to Claribell relide [3]:
So all afresh gan former fight renew.
As when two barks, this carried with the tide,
That with the wind, contráry courses sew,[4]
If wind and tide do change, their courses change anew.

6 Thenceforth they much more furiously gan fare,[5]
As if but then the battle had begun;
Ne helmets bright ne hauberks strong did spare,
That through the clifts [6] the vermeil [7] blood out-spun,
And all adown their riven [8] sides did run.
Such mortal [9] malice wonder was to see
In friends professed, and so great outrage done:
But sooth is said,[10] and tried in each degree,[11]
Faint friends when they fall out most cruel foemen be.

---

[1] *Unneath*, with difficulty.
[2] *Envied*, i.e. had a grudge against.
[3] *Relide*, joined himself.
[4] *Sew*, pursue.
[5] *Gan fare*, did proceed.
[6] *Clifts*, openings.
[7] *Vermeil*, vermillion.
[8] *Riven*, torn, wounded.
[9] *Mortal*, deadly.
[10] *Sooth is said*, i.e. it is truly said.
[11] *Tried in each degree*, experienced in every station in life.

7 Thus they long while continuèd in fight;
   Till Scudamour and that same Briton maid
   By fortune in that place did chance to light:
   Whom soon as they with wrathful eye bewrayed,[1]
   They gan remember of the foul upbraid,[2]
   The which that Britoness had to them done
   In that late tourney for the snowy maid;
   Where she had them both shamefully fordonne,[3]
   And eke[4] the famous prize of beauty from them won.

8 Eftsoones all burning with a fresh desire
   Of fell[5] revenge, in their malicious mood
   They from themselves gan turn their furious ire,
   And cruel blades yet steaming with hot blood
   Against those two let drive, as[6] they were wood[7]:
   Who wond'ring much at that so sudden fit,[8]
   Yet nought dismayed, them stoutly well withstood;
   Ne yielded foot, ne once aback did flit,
   But, being doubly smitten, likewise doubly smit.

9 The warlike dame was on her part assayed
   Of Claribell and Blandamour attone[9];
   And Paridell and Druon fiercely laid
   At Scudamour, both his professèd fone[10]:
   Four chargèd two, and two surchargèd[11] one;

---

[1] *Bewrayed*, discovered.
[2] *Upbraid*, injury.
[3] *Fordonne*, undone, means here, utterly defeated.
[4] *Eke*, also.
[5] *Fell*, fierce.
[6] *As*, as though.
[7] *Wood*, mad.
[8] *Fit*, attack.
[9] *Attone*, at once.
[10] *Fone*, foes.
[11] *Surcharged*, attacked with superior force.

Yet did those two themselves so bravely beare,
That the other little gainèd by the loan,
But with their own repayèd duly weare,
And usury withal : such gain was gotten deare.

10 Full oftentimes did Britomart assay
To speak to them, and some emparlance[1] move ;
But they for nought their cruel hands would stay,
Ne lend an ear to ought that might behove[2] :
As when an eager mastiff once doth prove[3]
The taste of blood of some engorèd beast,
No words may rate,[4] nor rigour him remove
From greedy hold of that his bloody feast,—
So little did they hearken to her sweet beheast.[5]

11 Whom when the Briton prince[6] afar beheld
With odds of so unequal match oppressed,
His mighty heart with indignation swelled,
And inward grudge filled his heroic breast :
Eftsoones himself he to their aid addressed,
And, thrusting fierce into the thickest preace,[7]
Divided them, however loath to rest ;
And would them fain from battle to surceasse,[8]
With gentle words persuading them to friendly peace :

12 But they so far from peace or patience were,
That all at once at him gan fiercely fly,

[1] *Emparlance*, parley.
[2] *That might behove*, that was fitting.
[3] *Prove*, experience.
[4] *Rate*, check by chiding.
[5] *Beheast*, behest.
[6] *Briton prince*, Prince Arthur.
[7] *Preace*, press.
[8] *Surceasse*, desist.

And lay on load, as they him down would bear:
Like to a storm which hovers under sky,
Long here and there and round about doth sty,[1]
At length breaks down in rain, and hail, and sleet,
First from one coast,[2] till nought thereof be dry;
And then another, till that likewise fleet[3];
And so from side to side till all the world it weet.[4]

13 But now their forces greatly were decayed,[5]
The prince yet being fresh untouched afore;
Who them with speeches mild gan first dissuade
From such foul outrage, and them long forbore[6]:
Till, seeing them through suff'rance[7] heartnèd[8] more,
Himself he bent their furies to abate,
And laid at[9] them so sharply and so sore,
That shortly them compellèd to retrate,
And being brought in danger to relent too late.

14 But now his courage being throughly[10] fired,
He meant to make them know their folly's prise,[11]
Had not those two[12] him instantly[13] desired
T' assuage his wrath, and pardon their mesprise[14]:
At whose request he gan himself advise
To stay his hand, and of a truce to treat

---

[1] *Sty*, rise.
[2] *Coast*, side.
[3] *Fleet*, float.
[4] *Weet*, wet.
[5] *Decayed*, weakened.
[6] *Forbore*, kept away from.
[7] *Sufferance, i.e.* his patience.
[8] *Heartened*, encouraged.
[9] *Laid at*, struck at.
[10] *Throughly*, thoroughly.
[11] *Prise*, price.
[12] *Those two, i.e.* Britomart and Scudamour.
[13] *Instantly*, urgently.
[14] *Mesprise*, contempt.

In milder terms, as list them¹ to devise;
Mongst which the cause of their so cruel heat
He did them ask; who all that passèd gan repeat;

15. And told at large how that same errant knight,
To weet,² fair Britomart, them late had foiled
In open tourney, and by wrongful fight
Both of their public praise had them despoiled,
And also of their private loves beguiled;
Of two full hard to read³ the harder theft.
But she that wrongful challenge⁴ soon assoiled,⁵
And shewed that she had not that lady⁶ reft,⁷
(As they supposed,) but her had to her liking left.

16 To whom the prince thus goodly well replied:
"Certes,⁸ Sir knights, ye seemen⁹ much to blame
To rip up wrong that battle once hath tried;
Wherein the honor both of arms ye shame,
And eke the love of ladies foul defame;
To whom the world this franchise¹⁰ ever yielded,
That of their loves' choice they might freedom claim,
And in that right should by all knights be shielded:
Gainst which, me seems, this war ye wrongfully have wielded." ¹¹

¹ *List them*, they pleased.
² *To weet*, to wit.
³ *Read*, declare.
⁴ *Challenge*, charge, accusation.
⁵ *Assoiled*, cleared herself of.
⁶ *That lady;* that is, the false Florimell.
⁷ *Reft*, taken away.
⁸ *Certes*, certainly.
⁹ *Seemen*, seem.
¹⁰ *Franchise*, liberty.
¹¹ *Wielded*, waged.

17 "And yet," quoth she, "a greater wrong remains:
For I thereby my former love have lost;
Whom seeking ever since with endless pains
Hath me much sorrow and much travel[1] cost:
Aye me, to see that gentle maid so tossed!"
But Scudamour then, sighing deep, thus said:
"Certes her loss ought me to sorrow[2] most,
Whose right she is, wherever she be strayed,
Through many perils won, and many fortunes waide[3]:

18 "For from the first that I her love professed,
Unto this hour, this present luckless hour,
I never joyèd[4] happiness nor rest;
But thus turmoiled[5] from one to other stowre[6]
I waste my life, and do my days devour
In wretched anguish and incessant woe,
Passing the measure of my feeble power;
That, living thus a wretch and loving so,
I neither can my love ne yet my life forego."

* * *

19 Then good Sir Claribell him thus bespake:
"Now were it not, Sir Scudamour, to you
Dislikeful[7] pain so sad a task to take,
Mote we[8] entreat you, sith this gentle crew[9]
Is now so well accorded all anew,

---

[1] *Travel*, labor.
[2] *Sorrow*, grieve.
[3] *Waide*, weighed; esteemed.
[4] *Joyed*, enjoyed.
[5] *Turmoiled*, disquieted.
[6] *Stowre*, disturbance.
[7] *Dislikeful*, disagreeable.
[8] *Mote we*, i.e. we should like to.
[9] *Gentle crew*, noble company.

That, as we ride together on our way,
Ye will recount to us in order due
All that adventure which ye did assay
For that fair lady's love: past perils well appay." [1]

20 So gan the rest him likewise to require [2]:
But Britomart did him impórtune hard
To take on him that pain; whose great desire
He glad to satisfy, himself prepar'd
To tell through what misfortune he had far'd
In that achievement, as to him befell,
And all those dangers unto them declar'd;
Which sith they cannot in this canto well
Comprisèd be, I will them in another tell.

Where Amoret was all this while it is not easy to guess. Doubtles Prince Arthur left her in some place of safety while he joined in the struggle just described. In the following canto — canto X, book IV — Scudamour tells how he gained the hand of his lovely wife. This is the last that we hear of Amoret. Had Spenser finished the "Faery Queene" we may believe that he would have described the happy reunion of this sorely tried pair.

[1] *Appay*, please, satisfy. [2] *Require*, request.

XIV.

The poet goes back in his narrative to tell of the education of Artegall, the knight of Justice. Artegall starts out to deliver Irena from the giant Grantorto. After a number of adventures, the young knight frees Sir Terpin from the Amazons and has an encounter with Radigund, the Amazonian queen.

1 Though virtue then were held in highest price,
　In those old times of which I do intreat,[1]
　Yet then likewise the wicked seed of vice
　Began to spring; which shortly grew full great,
　And with their boughs the gentle plants did beat:
　But evermore some of the virtuous race
　Rose up, inspirèd with heroic heat,
　That cropped the branches of the sient[2] base,
　And with strong hand their fruitful rankness did deface.

2 Such first was Bacchus, that with furious might
　All th' east, before untamed, did overrun,
　And wrong repressèd, and established right
　Which lawless men had formerly fordone[3]:
　There Justice first her princely rule begun.
　Next Hercules his like ensample showed,
　Who all the west with equal conquest won,
　And monstrous tyrants with his club subdued;
　The club of justice dread, with kingly pow'r endued.

[1] *Intreat*, treat.   [2] *Sient*, scion.
[3] *Fordone*, destroyed.

3 And such was he of whom I have to tell,
   The champion of true justice, Artegall[1]:
   Whom (as ye lately mote remember well)
   An hard adventure, which did then befall
   Into redoubted peril forth did call;
   That was, to succour a distressèd dame
   Whom a strong tyrant did unjustly thrall,[2]
   And from the heritage which she did claim
   Did with strong hand withhold; Grantorto[3] was his
      name.

4 Wherefore the lady, which Irena[4] hight,[5]
   Did to the Faery Queen her way address,
   To whom complaining her afflicted plight,
   She her besought of gracious redress:
   That sovereign queen, that mighty emperesse,
   Whose glory is to aid all suppliants pore,[6]
   And of weak princes to be patroness,
   Chose Artegall to right her to restore;
   For that to her he seemed best skilled in righteous
      lore.

5 For Artegall in justice was upbrought
   Even from the cradle of his infancy,
   And all the depth of rightful doom[7] was taught

---

[1] *Artegall.* Spenser was secretary to Arthur, Lord Grey of Wilton, Lord Lieutenant of Ireland. The poet was a warm friend and admirer of Lord Grey's, and expressed his admiration by portraying his character in the knight of Justice, Artegall.

[2] *Thrall*, imprison.
[3] *Grantorto, i.e.* great wrong.
[4] *Irena.* Irena, or Irene, is an anagram of *Ierne*, the ancient name of Ireland. Church.
[5] *Hight*, was called.
[6] *Pore*, poor.
[7] *Doom*, judgment.

By fair Astræa,[1] with great industry,
Whilst here on earth she livèd mortally:
For, till the world from his perfection fell
Into all filth and foul iniquity,
Astræa here mongst earthly men did dwell,
And in the rules of justice them instructed well.

6 Whiles through the world she walkèd in this sort,
Upon a day she found this gentle child
Amongst his peers playing his childish sport;
Whom seeing fit, and with no crime defiled,
She did allure with gifts and speeches mild
To wend with her: so thence him far she brought
Into a cave from company exiled,
In which she nursled him, till years he raught[2];
And all the discipline of justice there him taught.

7 There she him taught to weigh both right and wrong
In equal balance with due recompense,
And equity to measure out along
According to the line of conscience,
Whenso it needs with rigor to dispense:
Of all the which, for want there of mankind,
She causèd him to make experiencè
Upon wild beasts which she in woods did find
With wrongful pow'r oppressing others of their kind.

8 Thus she him trainèd, and thus she him taught
In all the skill of deeming[3] wrong and right,

---

[1] *Astræa*, the goddess of Justice who during the golden age lived on the earth.

[2] *Raught*, reached.

[3] *Deeming*, judging.

Until the ripeness of man's years he raught;
That even wild beasts did fear his awful sight,
And men admired [1] his over-ruling might;
Ne any lived on ground that durst withstand
His dreadful hest,[2] much less him match in fight,
Or bide the horror of his wreakful [3] hand,
Whenso he list in wrath lift up his steely brand:

9 Which steely brand, to make him dreaded more,
She gave unto him, gotten by her sleight [4]
And earnest search, where it was kept in store
In Jove's eternal house, unwist of wight,[5]
Since he himself it used in that great fight
Against the Titans,[6] that whilom rebelled
Gainst highest heaven; Chrysaor [7] it was hight;
Chrysaor, that all other swords excelled,
Well proved in that same day when Jove those giants quelled:

10 For of most perfect metal it was made,
Temp'red with adamant [8] amongst the same,
And garnished all with gold upon the blade
In goodly wise, whereof it took his [9] name,
And was of no less virtue than of fame:

[1] *Admired*, wondered at.
[2] *Hest*, command.
[3] *Wreakful*, avengeful.
[4] *Sleight*, art, skill.
[5] *Unwist of wight*, unbeknown to any one.
[6] *That great fight*, etc. The Titans, the old gods, rebelled against Jupiter after he had wrested the power from his father, Saturn.
[7] *Chrysaor*, i.e. golden sword.
[8] *Adamant*, a stone supposed to be of impenetrable hardness. The name is not used in modern mineralogy.
[9] *His*, commonly used for its in Spenser's time.

For there no substance was so firm and hard,
But it would pierce or cleave whereso it came;
Ne any armour could his dint out-ward[1];
But wheresoever it did light, it throughly shard.[2]

11 Now when the world with sin gan to abound,
Astræa loathing lenger here to space[3]
Mongst wicked men, in whom no truth she found,
Returned to heaven, whence she derived her race[4];
Where she hath now an everlasting place
Mongst those twelve signs which nightly we do see
The heaven's bright-shining baldric[5] to enchase[6];
And is the Virgin, sixt in her degree,[7]
And next herself her righteous balance[8] hanging be.

12 But when she parted hence she left her groom,[9]
An iron man, which did on her attend
Always, to execute her steadfast doom,
And willèd him with Artegall to wend,
And do whatever thing he did intend:
His name was Talus,[10] made of iron mould,
Immoveable, resistless, without end;

[1] *Could his dint out-ward, i.e.* could ward off its blow.
[2] *Throughly shard, i.e.* cut through entirely.
[3] *Space*, walk.
[4] *Whence she derived her race, i.e.* where she originated.
[5] *Baldric*, belt worn over one shoulder.
[6] *Enchase*, ornament.
[7] *The Virgin, sixt in her degree.* The Virgin signifies the constellation Virgo. August, in which the sun enters the constellation Virgo, was the sixth month in Spenser's time, because from the fourteenth century to the middle of the eighteenth, the year began on the 25th of March.
[8] *Balance;* here plural.
[9] *Groom*, servant.
[10] *Talus* represents power.

Who in his hand an iron flail did hold,
With which he threshed out falsehood and did truth
   unfold.

13 He now went with him in this new inquest,[1]
Him for to aid, if aid he chanced to need,
Against that cruel tyrant, which oppressed
The fair Irena with his foul misdeed,
And kept the crown in which she should succeed:

  .   .   .   .

While passing on his way, the knight met with several adventures in which he gave proof of his bravery and of his good judgment as well. He then —

Departed on his way, as did befall.
To follow his old quest, the which him forth did call.

14 So as he travellèd upon the way,
He chanced to come, where happily[2] he spied
A rout of many people far away;
To whom his course he hastily applied,[3]
To weet[4] the cause of their assemblance wide:
To whom when he approachèd near in sight,
(An uncouth[5] sight,) he plainly then descried
To be a troop of women, warlike dight,[6]
With weapons in their hands, as ready for a fight:

15 And in the midst of them he saw a knight,
With both his hands behind him pinnoed[7] hard,

---

[1] *In this new inquest*, on the new quest.
[2] *Happily*, by chance.
[3] *Applied*, directed.
[4] *Weet*, know.
[5] *Uncouth*, strange.
[6] *Warlike dight*, arrayed in a warlike manner.
[7] *Pinnoed*, pinioned.

And round about his neck an halter tight,
And ready for the gallow tree prepard[1]:
His face was covered, and his head was bar'd,
That who he was uneath[2] was to descry;
And with full heavy heart with them he far'd,[3]
Grieved to the soul, and groaning inwardly,
That he of women's hands so base a death should die.

16 But they, like tyrants merciless, the more
Rejoicèd at his miserable case,
And him revilèd and reproachèd sore
With bitter taunts and terms of vile disgrace.
Now when as Artegall, arrived in place,
Did ask what cause brought that man to decay,[4]
They round about him gan to swarm apace,
Meaning on him their cruel hands to lay,
And to have wrought unwares some villainous assay.[5]

17 But he was soon aware of their ill mind,
And, drawing back, deceivèd their intent:
Yet, though himself did shame on womankind
His mighty hand to shend,[6] he Talus sent
To wreck[7] on them their folly's hardiment[8]:
Who with few souses[9] of his iron flail
Dispersèd all their troop incontinent,[10]
And sent them home to tell a piteous tale
Of their vain prowess turnèd to their proper bale.[11]

---

[1] *Prepard*, prepared.
[2] *Uneath*, not easy.
[3] *Fared*, went.
[4] *Decay*, destruction.
[5] *Assay*, assault.
[6] *Shend*, disgrace.
[7] *Wreck*, wreak, revenge.
[8] *Hardiment*, boldness.
[9] *Souses*, blows.
[10] *Incontinent*, instantly.
[11] *Their proper bale*, their own sorrow.

18 But that same wretched man, ordained to die,
   They left behind them, glad to be so quit:
   Him Talus took out of perplexity,
   And horror of foul death for knight unfit,
   Who more then loss of life ydreaded it;
   And, him restoring unto living light,
   So brought unto his lord, where he did sit
   Beholding all that womanish weak fight;
   Whom soon as he beheld he knew, and thus behight[1]:

19 "Sir Terpin, hapless man, what make you here[2]?
   Or have you lost yourself and your discretion,
   That ever in this wretched case ye were[3]?
   Or have ye yielded you to proud oppression
   Of women's pow'r, that boast of men's subjection?
   Or else what other deadly dismal day
   Is fall'n on you by heaven's hard direction,
   That ye were run so fondly[4] far astray,
   As for to lead yourself unto your own decay?"

20 Much was the man confounded in his mind,
   Partly with shame, and partly with dismay,
   That all astonished he himself did find,
   And little had for his excuse to say,
   But only thus: "Most hapless well ye may
   Me justly term, that to this shame am brought,
   And made the scorn of knighthood this same day:
   But who can scape what his own fate hath wrought?
   The work of heaven's will surpasseth human thought."

---

[1] *Behight*, addressed.
[2] *What make you here, i.e.* what are you doing here.
[3] *That ever in this wretched case ye were, i.e.* that you should have got into this wretched plight.
[4] *Fondly*, foolishly.

21 "Right true: but faulty men use oftentimes
   To áttribute their folly unto fate,
   And lay on heaven the guilt of their own crimes.
   But tell, Sir Terpin, ne let you amate
   Your misery,[1] how fell ye in this state?"
   "Then sith ye needs," quoth he, "will know my shame,
   And all the ill which chanced to me of late,
   I shortly will to you rehearse the same,
   In hope you will not turn misfortune to my blame.

22 "Being desirous (as all knights are wont)
   Through hard adventures deeds of arms to try,
   And after fame and honour for to hunt,
   I heard report that far abroad did fly,
   That a proud amazon did late defy
   All the brave knights that hold of Maidenhead,[2]
   And unto them wrought all the villainy
   That she could forge in her malicious head,
   Which some hath put to shame, and many done be dead.[3]

23 "The cause, they say, of this her cruel hate,
   Is for the sake of Bellodant the bold,
   To whom she bore most fervent love of late,
   And wooèd him by all the ways she could:
   But, when she saw at last that he ne would
   For ought or nought be won unto her will,

---

[1] *Ne let you amate your misery,* i.e. nor let your misery confound you, overwhelm you.

[2] *That hold of Maidenhead, i.e.* that acknowledge allegiance to the maiden queen, Gloriana.

[3] *Done be dead, i.e.* caused to be put to death.

She turned her love to hatred manifold,
And for his sake vowed to do all the ill
Which she could do to knights; which now she
    doth fulfil.

24 "For all those knights, the which by force or guile
She doth subdue, she foully doth entreat[1]:
First, she doth them of warlike arms despoil,
And clothe in women weeds[2]; and then with threat
Doth them compel to work, to earn their meat,[3]
To spin, to card, to sew, to wash, to wring;
Ne doth she give them other thing to eat
But bread and water, or like feeble thing;
Them to disable from revenge adventuring.[4]

25 "But if through stout disdain of manly mind
Any her proud observance[5] will withstand,
Upon that gibbet, which is there behind,
She causeth them be hanged up out of hand[6];
In which condition I right now did stand:
For, being overcome by her in fight,
And put to that base service of her band,
I rather chose to die in live's despite,[7]
Then lead that shameful life, unworthy of a knight."

26 "How hight that amazon," said Artegall,
"And where and how far hence does she abide?"
"Her name," quoth he, "they Radigund do call,
A princess of great power and greater pride,

---

[1] *Entreat*, treat.
[2] *Weeds*, garments.
[3] *Meat*, food.
[4] *Adventuring*, attempting.
[5] *Observance*, order.
[6] *Out of hand*, forthwith.
[7] *In live's despite*, i.e. despising life.

And queen of amazons, in arms well tried
And sundry battles, which she hath achieved
With great success, that her hath glorified,
And made her famous, more then is believed ;
Ne would I it have weened[1] had I not late it prieved.[2]"

27 "Now, sure," said he, "and by the faith that I
To Maidenhead[3] and noble knighthood owe,
I will not rest till I her might do try,
And venge[4] the shame that she to knights doth show.
Therefore, Sir Terpin, from you lightly throw
This squalid weed,[5] the pattern of despair,
And wend with me, that ye may see and know
How fortune will your ruined name repair
And knights of Maidenhead, whose praise she would impair."

28 With that, like one that hopeless was repryved[6]
From deathës door at which he lately lay,
Those iron fetters with which he was gyved,[7]
The badges of reproach, he threw away,
And nimbly did him dight[8] to guide the way
Unto the dwelling of that amazone :
Which was from thence not past a mile or tway,[9]
A goodly city and a mighty one,
The which, of her own name, she callèd Radegone.

---

[1] *Weened*, believed.
[2] *Prieved*, proved.
[3] *Maidenhead*, maidenhood ; *i.e.* Gloriana.
[4] *Venge*, revenge.
[5] *Weed*, garment.
[6] *Repryved*, reprieved.
[7] *Gyved*, fettered.
[8] *Dight*, make ready.
[9] *Tway*, two.

29 Where they arriving by the watchman were
　　Descrièd straight ; who all the city warned
　　How that three warlike persons did appear,
　　Of which the one him seemed a knight all armed,
　　And th' other two well likely to have harmed.
　　Eftsoones [1] the people all to harness ran,
　　And like a sort [2] of bees in clusters swarmed :
　　Ere long their queen herself, half like a man,
　　Came forth into the rout, and them t' array [3] began.

30 And now the knights, being arrivèd near,
　　Did beat upon the gates to enter in ;
　　And at the porter, scorning them so few,
　　Threw many threats, if they the town did win,
　　To tear his flesh in pieces for his sin :
　　Which when as Radigund there coming heard,
　　Her heart for rage did grate,[4] and teeth did grin [5]:
　　She bade that straight the gate should be unbarred,
　　And to them way to make with weapons well prepard.

31 Soon as the gates were open to them set,
　　They pressèd forward, entrance to have made :
　　But in the middle way they were ymet
　　With a sharp shower of arrows, which them stayed
　　And better bade advise,[6] ere they assayed
　　Unknowën peril of bold women's pride.
　　Then all that rout upon them rudely laid,

---

[1] *Eftsoones*, immediately.
[2] *Sort*, company, swarm.
[3] *T'array*, to draw up, ready for battle.
[4] *Did grate*, became irritated, enraged.
[5] *Teeth did grin*, i.e. she showed her teeth as if grinning with rage.
[6] *Advise*, consider.

And heapèd strokes so fast on every side,
And arrows hailed so thick, that they could not
   abide.

32 But Radigund herself, when she espied
Sir Terpin, from her direful doom acquit,
So cruel dole amongst her maids divide,[1]
T' avenge that shame they did on him commit,
All suddenly enflamed with furious fit,
Like a fell lioness at him she flew,
And on his head-piece him so fiercely smit,
That to the ground him quite she overthrew,
Dismayed so with the stroke that he no colours
   knew.[2]

33 Soon as she saw him on the ground to grovel,
She lightly to him leapt ; and, in his neck
Her proud foot setting, at his head did level,
Weening at once her wrath on him to wreak,
And his contempt, that did her judgment break :
As when a bear hath seized[3] her cruel claws
Upon the carcass of some beast too weak,
Proudly stands over, and awhile doth pause
To hear the piteous beast pleading her plaintiffe
   cause.

34 Whom when as Artegall in that distress
By chance beheld, he left the bloody slaughter
In which he swam, and ran to his redress :

---

[1] *So cruel dole amongst her maids divide*, *i.e.* bringing such suffering upon her maids.

[2] *He no colours knew*, *i.e* everything looked dark to him.

[3] *Seized*, fastened.

There her assailing fiercely fresh, he raught[1] her
Such an huge stroke, that it of sense distraught[2]
    her;
And, had she not it warded warily,
It had deprived her mother of a daughter:
Nathless for all the pow'r she did apply
It made her stagger oft, and stare with ghastly eye.

35 Like to an eagle, in his kingly pride
Soaring through his wide empire of the air,
To weather[3] his broad sails, by chance hath spied
A goshawk, which hath seizèd for her share
Upon some fowl, that should her feast prepare;
With dreadful force he flies at her bylive,[4]
That with his souse,[5] which none enduren dare,
Her from the quarry[6] he away doth drive,
And from her griping pounce the greedy prey doth
    rive.[7]

36 But, soon as she her sense recovered had,
She fiercely towards him herself gan dight,[8]
Through vengeful wrath and 'sdainful pride half
    mad;
For never had she suff'red such despite:
But, ere she could join hand with him to fight,
Her warlike maids about her flocked so fast,
That they disparted them, maugre[9] their might,

---

[1] *Raught*, dealt.
[2] *Distraught*, deprived.
[3] *Weather*, air.
[4] *Bylive*, quickly.
[5] *Souse*, sudden swoop.
[6] *Quarry*, prey.
[7] *Rive*, tear away.
[8] *Gan dight*, began to prepare.
[9] *Maugre*, in spite of.

And with their troops did far asunder cast:
But mongst the rest the fight did until evening last.

37 And every while that mighty iron man
With his strange weapon, never wont[1] in war,
Them sorely vexed, and coursed, and overran,
And broke their bows, and did their shooting mar,
That none of all the many once did darre
Him to assault, nor once approach him nigh;
But like a sort[2] of sheep dispersèd far,
For dread of their devouring enemy,
Through all the fields and valleys did before him fly.

38 But whenas day's fair shiny beam, yclouded
With fearful shadows of deformèd night,
Warned man and beast in quiet rest be shrouded,
Bold Radigund, with sound of trump on hight,[3]
Caused all her people to surcease[4] from fight;
And, gathering them unto her city's gate,
Made them all enter in before her sight;
And all the wounded, and the weak in state,
To be conveyèd in, ere she would once retrate.

39 When thus the field was voided[5] all away,
And all things quieted, the elfin knight,[6]
Weary of toil and travel of that day,
Caused his pavilion to be richly pight[7]

---

[1] *Wont*, used.
[2] *Sort*, company, flock.
[3] *On hight*, aloud.
[4] *Surcease*, cease entirely.
[5] *Voided*, cleared.
[6] *Elfin knight*, i.e. faery knight, because he serves the Faery Queen.
[7] *Pight*, pitched.

Before the city gate, in open sight;
Where he himself did rest in safëty,
Together with Sir Terpin, all that night:
But Talus used, in times of jeopardy,
To keep a nightly watch for dread of treachery.

40 But Radigund, full of heart-gnawing grief
For the rebuke which she sustained that day,
Could take no rest, ne would receive relief;
But tossèd in her troublous mind what way
She mote revenge that blot which on her lay.
There she resolved herself in single fight
To try her fortune, and his force assay,
Rather then see her people spoilèd quite,
As she had seen that day, a disaventerous[1] sight.

41 She callèd forth to her a trusty maid,
Whom she thought fittest for that business,
(Her name was Clarin,) and thus to her said:
"Go, damsel, quickly, do thyself address[2]
To do the message which I shall express.
Go thou unto that stranger faery knight,
Who yesterday drove us to such distress;
Tell that tomorrow I with him will fight,
And try in equal field whether[3] hath greater might.

42 "But these conditions do to him propound;
That, if I vanquish him, he shall obey
My law, and ever to my lore[4] be bound;
And so will I, if me he vanquish may,

---

[1] *Disaventerous*, unhappy.
[2] *Address*, make ready.
[3] *Whether*, which of the two.
[4] *Lore*, command.

> Whatever he shall like to do or say:
> Go straight, and take with thee to witness it
> Six of thy fellows of the best array,
> And bear with you both wine and junkets[1] fit,
> And bid him eat: henceforth he oft shall hungry sit."

43 The damsel straight[2] obeyed: and, putting all
In readiness, forth to the town-gate went;
Where, sounding loud a trumpet from the wall,
Unto those warlike knights she warning sent.
Then Talus, forth issùing from the tent,
Unto the wall his way did fearless take,
To weeten[3] what that trumpet's sounding meant:
Where that same damsel loudly him bespake,
And showed that with his lord she would emparlance[4] make.

44 So he them straight conducted to his lord;
Who, as he could, them goodly well did greet,
Till they had told their message word by word:
Which he accepting well, as he could weet,[5]
Them fairly entertained with curt'sies meet,
And gave them gifts and things of dear delight.
So back again they homeward turned their feet;
But Artegall himself to rest did dight,[6]
That he mote fresher be against the next day's fight.

[1] *Junkets*, sweetmeats.
[2] *Straight*, straightway.
[3] *To weeten*, to learn.
[4] *Emparlance*, parley.
[5] *As he could weet*, as he knew how.
[6] *Dight*, prepare.

XV.

Artegall meets Radigund in single combat and yields himself her vassal. His degradation.

1 So soon as day forth dawning from the east
  Night's humid curtain from the heavens withdrew,
  And early calling forth both man and beast,
  Commanded them their daily works renew;
  These noble warriors, mindful to pursue
  The last day's purpose of their vowèd fight,
  Themselves thereto prepared in order due;
  The knight, as best was seeming for a knight,
  And th' amazon, as best it liked herself to dight[1]:

2 All in a camis[2] light of purple silk
  Woven upon with silver, subtly wrought,
  And quilted upon satin white as milk;
  Trailèd with ribbons diversely distraught,[3]
  Like as the workman had their courses taught;
  Which was short tuckèd for light motion
  Up to her ham[4]; but, when she list,[5] it raught[6]
  Down to her lowest heel, and thereupon
  She wore for her defence a mailed habergeon.[7]

---

[1] *As best it liked herself to dight,* i.e. as she liked best to array herself.
[2] *Camis,* a loose robe.
[3] *Trailed with ribbons diversely distraught,* i.e. with ribbons running over it in different directions.
[4] *Ham,* thigh.
[5] *List,* pleased.
[6] *Raught,* reached.
[7] *Habergeon,* sleeveless coat of mail.

3 And on her legs she painted buskins[1] wore,
  Basted with bands of gold[2] on every side,
  And mails[3] between, and lacèd close afore;
  Upon her thigh her scimitar was tied
  With an embroidered belt of mickle pride[4];
  And on her shoulder hung her shield, bedecked
  Upon the boss[5] with stones that shinèd wide,
  As the fair moon in her most full aspect;
  That to the moon it mote be like in each respect.

4 So forth she came out of the city-gate
  With stately port and proud magnificence,
  Guarded with many damsels that did wait
  Upon her person for her sure defence,
  Playing on shawms[6] and trumpets, that from hence
  Their sound did reach unto the heaven's height:
  So forth into the field she marchèd thence,
  Where was a rich pavilion ready pight
  Her to receive, till time they should begin the fight.

5 Then forth came Artegall out of his tent,
  All armed to point,[7] and first the lists did enter:
  Soon after eke[8] came she with full intent
  And countenance fierce, as having fully bent her
  That battle's utmost trial to adventer.[9]

---

[1] *Buskins*, coverings for the feet, coming some distance up the leg.

[2] *Basted with bands of gold*, i.e. with bands of gold sewed on.

[3] *Mails*, metal rings interlinked.

[4] *Belt of mickle pride*, i.e. a rich, showy belt.

[5] *Boss*, any protuberant part.

[6] *Shawms*, pipes.

[7] *To point*, i.e. at all points, completely.

[8] *Eke*, likewise.

[9] *Adventer*, try.

The lists were closèd fast, to bar the rout
From rudely pressing on the middle centre;
Which in great heaps them circled all about,
Waiting how fortune would resolve that dangerous doubt.[1]

6 The trumpets sounded, and the field[2] began;
With bitter strokes it both began and ended.
She at the first encounter on him ran
With furious rage, as if she had intended
Out of his breast the very heart have rended:
But he, that had like tempests often tried,
From that first flaw himself right well defended.
The more she raged, the more he did abide:
She hewed, she foined,[3] she lashed, she laid on every side.

7 Yet still her blows he bore, and her forbore,
Weening at last to win advantage new;
Yet still her cruelty increasèd more,
And, though pow'r failed, her courage did accrue[4];
Which failing, he gan fiercely her pursue:
Like as a smith that to his cunning feat
The stubborn metal seeketh to subdue,
Soon as he feels it mollified with heat,
With his great iron sledge doth strongly on it beat.

8 So did Sir Artegall upon her lay,
As if she had an iron andvile[5] been,

---

[1] *Dangerous doubt, i.e.* doubtful contest.
[2] *Field,* battle.
[3] *Foined,* thrust.
[4] *Accrue,* increase.
[5] *Andvile,* anvil.

That flakes of fire, bright as the sunny ray,
Out of her steely arms were flashing seen,
That all on fire ye would her surely ween:
But with her shield so well herself she warded
From the dread danger of his weapon keen,
That all that while her life she safely guarded;
But he that help from her against her will discarded:

9 For with his trenchant blade at the next blow
Half of her shield he sharèd[1] quite away,
That half her side itself did naked show,
And thenceforth unto danger opened way.
Much was she movèd with the mighty sway
Of that sad[2] stroke, that half enraged she grew;
And like a greedy bear unto her prey
With her sharp scimitar at him she flew,
That glancing down his thigh the purple blood forth drew.

10 Thereat she gan to triumph with great boast,
And to upbraid that chance which him misfell,
As if the prize she gotten had almost,
With spiteful speeches, fitting with her well;
That his great heart gan inwardly to swell
With indignation at her vaunting vain,
And at her strook with puissance fearful fell[3];
Yet with her shield she warded it again,
That shattered all to pieces round about the plain.

11 Having her thus disarmèd of her shield,
Upon her helmet he again her strook,

---

[1] *Shared*, cut.   [2] *Sad*, heavy.   [3] *Fell*, fierce.

That down she fell upon the grassy field
In senseless swoon, as if her life forsook,
And pangs of death her spirit overtook :
Whom when he saw before·his foot prostrated,
He to her leapt with deadly dreadful look,
And her sun-shiny helmet soon unlacèd,
Thinking at once both head and helmet to have racèd.[1]

12 But, whenas he discovered had her face,
He saw, his senses' strange astonishment,
A miracle of nature's goodly grace
In her fair visage void of ornament,
But bathed in blood and sweat together ment[2];
Which, in the rudeness of that evil plight,
Bewrayed[3] the signs of feature excellent :
Like as the moon, in foggy winter's night,
Doth seem to be herself, though dark'ned be her light.

13 At sight thereof his cruel minded heart
Empiercèd was with pitiful regard,
That his sharp sword he threw from him apart,
Cursing his hand that had that visage marred :
No hand so cruel, nor no heart so hard,
But ruth[4] of beauty will it mollify.
By this, upstarting from her swoon she star'd
A while about her with confusèd eye ;
Like one that from his dream is wakèd suddenly.

---

[1] *Raced*, razed, cut off.   [3] *Bewrayed*, revealed.
[2] *Ment*, mingled.   [4] *Ruth*, pity.

14 Soon as the knight she there by her did spy
   Standing with empty hands all weaponless,
   With fresh assault upon him she did fly,
   And gan renew her former cruelness:
   And though he still retired, yet nathëless
   With huge redoubled strokes she on him laid;
   And more increased her outrage merciless,
   The more that he with meek entreaty prayed
   Her wrathful hand from greedy vengeance to have stayed.

15 Nought could he do but shun the dread despite
   Of her fierce wrath, and backward still retire;
   And with his single shield,[1] well as he might,
   Bear off the burden of her raging ire;
   And evermore he gently did desire
   To stay her strokes, and he himself would yield;
   Yet nould she heark,[2] ne let him once respire,
   Till he to her delivered had his shield,
   And to her mercy him submitted in plain[3] field.

16 So was he overcome; not overcome,
   But to her yielded of his own accord;
   Yet was he justly damnèd[4] by the doom[5]
   Of his own mouth, that spake so wareless[6] word,
   To be her thrall and service her afford:
   For though that he first victory obtained,
   Yet after, by abandoning his sword,

---

[1] *His single shield*, his shield alone.
[2] *Yet nould she heark*, yet she would not hearken.
[3] *Plain*, open.
[4] *Damned*, condemned.
[5] *Doom*, judgment.
[6] *Wareless*, unwary.

He wilful lost that he before attained :
No fairer conquest then that¹ with good will is gained.

17 Tho with her sword on him she flatling strook,
In sign of true subjection to her pow'r,
And as her vassal him to thraldom took :
But Terpin, born to 'a more unhappy hour,
As he on whom the luckless stars did lower,²
She caused to be attached and forthwith led
Unto the crook,³ t' abide the baleful stowre⁴
From which he lately had through rescue fled :
Where he full shamefully was hangèd by the head.

18 But, when they thought on Talus hands to lay,
He with his iron flail amonst them thondred,
That they were fain to let him scape away,
Glad from his company to be so sondred ;
Whose presence all their troops so much encombred,
That th' heaps of those which he did wound and slay,
Besides the rest dismayed,⁵ might not be nombred :
Yet all that while he would not once assay
To rescue his own lord, but thought it just t' obey.

19 Then took the amazon this noble knight,
Left to her will by his own wilful blame,

---

¹ *Then that*, i.e. than that which.
² *As he on whom*, etc. The belief in astrology — in the influence of the heavenly bodies upon the individual human life — was widespread in and before Spenser's time.
³ *Crook* (crux), gibbet.
⁴ *Baleful stowre, i.e.* sad fate.
⁵ *Dismayed*, here, disabled.

And causèd him to be disarmèd quite
Of all the ornaments of knightly name,
With which whilom he gotten had great fame:
Instead whereof she made him to be dight [1]
In woman's weeds, that is to manhood shame,
And put before his lap a napron [2] white,
Instead of curiets [3] and bases [4] fit for fight.

20 So being clad, she brought him from the field,
In which he had been trainèd many a day,
Into a long large chamber, which was ceiled
With moniments [5] of many knights' decay [6]
By her subduèd in victorious fray:
Amongst the which she caused his warlike arms
Be hanged on high, that mote his shame bewray [7];
And broke his sword for fear of further harms,
With which he wont to stir up battailous [8] alarms.

21 There ent'red in, he round about him saw
Many brave knights whose names right well he knew,
There bound t' obey that amazon's proud law,
Spinning and carding all in comely rew, [9]
That his big heart loathed so uncomely view:
But they were forced through penury [10] and pine, [11]

[1] *Dight*, arrayed.
[2] *Napron*, apron.
[3] *Curiets*, cuirasses.
[4] *Bases*, a kind of petticoats worn by knights on horseback.
[5] *Moniments*, monuments, reminders of some kind.
[6] *Decay*, destruction.
[7] *Bewray*, reveal.
[8] *Battailous*, warlike.
[9] *Rew*, row.
[10] *Penury*, i.e. want of food.
[11] *Pine*, torment, woe.

To do those works to them appointed due :
For nought was given them to sup or dine,
But what their hands could earn by twisting linen
  twine.

22 Amongst them all she placèd him most low,
And in his hand a distaff to him gave,
That he thereon should spin both flax and tow ;
A sordid office for a mind so brave :
So hard it is to be a woman's slave !
Yet he it took in his own self's despite,[1]
And thereto did himself right well behave[2]
Her to obey, sith he his faith had plight
Her vassal to become, if she him won in fight.

23 Who had seen him, imagine mote thereby
That whilom[3] hath of Hercules been told,
How for Iola's sake[4] he did apply
His mighty hands the distaff vile to hold
For[5] his huge club, which had subdued of old
So many monsters which the world annoyed ;
His lion's skin changed to a pall[6] of gold,
In which, forgetting wars, he only joyed
In combats of sweet love, and with his mistress
  toyed.

---

[1] *In his own self's despite*, i.e. in defiance or contempt of his own inclination.

[2] *Behave*, apply.

[3] *Whilom*, formerly.

[4] *Iola's sake*. Iole, the daughter of Eurytus, king of Œchalia, was beloved of Hercules. In order to win Iole, Hercules served Omphale, queen of Lydia ; and while serving her he dressed as a woman and did a woman's work.

[5] *For*, in place of.

[6] *Pall*, mantle.

24 Such is the cruelty of womenkind,
    When they have shaken off the shamefast[1] band,
    With which wise nature did them strongly bind
    T' obey the hests[2] of man's well-ruling hand,
    That then all rule and reason they withstand
    To purchase a licentious liberty:
    But virtuous women wisely understand,
    That they were born to base humility,[3]
    Unless the heavens them lift to lawful sovereignty.[4]

25 Thus there long while continued Artegall,
    Serving proud Radigund with true subjection:
    However it his noble heart did gall
    T' obey a woman's tyrannous direction,
    That might have had of life or death election:
    But, having chosen, now he might not change.

. . . .

   To add to Artegall's discomfort, his mistress conceived a liking for her noble captive and used every means at her command to gain his affection. Her maid Clarinda also persecuted him with her attentions. However, steadfast in his love for Britomart, the knight withstood both threats and entreaties, and endured in stubborn patience his hard lot.

[1] *Shamefast*, modest.
[2] *Hests*, commands.
[3] *Base humility*, humble subordination.
[4] *Unless the heavens them*, etc. Spenser wisely makes an exception in favor of female sovereigns.

XVI.

Informed by Talus, Artegall's servant, of his master's sad plight, Britomart sets out to deliver her lover. The treachery of Dolon and Britomart's combat with his sons.

1 Some men, I wote, will deem in Artegall
   Great weakness, and report of him much ill,
   For yielding so himself a wretched thrall
   To th' insolent command of women's will;
   That all his former praise doth foully spill[1]:
   But he, the man that say or do so dare,
   Be well advised that he stand steadfast still;
   For never yet was wight so well aware,
   But he at first or last was trapped in women's snare.

2 Yet in the straitness[2] of that captive state
   This gentle[3] knight himself so well behaved,
   That notwithstanding all the subtile[4] bait,
   With which those amazons his love still craved,
   To his own love his loyalty he saved:
   Whose character[5] in th' adamantine mould[6]
   Of his true heart so firmly was engraved,
   That no new love's impression ever could
   Bereave it[7] thence: such blot his honour blemish should.

[1] *Spill*, spoil.
[2] *Straitness*, narrowness, restraint.
[3] *Gentle*, high-born, noble.
[4] *Subtile*, sly, artful.
[5] *Character*, image.
[6] *Th' adamantine mould*, the adamantine (or extremely hard) substance.
[7] *Bereave it*, take it away from.

3 Yet his own love, the noble Britomart,
  Scarce so conceivèd in her jealous thought,
  What time sad tidings of his baleful smart
  In woman's bondage Talus to her brought;
  Brought in untimely hour, ere it was sought:
  For, after that the utmost date assigned
  For his return she waited had for nought,
  She gan to cast[1] in her misdoubtful[2] mind
  A thousand fears, that love-sick fancies fain[3] to find.

4 Sometime she fearèd lest some hard mishap
  Had him misfall'n in his adventurous quest;
  Sometime lest his false foe did him entrap
  In traitrous traine,[4] or had unawares opprest;
  But most she did her troubled mind molest,
  And secretly afflict with jealous fear,
  Lest some new love had him from her possessed;
  Yet loath she was, since she no ill did hear,
  To think of him so ill; yet could she not forbear.

5 One while she blamed herself; another while
  She him condemned as trustless and untrue:
  And then, her grief with error to beguile,
  She fained to count the time again anew,
  As if before she had not counted true:
  For hours, but days; for weeks that passèd were,
  She told but months, to make them seem more few:
  Yet, when she reck'ned them still drawing near,
  Each hour did seem a month, and every month a year.

---

[1] *Cast*, plan.
[2] *Misdoubtful*, apprehensive.
[3] *Fain*, pretend.
[4] *Traine*, snare.

6 But, when as yet she saw him not return,
   She thought to send some one to seek him out;
   But none she found so fit to serve that turn
   As her own self, to ease herself of doubt.
   Now she devised, amongst the warlike rout
   Of errant knights, to seek her errant knight;
   And then again resolved to hunt him out
   Amongst loose ladies lappèd in delight:
   And then both knights envíed,[1] and ladies eke did spite.

7 One day whenas she long had sought for ease
   In every place, and every place thought best,
   Yet found no place that could her liking please,
   She to a window came, that opened west,
   Towards which coast her love his way addressed
   There looking forth she in her heart did find
   Many vain fancies working her unrest;
   And sent her wingèd thoughts more swift than wind
   To bear unto her love the message of her mind.

8 There as she lookèd long, at last she spied
   One coming towards her with hasty speed;
   Well weened she then, ere him she plain descried,
   That it was one sent from her love indeed:
   Who when he nigh approached, she mote aread[2]
   That it was Talus, Artegall his groom[3]:
   Whereat her heart was filled with hope and dread;

---

[1] *Envied*, felt a grudge against, hated.

[2] *Mote aread*, could perceive.

[3] *Artegall his groom*, i.e. Artegall's servant.

Ne would she stay till he in place could come,
But ran to meet him forth to know his tidings' sum.

9. Even in the door him meeting, she begun :
"And where is he thy lord, and how far hence?
Declare at once : and hath he lost or won?"
The iron man, albe he wanted sense
And sorrow's feeling, yet, with conscience [1]
Of his ill news, did inly chill and quake,
And stood still mute, as one in great suspense ;
As if that by his silence he would make
Her rather read his meaning then himself it spake.[2]

10. Till she again thus said : "Talus, be bold,
And tell whatever it be, good or bad,
That from thy tongue thy heart's intent doth hold."
To whom he thus at length : "The tidings sad,
That I would hide, will needs, I see, be rad.[3]
My lord, your love, by hard mishap doth lie
In wretched bondage, wofully bestad."[4]
"Ay me," quoth she, "what wicked destiny !
And is he vanquished by his tyrant enemy?"

11. "Not by that tyrant, his intended foe[5];
But by a tyranness," he then replied,
"That him captivèd hath in hapless woe."
"Cease, thou bad news-man ; badly dost thou hide
Thy master's shame, ...
. . . .

---

[1] *Conscience*, consciousness.
[2] *Then himself it spake*, than himself disclose it.
[3] *Rad*, uttered.
[4] *Bestad*, bestead, beset.
[5] *His intended foe, i.e.* Grantorto from whose power he was to release Irena.

With that in rage she turned from him aside,
Forcing in vain the rest to her to tell;
And to her chamber went like solitary cell.

12 There she began to make her moanful plaint
Against her knight for being so untrue;
And him to touch with falsehood's foul attaint,
That all his other honour overthrew.
Oft did she blame herself, and often rue,[1]
For yielding to a stranger's love so light,
Whose life and manners strange she never knew;
And evermore she did him sharply twight[2]
For breach of faith to her, which he had firmly plight.

13 And then she in her wrathful will did cast
How to revenge that blot of honour blent,[3]
To fight with him, and goodly die her last:
And then again she did herself torment,
Inflicting on herself his punishment.
Awhile she walked, and chauft[4]; awhile she threw
Herself upon her bed and did lament:
Yet did she not lament with loud alew,[5]
As women wont, but with deep sighs and singulfs[6] few.

14 Like as a wayward child, whose sounder sleep
Is broken with some fearful dream's affright,
With froward[7] will doth set himself to weep,

---

[1] *Rue*, grieve, repent.
[2] *Twight*, twit, reproach.
[3] *Blent*, stained.
[4] *Chauft*, chafed.
[5] *Alew*, halloo, outcry.
[6] *Singulfs*, singults, sobs.
[7] *Froward*, perverse.

Ne can be stilled for all his nurse's might,
But kicks, and squalls, and shrieks for fell despite [1];
Now scratching her, and her loose locks misusing,
Now seeking darkness, and now seeking light,

. . . .

Such was this lady's fit [2] in her love's fond [3] accusing.

15 But when she had with such unquiet fits
Herself there close [4] afflicted long in vain,
Yet found no easement in her troubled wits,
She unto Talus forth returned again,
By change of place seeking to ease her pain;
And gan enquire of him with milder mood
The certain cause of Artegall's detain,[5]
And what he did, and in what state he stood,
And whether he did woo, or whether he were wooed.

16 "Ah wellaway!" said then the iron man,
"That he is not the while in state to woo;
But lies in wretched thraldom, weak and wan,
Not by strong hand compellèd thereunto,
But his own doom [6] that none can now undo."
"Said I not then," quoth she, "ere-while aright,
That this is thing compact betwixt you two,
Me to deceive of faith unto me plight,
Since that he was not forced, nor overcome in fight?"

---

[1] *Fell despite*, fierce vexation.
[2] *Fit*, state of mind, mood.
[3] *Fond*, foolish.
[4] *Close*, secretly.
[5] *Detain*, detention.
[6] *Doom*, judgment.

17 With that he gan at large to her dilate
   The whole discourse of his captivance sad,
   In sort as ye have heard the same of late :
   All which when she with hård endurance had
   Heard to the end, she was right sore bestad,
   With sudden stounds [1] of wrath and grief attone [2];
   Ne would abide, till she had answer made ;
   But straight herself did dight,[3] and armour don,
   And mounting to her steed bade Talus guide her on.

18 So forth she rode upon her ready way,
   To seek her knight, as Talus her did guide :
   Sadly she rode, and never word did say
   Nor good nor bad, ne ever looked aside,
   But still right down ; and in her thought did hide
   The fellness [4] of her heart, right fully bent
   To fierce avengement of that woman's pride,
   Which had her lord in her base prison pent,
   And so great honour with so foul reproach had blent.[5]

19 So as she thus melåncholic did ride,
   Chawing the cud of grief and inward pain,
   She chanced to meet toward the eventide
   A knight, that softly pacéd on the plain,
   As if himself to solace he were fain ;
   Well shot [6] in years he seemed, and rather bent
   To peace then needless trouble to constrain ;

[1] *Stounds*, paroxysms.
[2] *Attone*, at once.
[3] *Dight*, prepare.
[4] *Fellness*, fierceness, anger.
[5] *Blent*, stained.
[6] *Shot*, shot up, grown up.

As well by view of that his vestiment,
As by his modest semblant, that no evil meant.

20 He coming near gan gently her salute
With courteous words, in the most comely wise;
Who though desirous rather to rest mute,
Then terms to entertain of common guise,
Yet rather then she kindness would despise,
She would herself displease, so him requite.
Then gan the other further to devise
Of things abroad, as next to hand did light,
And many things demand, to which she answered light:

21 For little lust[1] had she to talk of ought,
Or ought to hear that mote delightful be;
Her mind was whole possessèd of one thought,
That gave none other place. Which when as he
By outward signs (as well he might) did see,
He list no lenger to use loathful speech,
But her besought to take it well in gree,[2]
Sith shady damp had dimmed the heaven's reach,[3]
To lodge with him that night, unless good cause empeach.[4]

22 The championess, now seeing night at door,
Was glad to yield unto his good request;
And with him went without gainsaying more.
Not far away, but little wide[5] by west,

---

[1] *Lust*, inclination.
[2] *In gree*, in liking.
[3] *Reach*, extent.
[4] *Empeach*, prevent.
[5] *Wide*, aside.

His dwelling was, to which he him addressed;
Where soon arriving, they receivèd were
In seemly wise, as them beseemèd best;
For he their host them goodly well did cheer,
And talked of pleasant things the night away to wear.

23 Thus passing th' evening well, till time of rest,
Then Britomart unto a bow'r[1] was brought;
Where grooms awaited her to have undressed:
But she ne would undressèd be for ought,
Ne doff her arms, though he her much besought:
For she had vowed, she said, not to forego
Those warlike weeds,[2] till she revenge had wrought
Of a late wrong upon a mortal foe;
Which she would sure perform, betide her weal or woe.

24 Which when their host perceived, right discontent
In mind he grew, for fear lest by that art[3]
He should his purpose miss, which close he meant[4]:
Yet, taking leave of her, he did depart:
There all that night remainèd Britomart,
Restless, recomfortless, with heart deep-grieved,
Not suffering the least twinkling sleep to start
Into her eye, which th' heart mote have relieved;
But if the least appeared, her eyes she straight reprieved.[5]

---

[1] *Bower*, chamber.
[2] *Weeds*, garments.
[3] *Art*, way, means.
[4] *Close he meant*, secretly he proposed.
[5] *Reprieved*, reproved.

25 "Ye guilty eyes," said she, "the which with guile
   My heart at first betrayed, will ye betray
   My life now too, for which a little while
   Ye will not watch? False watches, wellaway!
   I wote[1] when ye did watch both night and day
   Unto your loss; and now needs will ye sleep?
   Now ye have made my heart to wake alway,
   Now will ye sleep? ah! wake, and rather weep
   To think of your night's[2] want, that should ye waking keep."

26 Thus did she watch, and wear the weary night
   In wailful plaints, that none was to appease;
   Now walking soft, now sitting still upright,
   As sundry change her seemèd best to ease.
   Ne less did Talus suffer sleep to seize
   His eyelids sad,[3] but watched continually,
   Lying without her door in great disease[4];
   Like to a spaniel waiting carefully
   Lest any should betray his lady treacherously.

27 What time the native bellman of the night,
   The bird that warnèd Peter of his fall,
   First rings his silver bell t' each sleepy wight,
   That should their minds up to devotion call,
   She heard a wondrous noise below the hall:
   All suddenly the bed, where she should lie,
   By a false trap was let adown to fall

---

[1] *I wote*, I know.
[2] *Night's*, should perhaps be knight's.
[3] *Sad*, heavy.
[4] *Disease*, uneasiness.

Into a lower room, and by and by
The loft[1] was raised again, that[2] no man could it spy.

28 With sight whereof she was dismayed right sore,
Perceiving well the treason which was meant:
Yet stirrèd not at all for doubt[3] of more,
But kept her place with courage confident,
Waiting what would ensue of that event.
It was not long before she heard the sound
Of armèd men coming with close intent
Towards her chamber; at which dreadful stound[4]
She quickly caught her sword, and shield about her bound.

29 With that there came unto her chamber door
Two knights all armèd ready for to fight;
And after them full many other more,
A rascal rout,[5] with weapons rudely dight[6]:
Whom soon as Talus spied by glims[7] of night,
He started up, there where on ground he lay,
And in his hand his thresher ready keight[8]:
They, seeing that, let drive at him straightway,
And round about him press in riotous array.

30 But, soon as he began to lay about
With his rude iron flail, they gan to fly,
Both armèd knights and eke unarmèd rout:

---

[1] *Loft*, flooring.
[2] *That*, so that.
[3] *Doubt*, fear, dread.
[4] *Stound*, exigency.
[5] *Rascal rout*, base multitude.
[6] *Dight*, furnished, armed.
[7] *Glims*, gleams.
[8] *Keight*, caught.

Yet Talus after them apace did ply,
Wherever in the dark he could them spy;
That here and there like scatt'red sheep they lay.
Then, back returning where his dame did lie,
He to her told the story of that fray,
And all that treason there intended did bewray.[1]

31 Wherewith though wondrous wroth, and inly burning
To be avengèd for so foul a deed,
Yet, being forced to abide the day's returning,
She there remained; but with right wary heed,
Lest any more such practice[2] should proceed.
Now mote ye know (that which to Britomart
Unknowen was) whence all this did proceed;
And for what cause so great mischiévous smart
Was meant to her that never evil meant in heart.

32 The goodman of this house was Dolon[3] hight;
A man of subtile[4] wit and wicked mind,
That whilom[5] in his youth had been a knight,
And arms had borne, but little good could find,
And much less honour by that warlike kind
Of life: for he was nothing valorous,
But with sly shifts and wiles did[6] undermined
All noble knights which were adventurous,
And many brought to shame by treason treacherous.

[1] *Bewray*, reveal.
[2] *Practice*, plot.
[3] *Dolon*, goodman, master.
[4] *Subtile*, subtle.
[5] *Whilom*, formerly.
[6] *Did*, probably a misprint for had.

33 He had three sons, all three like father's sons,
   Like treacherous, like full of fraud and guile,
   Of all that on this earthly compass wonnes[1] :
   The eldest of the which was slain erewhile
   By Artegall, through his own guilty wile ;
   His name was Guizor ; whose untimely fate
   For to avenge, full many treasons vile
   His father Dolon had devised of late
   With these his wicked sons, and showed his cank'red hate.

34 For sure he weened that this his present guest
   Was Artegall, by many tokens plain ;
   But chiefly by that iron page he guessed
   Which still was wont with Artegall remain ;
   And therefore meant him surely to have slain :
   But by God's grace and her good heediness,
   She was preservèd from their traitrous traine.[2]
   Thus she all night wore out in watchfulness,
   Ne suff'red slothful sleep her eyelids to oppress.

35 The morrow next, so soon as dawning hour
   Discovered had the light to living eye,
   She forth issued out of her loathed bow'r,[3]
   With full intent t' avenge that villany
   On that vilde[4] man and all his family :
   And, coming down to seek them where they wonned,
   Nor sire, nor sons, nor any could she spy ;

[1] *Wonnes*, dwells.
[2] *Traine*, artifice, snare.
[3] *Bower*, chamber.
[4] *Vilde*, vile.

Each room she sought, but them all empty fond:
They all were fled for fear; but whether, nether
kond.[1]

36 She saw it vain to make there lenger stay,
But took her steed; and thereon mounting light,
Gan her address unto her former way.
She had not rid the mountenance of a flight,[2]
But that she saw there present in her sight
Those two false brethren on that perilous bridge,
On which Pollente with Artegall did fight.
Strait[3] was the passage, like a ploughèd ridge.
That, if two met, the one mote needs fall over the
lidge.[4]

37 There they did think themselves on her to wreak[5];
Who as she nigh unto them drew, the one
These vile reproaches gan unto her speak:
"Thou recreant false traitor, that with loan
Of arms hast knighthood stol'n, yet knight art none,
No more shall now the darkness of the night
Defend thee from the vengeance of thy fone[6]:
But with thy blood thou shalt appease the sprite[7]
Of Guizor, by thee slain and murd'red by thy
sleight."[8]

38 Strange were the words in Britomartis ear;
Yet stayed she not for them, but forward fared,[9]

---

[1] *Nether kond*, neither knew.
[2] *The mountenance of a flight*, i.e. a bow-shot.
[3] *Strait*, narrow.
[4] *Lidge*, ledge.
[5] *Wreak*, revenge.
[6] *Fone*, foes.
[7] *Sprite*, spirit.
[8] *Sleight*, artful trick.
[9] *Fared*, proceeded.

Till to the perilous bridge she came ; and there
Talus desired that he might have prepared
The way to her, and those two losels[1] scared :
But she thereat was wroth, that for despite[2]
The glancing sparkles through her beaver glared,
And from her eyes did flash out fiery light,
Like coals that through a silver censer sparkle
  bright.

39 She stayed not to advise which way to take ;
But, putting spurs unto her fiery beast,
Thorough the midst of them she way did make.
The one of them, which most her wrath increased,
Upon her spear she bore before her breast,
Till to the bridge's further end she passed ;
Where falling down his challenge he released[3] :
The other over side the bridge she cast
Into the river, where he drunk his deadly last.

40 As when the flashing levin[4] haps to light
Upon two stubborn oaks, which stand so near
That way betwixt them none appears in sight ;
The engine, fiercely flying forth, doth tear
Th' one from the earth, and through the air doth
  bear ;
The other it with force doth overthrow
Upon one side, and from his roots doth rear :
So did the championess these two there strow,
And to their sire their carcasses left to bestow.

[1] *Losels*, good-for-nothings.
[2] *Despite*, vexation.
[3] *His challenge he released, i.e.* he withdrew his accusation.
[4] *Levin*, lightning.

XVII.

After visiting the temple of Isis, Britomart slays Radigund and frees her lover.

1   NOUGHT is on earth more sacred or divine,
    That gods and men do equally adore,
    Then this same virtue that doth right define :
    For th' heavens themselves, whence mortal men implore
    Right in their wrongs, are ruled by righteous lore
    Of highest Jove, who doth true justice deal
    To his inferior gods, and evermore
    Therewith contains[1] his heavenly common-weal :
    The skill whereof to princes' hearts he doth reveal.

2   Well therefore did the antique world invent
    That Justice was a god of sovereign grace,
    And altars unto him and temples lent,[2]
    And heavenly honours in the highest place ;
    Calling him great Osiris,[3] of the race
    Of th' old Ægyptian kings that whilom were ;
    With feignèd colors shading.[4] a true case ;
    For that Osiris, whilst he livèd here,
    The justest man alive and truest did appear.

---

[1] *Contains*, restrains, governs.
[2] *Lent*, furnished.
[3] *Osiris*, one of the principal divinities of Egypt ; the husband and brother of Isis.
[4] *Shading*, shadowing forth.

3 His wife was Isis; whom they likewise made
   A goddess of great pow'r and sovereignty,
   And in her person cunningly did shade
   That part of justice which is equity,
   Whereof I have to treat here presently:
   Unto whose temple whenas Britomart
   Arrivèd, she with great humility
   Did enter in, ne would that night depart;
   But Talus mote not be admitted to her part.

4 There she receivèd was in goodly wise
   Of many priests, which duly did attend
   Upon the rites and daily sacrifice,
   All clad in linen robes with silver hemmed[1];
   And on their heads with long locks comely kembed[2]
   They wore rich mitres shapèd like the moon,
   To show that Isis doth the moon portend;
   Like as Osiris signifies the sun:
   For that they both like race in equal justice[3] run.

5 The championess them greeting, as she could,[4]
   Was thence by them into the temple led;
   Whose goodly building when she did behold
   Borne upon stately pillars, all dispread
   With shining gold, and archèd over head,
   She wond'red at the workman's passing[5] skill,
   Whose like before she never saw nor read;

---

[1] *Hemmed*, edged.
[2] *Kembed*, combed. Prof. Child says: "The Egyptian priests were bald, while the Jewish priests, as Upton remarks, were forbidden to shave their heads."
[3] *In equal justice*, i.e. with the same regularity.
[4] *As she could*, as she knew how.
[5] *Passing*, surpassing.

And thereupon long while stood gazing still,
But thought that she thereon could never gaze her fill.

6   Thenceforth unto the idol[1] they her brought;
The which was framèd all of silver fine,
So well as could with cunning hand be wrought,
And clothèd all in garments made of line,[2]
Hemmed all about with fringe of silver twine:
Upon her head she wore a crown of gold;
To show that she had pow'r in things divine:
And at her feet a crocodile was rolled,
That with her wreathèd tail her middle[3] did enfold.

7   One foot was set upon the crocodile,
And on the ground the other fast did stand;
So meaning to suppress both forgèd guile
And open force: and in her other hand[4]
She stretchèd forth a long, white, slender wand.
Such was the goddess: whom when Britomart
Had long beheld, herself upon the land[5]
She did prostráte, and with right humble heart
Unto herself her silent prayers did impart.

8   To which the idol as it were inclining,
Her wand did move with amiable look,
By outward show her inward sense designing[6]:
Who well perceiving how her wand she shook,

---

[1] *The idol*, the image of Isis.
[2] *Line*, linen.
[3] *Middle*, waist.
[4] *In her other hand*, i.e. in one of her two hands.
[5] *Land*, ground.
[6] *Designing*, signifying.

It as a token of good fortune took.
By this the day with damp was overcast,
And joyous light the house of Jove forsook :
Which when she saw, her helmet she unlaced,
And by the altar's side herself to slumber placed.

9 For other beds the priests there usèd none,
But on their mother Earth's dear lap did lie,
And bake¹ their sides upon the cold hard stone,
T' enure themselves to sufferance² thereby,
And proud rebellious flesh to mortify :
For, by the vow of their religion,
They tièd were to steadfast chastity
And continence of life ; that, all forgon,³
They mote the better tend to their devotion.

10 Therefore they mote not taste of fleshly food,
Ne feed on ought the which doth blood contain,
Ne drink of wine⁴; for wine they say is blood,
Even the blood of giants, which were slain
By thund'ring Jove in the Phlegrean plain⁵:
For which the Earth, (as they the story tell,)
Wroth with the gods, which to perpetual pain
Had damned her sons which gainst them did rebel,
With inward grief and malice did against them swell :

---

¹ *Bake, i.e.* make hard.
² *Sufferance*, suffering.
³ *All forgon*, all foregone, *i.e.* everything given up.
⁴ *Therefore they mote not*, etc. The priests of Isis did not abstain from flesh of all kinds, and they drank wine sparingly.
⁵ *Phlegrean plain :* the volcanic plain extending along the coast of Campania, Italy, from Cumæ to Capua.

11 And of their vital blood, the which was shed
   Into her pregnant bosom, forth she brought
   The fruitful vine; whose liquor bloody red,
   Having the minds of men with fury fraught,[1]
   Mote in them stir up old rebellious thought
   To make new war against the gods again:
   Such is the pow'r of that same fruit, that nought
   The fell[2] contagion may thereof restrain,
   Ne within reason's rule her madding mood contain.[3]

12 There did the warlike maid herself repose,
   Under the wings of Isis all that night;
   And with sweet rest her heavy eyes did close,
   After that long day's toil and weary plight:
   Where whilst her earthly parts with soft delight
   Of senseless sleep did deeply drownèd lie,
   There did appear unto her heavenly sprite
   A wondrous vision, which did close imply[4]
   The course of all her fortune and posterity.

The maiden dreamed of flame and tempest, and saw in her dream first a crocodile, and then

13 .   .   .   a lion of great might,
   That shortly did all other beasts subdue:
   With that she wakèd full of fearful fright,
   And doubtfully dismayed through that so uncouth[5]
      sight.

14 So thereupon long while she musing lay,
   With thousand thoughts feeding her fantasy;

[1] *Fraught*, filled. [3] *Contain*, restrain.
[2] *Fell*, fierce.   [4] *Close imply*, secretly infold.
      [5] *Uncouth*, strange.

Until she spied the lamp of lightsome day
   Up-lifted in the porch of heaven high:
   Then up she rose, fraught with meláncholy,
   And forth into the lower parts did pass,
   Whereas, the priests she found full busily
   About their holy things for morrow mass;
   Whom she saluting fair, fair resaluted was:

15 But, by the change of her uncheerful look,
   They might perceive she was not well in plight,
   Or that some pensiveness to heart she took:
   Therefore thus one of them, who seemed in sight
   To be the greatest and the gravest wight,
   To her bespake: "Sir knight, it seems to me
   That, thorough evil rest of this last night,
   Or ill apayed¹ or much dismayed ye be;
   That by your change of cheer is easy for to see."

16 "Certes,"² said she, "sith ye so well have spied
   The troublous passion of my pensive mind,
   I will not seek the same from you to hide;
   But will my cares unfold in hope to find
   Your aid to guide me out of error blind."
   "Say on," quoth he, "the secret of your heart
   For, by the holy vow which me doth bind,
   I am adjured best counsel to impart
   To all that shall require my comfort in their smart."

17 Then gan she to declare the whole discourse
   Of all that vision which to her appeared,

---

¹ *Ill apayed*, ill content.   ² *Certes*, truly.

As well as to her mind it had recourse.[1]
All which when he unto the end had heard,
Like to a weak, faint-hearted man he fared,[2]
Through great astonishment of that strange sight;
And, with long locks up-standing, stiffly, stared
Like one adawèd[3] with some dreadful sprite[4]:
So filled with heavenly fury, thus he her behight[5]:

18 "Magnifick virgin, that in quaint[6] disguise
Of British arms dost mask thy royal blood,
So to pursue a perilous emprise[7];
How couldst thou ween, through that disguisèd hood,[8]
To hide thy state from being understood?
Can from th' immortal gods ought hidden be?
They do thy linage, and thy lordly brood,
They do thy sire lamenting sore for thee,
They do thy love forlorn in women's thraldom see.

19 "The end whereof, and all the long event,
They do to thee in this same dream discover:
For that same crocodile doth represent
The righteous knight that is thy faithful lover,
Like to Osiris in all just endeavor:
For that same crocodile Osiris is,
That under Isis' feet doth sleep forever;
To show that clemence oft, in things amiss,
Restrains those stern behests and cruel dooms of his.

---

[1] *It had recourse*, it did recur.
[2] *He fared*, he was affected.
[3] *Adawed*, confounded.
[4] *Sprite*, spirit.
[5] *Behight*, addressed.
[6] *Quaint*, ingenious.
[7] *Emprise*, enterprise.
[8] *Hood*, mask.

20 "That knight shall all the troublous storms
 assuage
And raging flames, that many foes shall rear [1]
To hinder thee from the just heritage
Of thy sire's crown, and from thy country dear:
Then shalt thou take him to thy lovèd fere,[2]
And join in equal portion of thy realm:
And afterwards a son to him shalt bear,
That lion-like shall show his pow'r extreme.
So bless thee God, and give thee joyance of thy
 dream!"

21 All which when she unto the end had heard,
She much was easèd in her troublous thought,
And on those priests bestowèd rich reward;
And royal gifts of gold and silver wrought
She for a present to their goddess brought.
Then taking leave of them, she forward went,
To seek her love, where he was to be sought,
Ne rested till she came without relent [3]
Unto the land of amazons, as she was bent.

22 Whereof when news to Radigund was brought,
Not with amaze, as women wonted be,
She was confusèd in her troublous thought,
But filled with courage and with joyous glee,
As glad to hear of arms, the which now she
Had long surceased,[4] she bade to open bold,
That she the face of her new foe might see:

---

[1] *Rear*, raise, excite.
[2] *Fere*, mate, companion.
[3] *Relent*, delay.
[4] *Surceased, i.e.* ceased using.

But when they of that iron man had told,
Which late her folk had slain, she bade them forth to hold.[1]

23 So there without the gate, as seemèd best,
She causèd her pavilion be pight[2];
In which stout[3] Britomart herself did rest,
Whiles Talus watchèd at the door all night.
All night likewise they of the town in fright
Upon their wall good watch and ward did keep.
The morrow next, so soon as dawning light
Bade do away the damp of drowsy sleep,
The warlike amazon out of her bow'r did peep;

24 And causèd straight a trumpet loud to shrill,
To warn her foe to battle soon be prest[4];
Who, long before awoke, (for she full ill
Could sleep all night, that in unquiet breast
Did closely[5] harbour such a jealous[6] guest,)
Was to the battle whilom[7] ready dight,[8]
Eftsoones[9] that warrioress with haughty crest
Did forth issúe, all ready for the fight;
On th' other side the foe appearèd soon in sight.

25 But, ere they rearèd hand, the amazone
Began the strait[10] conditions to propound,

---

[1] *She bade them forth to hold*, i.e. she bade them to proceed, to go outside the walls. As she feared Talus, she would not allow him to enter the city.
[2] *Pight*, pitched.
[3] *Stout*, dauntless.
[4] *Prest*, ready.
[5] *Closely*, secretly.
[6] *Jealous*, suspicious.
[7] *Whilom*, means here, some time before.
[8] *Dight*, prepared.
[9] *Eftsoones*, immediately.
[10] *Strait*, strict, severe.

With which she usèd still to tie her fone,[1]
To serve her so, as she the rest had bound:
Which when the other heard, she sternly frowned
For high disdain of such indignity,
And would no longer treat, but bade them sound:
For her no other terms should ever tie
Then what prescribèd were by laws of chivalry.

26 The trumpets sound, and they together run
   With greedy rage, and with their falchions smot;
   Ne either sought the other's strokes to shun,
   But through great fury both their skill forgot,
   And practicke[2] use in arms; · . .
   . . . .

27 As when a tiger and a lioness
   Are met at spoiling of some hungry prey,
   Both challenge[3] it with equal greediness:
   But first the tiger claws thereon did lay;
   And therefore, loath to lose her right away,
   Doth in defence thereof full stoutly stond:
   To which the lion strongly doth gainsay,
   That she to hunt the beast first took in hond,
   And therefore ought it have wherever she it fond.

28 Full fiercely laid the amazon about,
   And dealt her blows unmercifully sore;
   Which Britomart withstood with courage stout,
   And then repaid again with double more.
   So long they fought, that all the grassy floor

---

[1] *Fone*, foes.   [2] *Practicke*, practiced.
[3] *Challenge*, claim.

> Was filled with blood which from their sides did flow,
> And gushèd through their arms, that all in gore
> They trode, and on the ground their lives did strow,
> Like fruitless seed, of which untimely death should grow.

29 At last proud Radigund with fell despite,[1]
  Having by chance espied advantage near,
  Let drive at her with all her dreadful might,
  And thus upbraiding said : "This token bear
  Unto the man whom thou dost love so dear ;
  And tell him for his sake thy life thou gavest."
  Which spiteful words she sore engrieved to hear,
  Thus answered : "Lewdly[2] thou my love depravest,[3]
  Who shortly must repent that now so vainly bravest."

30 Nathless that stroke so cruel passage found,
  That, glancing on her shoulder-plate, it bit
  Unto the bone, and made a grisly[4] wound,
  That she her shield through raging smart of it
  Could scarce uphold ; yet soon she it requit ;
  For, having force increased through furious pain,
  She her so rudely on the helmet smit,
  That it empiercèd to the very brain,
  And her proud person low prostráted on the plain.

31 Where being laid, the wrothful Britoness
  Stayed not till she came to herself again ;
  But in revenge both of her love's distress

---

[1] *Fell despite*, fierce hatred.
[2] *Lewdly*, impudently.
[3] *Depravest*, defamest.
[4] *Grisly*, dreadful.

And her late vile reproach, though vaunted vain,
And also of her wound, which sore did pain,
She with one stroke both head and helmet cleft :
Which dreadful sight when all her [1] warlike train
There present saw, each one, of sense bereft,
Fled fast into the town, and her sole victor left.

32 But yet so fast they could not home retrate,
But that swift Talus did the foremost win [2];
And, pressing through the preace [3] unto the gate,
Pellmell with them at once did enter in :
There then a piteous slaughter did begin ;
For all that ever came within his reach
He with his iron flail did thresh so thin,
That he no work at all left for the leech [4];
Like to an hideous storm which nothing may empeach.[5]

33 And now by this the noble conqueress
Herself came in, her glory to partake ;
Where though revengeful vows she did profess,
Yet, when she saw the heaps which he did make
Of slaught'red carcasses, her heart did quake
For very ruth,[6] which did it almost rive,[7]
That she his fury willèd him to slake [8]:
For else he sure had left not one alive ;
But all, in his revenge, of spirit [9] would deprive.

[1] *Her*, i.e. Radigund's.
[2] *Win*, overtake.
[3] *Preace*, press.
[4] *Leech*, physician.
[5] *Empeach*, hinder.
[6] *Ruth*, pity.
[7] *Rive*, rend.
[8] *Slake*, allay.
[9] *Spirit*, here, breath.

34 Tho,[1] when she had his execution stayed,
   She for that iron prison did inquire,
   In which her wretched love was captive laid:
   Which breaking open with indignant ire,
   She ent'red into all the parts entire[2]:
   Where when she saw that loathly uncouth[3] sight
   Of men disguised in womanish attire,
   Her heart gan grudge[4] for very deep despite
   Of so unmanly mask in misery misdight.[5]

35 At last whenas to her own love she came,
   Whom like disguise no less deformèd had,
   At sight thereof abashed with secret shame,
   She turned her head aside, as nothing glad
   To have beheld a spectacle so bad;
   And then too well believed that which tofore
   Jealous suspect as true untruly drad[6]:
   Which vain conceit now nourishing no more,
   She sought with ruth to salve his sad misfortune's
      sore.

36 Not so great wonder and astonishment
   Did the most chaste Penelope[7] possess,
   To see her lord, that was reported drent[8]
   And dead long since in dolorous distress,
   Come home to her in piteous wretchedness,

---

[1] *Tho*, then.
[2] *Entire*, interior.
[3] *Uncouth*, strange.
[4] *Grudge*, grow indignant.
[5] *Misdight*, wrongly clad.
[6] *Untruly drad*, i.e. suspected without reason. She at first believed that Artegall had been false to her and had given his affection to Radigund.
[7] *Penelope*, the wife of Ulysses, the hero of Homer's "Odyssey."
[8] *Drent*, drenched, drowned.

After long travel of full twenty years;
That she knew not his favor's likeliness,[1]
For many scars and many hoary hairs;
But stood long staring on him mongst uncertain fears.

37 "Ah! my dear lord, what sight is this?" quoth she;
"What May-game[2] hath misfortune made of you?
Where is that dreadful manly look? where be
Those mighty palms, the which ye wont t' embrue
In blood of kings, and great hosts to subdue?
Could ought on earth so wondrous change have wrought,
As to have robbed you of that manly hue?
Could so great courage stoopèd have to ought?
Then farewell, fleshly force; I see thy pride is naught!"

38 Thenceforth she straight unto a bow'r[3] him brought,
And caused him those uncomely weeds undight[4];
And in their stead for other raiment sought;
Whereof there was great store, and armors bright,
Which had been reft from[5] many a noble knight,
Whom that proud amazon subduèd had,
Whilst fortune favored her success in fight:
In which whenas she him anew had clad,
She was revived, and joyed much in his semblance[6] glad.

---

[1] *His favor's likeliness,* i.e. the likeness of his countenance.

[2] *May-game,* sport.

[3] *Bower,* room.

[4] *Those uncomely weeds undight,* i.e. to lay aside those unbecoming garments.

[5] *Reft from,* taken from.

[6] *Semblance,* appearance.

39 So there awhile they afterwards remained,
    Him to refresh, and her late wounds to heal:
    During which space she there as princess reigned;
    And, changing all that form of common-weal,
    The liberty of women did repeal,
    Which they had long usurped; and, them restoring
    To men's subjection, did true justice deal:
    That all they, as a goddess her adoring,
    Her wisdom did admire,[1] and heark'ned to her loring.[2]

40 For all those knights, which long in captive shade
    Had shrouded been, she did from thraldom free;
    And magistrates of all that city made,
    And gave to them great living and large fee[3]:
    And, that they should forever faithful be,
    Made them swear fealty to Artegall:
    Who when himself now well recured did see,
    He purposed to proceed, whatso befall,
    Upon his first adventure[4] which him forth did call.

41 Full sad and sorrowful was Britomart
    For his departure, her new cause of grief;
    Yet wisely moderated her own smart,
    Seeing his honor, which she tend'red chief,[5]
    Consisted much in that adventure's priefe[6]:
    The care whereof, and hope of his success,
    Gave unto her great comfort and relief,

---

[1] *Admire*, wonder at.
[2] *Loring*, teaching.
[3] *Fee*, possessions.
[4] *His first adventure;* this was to deliver Irena from the oppression of Grantorto.
[5] *Which she tend'red chief, i.e.* for which she had cared most of all.
[6] *Priefe*, proof, achievement.

That womanish complaints she did repress,
And temp'red for the time her present heaviness.

42 There she continued for a certain space,
　　Till through his want [1] her woe did more increase:
　　Then, hoping that the change of air and place
　　Would change her pain, and sorrow somewhat ease,
　　She parted thence, her anguish to appease.
　　Meanwhile her noble lord, Sir Artegall,
　　Went on his way, ne ever hour did cease,
　　Till he redeemèd had that lady thrall:
　　That for another canto will more fitly fall.

Spenser relates Artegall's further adventures, but does not again mention Britomart. However, since both Merlin and the priest of Isis have prophesied her happy union with the knight of Justice, we are not left in doubt regarding her future.

[1] *His want*, *i.e.* her want of him.

CLASSICS FOR CHILDREN.

Choice Literature; Judicious Notes; Large Type;
Firm Binding; Low Prices.

For a full description of these books, see our Common School Catalogue.

Aesop's Fables.
Andersen's Fairy Tales. First Series.
Andersen's Fairy Tales. Second Series.
Bunyan's Pilgrim's Progress.
Burt's Stories from Plato.
Chesterfield's Letters.
Church's Stories of the Old World.
Defoe's Robinson Crusoe.
Dickens' Tale of Two Cities.
Cervantes' Don Quixote of La Mancha.
Epictetus.
Fiske-Irving's Washington and His Country.
Francillon's Gods and Heroes.
Franklin: His Life by Himself.
Goldsmith's Vicar of Wakefield.
Grimm's Fairy Tales, Part I.
Grimm's Fairy Tales, Part II.
Grote and Ségur's Two Great Retreats.
Hale's Arabian Nights.
Hudson and Lamb's Merchant of Venice.
Hughes' Tom Brown at Rugby.
Irving's Alhambra.
Irving's Sketch-Book. (Six Selections.)
Johnson's Rasselas.
Kingsley's Greek Heroes.
Kingsley's Water Babies.
Lamb's Adventures of Ulysses.
Lamb's Tales from Shakespeare.
Marcus Aurelius.
Martineau's Peasant and the Prince.
Montgomery's Heroic Ballads.
Plutarch's Lives.
Ruskin's King of the Golden River.
Selections from Ruskin.
Scott's Guy Mannering.
 Ivanhoe.
 Lady of the Lake.
 Lay of the Last Minstrel.
 Marmion.
 Old Mortality.
 Quentin Durward.
 Rob Roy.
 Tales of a Grandfather.
 Talisman.
Swift's Gulliver's Travels.
Williams and Foster's Selections for Memorizing.
Wyss' Swiss Family Robinson.

GINN & COMPANY, Publishers,
BOSTON, NEW YORK, AND CHICAGO.

Ginn & Company's School Libraries.

No. 1. SCOTT'S NOVELS AND POEMS. Ten volumes for $5.75. Six great historical romances, three stirring and ever-popular poems, and the charming "Tales," — the masterpieces of this great magician. There are no better books to interest young people.

No. 2. OLD-TIME CLASSICS. Ten volumes for $4.75. — Ten old-time, ever-fresh, ever-interesting Classics which hold their sweetness and goodness as the years roll round. Other books come and go, but these abide.

No. 3. POPULAR FABLES AND STORIES. Ten volumes for $4.75. — Interesting and instructive fables, fairy tales and popular stories for young folks, written in an attractive style. They are as charming and instructive as the great masters of language can make them.

No. 4. STANDARD ENGLISH CLASSICS. Ten volumes for $5.25. — Staunch, sterling, sensible books by English classical writers. They are the finest and best known works of our world-famous authors.

No. 5. RUGBY LIBRARY FOR YOUNG MEN. Ten volumes for $5.60. — The best books are none too good as an incentive to young men who are ambitious to make a place for themselves in this world.

No. 6. REFERENCE LIBRARY FOR GRAMMAR SCHOOLS. Eighteen volumes for $14.50. — Every Grammar School that is abreast of the times should have these eighteen substantial works, arranged for easy reference in the schoolroom.

No. 7. REFERENCE LIBRARY FOR HIGH SCHOOLS. Fifteen volumes for $21.00. — The high school library cannot have too many sterling books for quick reference. These fifteen works will serve to round out your library and make it a better source of instruction and information.

No. 8. LIBRARY FOR UNGRADED SCHOOLS, No. 1. Fifteen volumes for $6.50. — The ungraded school library must provide a great variety of books. Fiction, history, natural science, romance, poetry, should be drawn from to provide a palatable and nutritious mental bill of fare.

No. 9. LIBRARY FOR UNGRADED SCHOOLS, No. 2. Twenty volumes for $11.50. — Every ungraded school needs an all-round, serviceable library — something interesting, instructive, and stimulating for all, from the youngest to the oldest scholar in school. This library will be found to meet this want.

No. 10. LIBRARY FOR UNGRADED SCHOOLS, No. 3. Thirty volumes for $17.50. — A strong and attractive library for ungraded schools. Thirty readable and instructive books for everyday reading and reference.

No. 11. A TEACHER'S LIBRARY. Sixteen volumes for $11.50. — A live teacher needs good tools in the shape of a well arranged, well selected library, to keep in touch with all that is fresh and choice in the educational world. This library will make a substantial working set of books.

No. 12. HUDSON'S SCHOOL SHAKESPEARE. Twenty-three volumes for $10.00. — The most convenient and scholarly school Shakespeare in the market. The convenient size and shape of the volumes, the clear type and attractive binding, the introductions and critical notes, all combine to make this a most fitting dress for the world's great dramatist.

No. 13. HUDSON'S HARVARD SHAKESPEARE. Twenty volumes for $25.00. — This is pre-eminently the edition for school libraries of an advanced grade. The type, paper, and binding are attractive and superior, and the introductions and notes represent the editor's ripest thought.

No. 14. HUDSON'S HARVARD SHAKESPEARE. Ten volumes for $20.00. — This library is exactly the same as the preceding one except that there are ten volumes instead of twenty. There are four plays in each volume.

No. 15. HOME AND SCHOOL LIBRARY. Thirty volumes for $14.50. — The cream of all that is attractive, sound and wholesome in classic literature. The judicious notes, large type, firm binding and low price are its strong features. There can be nothing better for a basal library for the average school or family.

The separate books of this library have been read and re-read by thousands of young people, in our "Classics for Children."

Our Portrait Catalogue of School Libraries sent free to any address.

GINN & COMPANY, Publishers, Boston, New York, Chicago.

James Parton, the Historian, called Jane Andrews, the author of these books, "the best teacher in the world."

THE JANE ANDREWS BOOKS

A remarkable series of attractive and interesting books for young people, — written in a clear, easy, and picturesque style. This is the famous Jane Andrews series which has been for many years an old-time favorite with young folks. Other juvenile books come and go, but the Jane Andrews books maintain the irresistible charm they always have had.

THE SEVEN LITTLE SISTERS WHO LIVE ON THE ROUND BALL THAT FLOATS IN THE AIR. 12mo. Cloth. 143 pages. Illustrated. For introduction, 50 cents.

EACH AND ALL; THE SEVEN LITTLE SISTERS PROVE THEIR SISTERHOOD. 12mo. Cloth. Illustrated. 162 pages. For introduction, 50 cents.

THE STORIES MOTHER NATURE TOLD HER CHILDREN. 12mo. Cloth. Illustrated. 161 pages. For introduction, 50 cents.

TEN BOYS WHO LIVED ON THE ROAD FROM LONG AGO TO NOW. 12mo. Cloth. 243 pages. Illustrated. For introduction, 50 cents.

GEOGRAPHICAL PLAYS. 12mo. Cloth. 140 pages. For Introduction, $1.00.

The "Seven Little Sisters" represent the seven races, and the book shows how people live in the various parts of the world, what their manners and customs are, what the products of each section are and how they are interchanged.

"Each and All" continues the story of Seven Little Sisters, and tells more of the peculiarities of the various races, especially in relation to childhood.

Dame Nature unfolds in "Stories Mother Nature Told" some of her most precious secrets. She tells about the amber, about the dragon-fly and its wonderful history, about water-lilies, how the Indian corn grows, what queer pranks the Frost Giants indulge in, about coral, and starfish, and coal mines, and many other things in which children take delight.

In "Ten Boys" the History of the World is summarized in the stories of Kabla the Aryan boy, Darius the Persian boy, Cleon the Greek boy, Horatius the Roman boy, Wulf the Saxon boy, Gilbert the Knight's page, Roger the English boy, Fuller the Puritan boy, Dawson the Yankee boy, and Frank Wilson the boy of 1885.

In "Ten Boys" one is struck with the peculiar excellence of its style, — clear, easy, graceful, and picturesque, — which a child cannot fail to comprehend, and in which "children of a larger growth" will find an irresistible charm. — **John G. Whittier.**

GINN & COMPANY, Publishers, Boston, New York, and Chicago.

Open Sesame!

About One Thousand Pieces of the Choicest Prose and Verse.

COMPILED BY

Blanche Wilder Bellamy and Maud Wilder Goodwin.

VOL. I. for children from four to ten years old.
VOL. II. for children from ten to fourteen years old.
VOL. III. for children of a larger growth.

Illustrated, and handsomely bound in cloth. Price of each to teachers, and for introduction, 75 cents.

No Eastern romancer ever dreamed of such a treasure-house as our English literature.

With this "Open Sesame" in his possession, a boy or girl has only to enter and make its wealth his own.

Every piece is believed to be worth carrying away in the memory.

The best writings of our classic authors are here, with selections from recent literature and not a few translations.

E. A. Sheldon, *Principal of State Normal School, Oswego, N.Y.:* It is very good indeed. We think it the best of all the collections.

F. B. Palmer, *Principal of State Normal School, Fredonia, N.Y.:* I think it by far the best collection of memory pieces I have ever seen.

W. E. Buck, *Superintendent of Public Schools, Manchester, N.H.:* It is a beauty, and of all similar works I have seen, it has the most desirable selections.

Chas. W. Cole, *Superintendent of Public Schools, Albany, N.Y.:* The book is a handsome specimen of the arts of typography and binding, while the selections and their arrangement speak well for the judgment and taste of the editors.

A. B. Poland, *Assistant Superintendent of Schools, New York City:* The selections are excellent. The editors have shown great literary judgment. The publishers have exhibited their usual good taste in the make-up of the books.

H. O. Wheeler, *Superintendent of Schools, Burlington, Vt.:* The work of selection and arrangement of materials in these books has been done with fine taste and good judgment.

O. H. Longwell, *President, Highland Park Normal College, Des Moines, Ia.:* I doubt if there is anything published that can be used to such good advantage in our school libraries as these three volumes. The selections are the best I have seen.

GINN & COMPANY, Publishers, Boston, New York, Chicago, Atlanta.

A BOOK OF THE RAREST EXCELLENCE.

The Knowledge of a Royal Astronomer

COMBINED WITH

The Happy Faculty of the Story-Teller.

STAR=LAND,

By Sir ROBERT S. BALL,

Royal Astronomer of Ireland.

Cloth. 384 pages. Fully Illustrated. For introduction, $1.00.

This fascinating book treats, in a manner equally true to science and attractive to children, all the chief topics of Astronomy: the sun, the moon, the planets, comets, meteors, and the stars.

TWO REPRESENTATIVE OPINIONS.

It pleases and satisfies the learned.

The Right Hon. W. E. GLADSTONE : — "I have now finished reading your luminous and delightful 'STAR-LAND,' and I am happy to be in a sense enrolled amongst your young pupils."

It instructs and delights the children.

A. W. MOREHOUSE, *State Normal School, Potsdam, N. Y.:* — "It is just the book we have wanted for a long time, and is calculated not only to interest and instruct, but to lead to greater effort, on the part of the learner, in the right direction."

For the regular study of Astronomy, one or another of Young's three books will be found precisely adapted to the requirements. *Send for a descriptive circular.*

GINN & COMPANY, Publishers,

BOSTON, NEW YORK, AND CHICAGO.

THE BEST SUPPLEMENTARY READING.

NATURE STUDY

THE JANE ANDREWS BOOKS. By JANE ANDREWS.
    The Seven Little Sisters. For introduction, 50 cents.
    Each and All. For introduction, 50 cents.
    Stories Mother Nature Told her Children. For introduction, 50 cents.

STUDY AND STORY NATURE READERS. By J. H. STICKNEY, Author of the Stickney Readers.
    Now Ready.
    Pets and Companions. For primary grades. Sq. 12mo. Cloth. Fully illustrated. 142 pages. For introduction, 30 cents.

ALL THE YEAR ROUND. By FRANCES L. STRONG of the Teachers' Training School, St. Paul, Minn.
    Part I. Autumn. *In press.*
    Part II. Winter. Sq. 12mo. Cloth. Fully illustrated. 102 pages. For introduction, 30 cents.
    Part III. Spring. Sq. 12mo. Cloth. Fully illustrated. 99 pages. For introduction, 30 cents.

LITTLE NATURE STUDIES FOR LITTLE PEOPLE. From the Essays of JOHN BURROUGHS. Edited by MARY E. BURT.
    Volume I. A Primer and a First Reader. Boards. 106 pages. Illustrated. For introduction, 25 cents.
    Volume II. A Second Reader and a Third Reader. Illustrated. Boards. 103 pages. For introduction, 25 cents.

GLIMPSES AT THE PLANT WORLD. By FANNY D. BERGEN. Fully illustrated. Cloth. 156 pages. For introduction, 50 cents.

SEED-BABIES. By MARGARET W. MORLEY, recently instructor in Biology, Armour Institute, Chicago. Boards. Illustrated. 75 pages. For introduction, 25 cents.

LITTLE FLOWER PEOPLE. By GERTRUDE ELISABETH HALE. Sq. 12mo. Cloth. Illustrated. 85 pages. For introduction, 40 cents.

STARLAND. By SIR ROBERT S. BALL, Royal Astronomer of Ireland. Illustrated. Cloth. 376 pages. For introduction, $1.00.

GINN & COMPANY, Publishers,
Boston. New York. Chicago. Atlanta. Dallas.

www.ingramcontent.com/pod-product-compliance
Lightning Source LLC
Chambersburg PA
CBHW030817230426
43667CB00008B/1254